Daily Ditties from Delron's Desk Volume VI

I0149550

Delron Shirley

2018

Cover design by Jeremy Shirley

For permission to quote material from this book, contact:
Delron Shirley
3210 Cathedral Spires Dr.
Colorado Springs, CO 80904
teachallnations@msn.com

Introduction
Ditties

A ditty is actually a poem or a song, but I grew up with the Carolina colloquialism of a ditty being any short, pithy saying or writing. Having written only one noteworthy poem in my life, I'm definitely not a poet, but I do hope that these few thoughts I'm sharing in this little book will prove to be short and pithy enough to inspire a little something into your life each day.

I once read that it's plagiarism if you steal from one person, but it's research if you steal from several writers. Another thing that I firmly believe is that none of us really has an original thought. Every thought we have is a result of all the input we have received. For most of us, the old saying might apply very aptly: GIGO – "garbage in, garbage out." If there is any good thought that comes out of our minds, it is because some good influences have entered our hearts; the most important of those positive influences would be the Word of God and the inspiration of the Holy Spirit.

As you read my little ditties each day, I encourage you to enjoy each place where I have plagiarized (ah, done some research) and each place where something other than garbage has come out due to the inspiration of the Holy Spirit.

Since some holidays do not occur on fixed dates, the message for each movable holiday is given on the earliest possible date on which it can be observed: Martin Luther King Day, January 15; State of the Union Address, January 25; Presidents' Day, February 15; Palm Sunday, March 15; Good Friday, March 20; Easter, March 22; Mothers Day, May 8; Pentecost, May 10; Fathers Day, June 15; and Thanksgiving, November 22.

Happy New Year

New Year's Day is always a time of reflection and projection. Portraying the previous year as an old man with a long gray beard and the upcoming year as a baby in a diaper, cartoonists like to project the idea that we have a chance to have a fresh start in life as we pull down one calendar and pin up a new one. That's why we all pull out our notepads and scribble down our list of resolutions – things that we are going to do differently this new year. Somehow, we really believe that we get a new chance just because we are in a new year. Of course, we have to remember that there is way too much truth to the old joke about how hard it is to find an empty treadmill at the gym for the first two weeks of January, but how easy it is by the time that half the month is over.

The truth is that life hasn't really changed just because we've updated the last figure on the date we write on our checks. After all, the new year is a totally arbitrary decision that was made centuries ago simply as a way to delineate the chronology of events. You may remember that in the Bible, time was calculated by the installation of a new king – thus, we read that certain events occurred in a certain year of a specific monarch's reign. Perhaps, we should follow the same pattern today – only with the true potentate, King Jesus. With each new year, each new month, each new day, each new minute that we yield the throne of our lives to Him, we can count it as a fresh start!

That way, we can live our lives fully by the little slogan, "Yesterday is history; tomorrow is a mystery; today is God's gift – that's why we call it the present."

January 2
A Happy and Healthy New Year
I always wish my friends a happy and healthy new year – and I especially hope that none of them wind up with any of the following real-life medical diagnoses:

Left nose is fractured, but right nose is okay.

She's okay; she just went into heart failure.

I think he has sleep apathy.

Patient had a Cadillac arrest.

The patient is tearful and crying constantly. She also appears to be depressed.

Discharge status: Alive but without my permission.

Healthy appearing decrepit sixty-nine-year-old male.

Mentally alert but forgetful.

The patient has no previous history of suicides.

Patient has left white blood cells at another hospital.

Patient's medical history has been remarkably insignificant with only a forty-pound weight gain in the past three days.

Patient had waffles for breakfast and anorexia for lunch.

She is numb from her toes down.

While in ER, she was examined, x-rated, and sent home.

The skin was moist and dry.

Occasional, constant infrequent headaches.

Patient was alert and unresponsive.

She stated that she had been constipated for most of her life, until she got a divorce.

I saw your patient today, who is still under our car for physical therapy.

The lab test indicated abnormal lover function.

Skin: somewhat pale but present.

Patient was seen in consultation by Dr. Blank, who felt we should sit on the abdomen and I agree.

January 3

Marriage

One item that we often find near the top of the New Year's resolutions list is to work on our marriages. Well, here are a few thoughts to keep in mind if that is on your list this year:

Although Lady Astor and Winston Churchill were not a couple, they were constantly at odds. But here's one conversation that they did have about matrimony:

Lady Astor: "If you were my husband, I'd put poison in your coffee."

Winston Churchill: "If you were my wife, I'd drink it."

Why does a woman work ten years trying to change her husband and then complain that he's not the man she married?

Men who have pierced ears are well prepared for marriage because they have already experienced pain and bought jewelry.

Actress Lee Grant, who was blacklisted from Hollywood for a period because of her marriages to men who were considered politically dangerous to the country, summed up her marriages with, "I've been married to a Marxist and to a Fascist, but neither one would take out the garbage."

The problem with women is that get excited about nothing and then marry him.

My wife and I lived happily for twenty years – then we met.

In olden times, sacrifices were made at the altar – a custom which is still very much practiced.

The most important four words for a successful marriage: I'll do the dishes.

Keep your eyes wide open before marriage, half shut afterwards. – Benjamin Franklin

January 4
New Perspectives for a New Year
I'm not presenting the following ideas as gospel, but they are points to ponder as we head into a new year:

Be careful about reading health books; you might die of a misprint.

An optimist is someone who falls out of the Empire State Building and after fifty floors says, "Well, so far so good."

The nice part about being a pessimist is that you are constantly being either proven right or pleasantly surprised.

I'm not offended by blonde jokes because I know that I'm not dumb…I also know that I'm not really blonde. – Dolly Parton

People who believe in predestination still look both ways before crossing the road.

The only people who call hurricanes acts of God are people who write insurance forms.

When you have bacon in your mouth, it doesn't matter who is President.

I was going to sue for defamation of character, but then I realized that I have no character.

He is a self-made man who worships his creator.

People who think they know everything are an annoyance to those of us who do.

An acceptable level of unemployment means that the economist to whom it is acceptable still has a job.

I'll never be an old man because an old man is fifteen years older than I am.

Makeup can only make you pretty on the outside. It doesn't help the ugly person you are inside, even if you eat it.

January 5

Dreams

In both the Old and New Testaments, we are told that it is old men who dream dreams while young men see visions. (Joel 2:28, Acts 2:17) In that case, I guess that I qualify as an old man since I often have dreams – sometimes just confusing images, but often answers to issues that I've been dealing with. The mechanics behind dreaming is that our brains do not become totally inactive during sleep; instead, they use that time when we are not consciously active for a myriad of unconscious activities including reorganizing all the bits of information that we have received during the day. In much the same way a computer has to determine where it will store all the data that has been entered into its memory bank, our brains have to take some time to organize all the thoughts that they are expected to retain. Since God is actively involved in the lives of believers one hundred percent of the time, He must also be actively involved in this nighttime subconscious brain activity as well. Therefore, He is actually in control of how our thoughts and memories get reorganized as we sleep. The result is that He can use the dreaming process to give us an enlightened perspective on everything that we have seen and heard the day before.

Interestingly, it has been proven that adults who attend church regularly dream less than those who do not. This is likely because they are actively relying on their faith to deal with life's big questions and they can, therefore, sleep more soundly.

It has also been proven that those who are close to death often dream of their departed friends and relatives. Again, proof that God is at work in their subconscious, getting them ready for their transition.

January 6
Your Children Shall be Taught of the Lord

The theme for today's meditation comes from Isaiah 54:13 – a passage which speaks of the restoration of creation through the establishment of order by the Lord. Imagine – a time when every man will have a personal revelation from God without any intermediates to misinterpret, dilute, or misrepresent His truth! Ever since the garden of Eden when the serpent caused Eve to question and then deny God's directives (Genesis 3:1-5), man has been on a downward spiral of refusal to retain the revelation that God has given him (Isaiah 5:20-21, Romans 1:19-22). But God has a plan to reverse this whole process of mental and spiritual degeneration. Hebrews 8:11 speaks of a time when no one will need to have his neighbor teach him the ways of the Lord since everyone – from the least to the greatest – will have a personal knowledge of God internally. Actually, this promise is a recurring theme in the scripture with Old Testament prophecy of a covenant in which God will put His law in our inward parts and write it in our hearts (Jeremiah 31:33-34) and Jesus' reaffirmation, *It is written in the prophets, And they shall be all taught of God. Every man therefore that hath heard, and hath learned of the Father, cometh unto me* (John 6:45).

But the wonderful truth is that even though we may not see this on a universal scale until the culmination of the human age, God is already doing it in the lives of those of us who are willing to receive it. In I Thessalonians 4:9, Paul declared that God had taught the believers how to love one another. John affirmed that the anointing of God teaches us so that we actually know all things. (I John 2:20, 2:27)

Tap into the spiritual instruction today!

January 7

Why Peter?

In the story of Jesus' prayer in the Garden of Gethsemane, Matthew 26:40 records that Jesus addressed the question, *Could you not watch with me one hour?* specifically to Peter rather than all the disciples. Why would Jesus single out just one disciple to bear the blame for something that all the disciples did? The answer seems to be related to Peter's tendency to step into a leadership role among the clan. In just this one gospel, we see repeated examples: in Matthew 14:28, it was Peter who wanted to try walking on water; in Matthew 15:15, it was Peter who spoke up for the whole team asking Jesus to explain the meaning of the parable of the sower; in Matthew 16:16, it was Peter who answered Jesus' question as to who they perceived Him to be; in Matthew 16:22, it was Peter who took it upon himself to scold Jesus for suggesting that His life was to end tragically; in Matthew 17:4, it was Peter who proposed to build three tabernacles on the Mount of Transfiguration; in Matthew 17:24, it was Peter who came forward with the question as to why Jesus hadn't paid His taxes; in Matthew 18:21, it was Peter who addressed the issue of how far believers were to go in forgiving those who offended them; in Matthew 19:27, it was Peter who boldly testified that he and the others had given up everything to become Jesus' disciples; and – most importantly of all – in Matthew 26:33-35, it was Peter who proclaimed that he would never abandon Jesus, no matter what everyone else might do.

His companion James summed up Peter's plight, *My brethren, be not many masters, knowing that we shall receive the greater condemnation.* (James 3:1)

January 8
Revel in His Holy Name

The Message version of the Bible renders I Chronicles 16:10, *Revel in his holy Name, God-seekers, be jubilant!* What an awesome way to express our relationship with the Lord! Usually we associate the word "revel" with the scene of drunken partiers in Times Square on New Year's Eve or in the French Quarter during Mardi Gras – but, in this case, King David is commanding that believers become so intense in their worship of God that their expression could be paralleled with the sensual abandon of these party-goers. Yes, other translations do soften the wording with terms such as "worship," "celebrate," "glory in," "be proud," and most frequently, "rejoice." However, I somehow think that Eugene Peterson is not so far off base with his wording in that – in this same event when David commanded the people to worship so demonstratively – he also celebrated with such exuberance that it embarrassed his wife. Furthermore, when she scolded him for his extravagance, he responded with the pledge to be even more expressive in his future worship. (I Chronicles 15:20, II Samuel 6:20-22)

But David did not encourage senseless partying. Notice that he goes on to tell the people that they should have an intelligent reason for their celebration, *Study God and his strength...Remember all the wonders he performed, the miracles and judgments that came out of his mouth...He keeps his commitments across thousands of generations...He posted it in big block letters...*

Yes, we should have radical celebration, but it must be based on a knowledge of who God is and what He has done – not just emotional exuberance.

January 9

Follow the Leader

Psalm 23 is so familiar to us that we can quote it essentially verbatim – unfortunately, such familiarity can often cause us to skim through the passage without stopping to notice some of the points that the Lord would want us to see in the psalm. That is exactly what happened to me the other day when I saw something, that now seems so obvious, but had eluded me all my life.

In verses two and three, David makes reference to the fact that the Lord is leading him. In verse six, he states that goodness and mercy follow him. For the first time in my life, I saw the psalm as a description of a parade – the Good Shepherd is out front, David is in second place, and goodness and mercy are bringing up the rear. The significance that I see in this arrangement is that we cannot expect goodness and mercy to be part of our lives unless we are following the Shepherd. How can they follow unless we are going somewhere? And how can we go where we should be heading unless we are following the Shepherd who knows the way? Unfortunately, too many believers anticipate that they will automatically accrue God's goodness and mercy without diligently following His direction for their lives.

When we get in our place in the parade, we actually have the benefit of the Lord's presence surrounding us.

The Lord will go before you, and the God of Israel will be your rear guard. (Isaiah 52:12 – English Standard Version)

The angel of the Lord encampeth round about them that fear him, and delivereth them. (Psalm 34:7)

January 10
Calling Upon the Name of the Lord

Genesis 4:26 states that people began to call upon the name of the Lord during the time of Seth's son Enos. This verse brings up a very perplexing question as to why people did not call on the Lord's name before this time – two hundred and forty years after the creation.

Of course, the first place to look for an answer to such a curious and puzzling question would be in the translations. Perhaps the King James simply worded the sentence in a misleading way. However, all the other translations are in uniform agreement with the concept with simple variations such as using the word "worship" or "pray."

Our next step to unraveling this conundrum must be to consider the passage in context. In doing so, we immediately see that there is a full legacy of individuals who communicated with God prior to this time; therefore, the uniqueness of this verse must lie in one or both of the characteristic words in this sentence – "people" and "call." Perhaps this passage is concluding that this was the first time that there was corporate worship as opposed to individual prayer and fellowship. Additionally, it could refer to the idea that man's abandonment of intimate communication with the Lord had forced him into a position of having to call out to Him rather than to experience His ever-present closeness. It seems likely that both of these concepts must play a role in explaining the verse.

In our New Testament relationship, God has restored that original close, personal fellowship between the believer and Himself and augmented it with the communal experience of corporate worship so that we have the best of both!

January 11
Five Ps for a Blessed Family
God's original intent for human families was that they would be blessed. (Genesis 1:28) Perhaps that is why there have been and continue to be so many attacks against the family unit. But actually, maintaining the blessing of God on our homes is not as difficult as we tend to believe. In fact, it seems that simply adopting a godly attitude and proactive faith can ensure that blessing. Try these five simple steps and watch your family be revolutionized.

1) Praise God that He has blessed you in the marriage, *Whoso findeth a wife findeth a good thing, and obtaineth favour of the Lord.* (Proverbs 18:22)

2) Proclaim God's enduring covenant over your family and posterity, *Know therefore that the Lord thy God, he is God, the faithful God, which keepeth covenant and mercy with them that love him and keep his commandments to a thousand generations.* (Deuteronomy 7:9)

3) Protection is yours to enjoy, *There shall no evil befall thee, neither shall any plague come nigh thy dwelling.* (Psalm 91:10)

4) God's promise is for blessing and increase even if you made your vows for richer or poorer, in sickness and in health, and for better or worse, *But the path of the just is as the shining light, that shineth more and more unto the perfect day.* (Proverbs 4:18)

5) Pray for the wisdom and courage to understand and follow God's plan for relationships in the extended family, *Therefore shall a man leave his father and his mother, and shall cleave unto his wife: and they shall be one flesh.* (Genesis 2:24)

January 12
When Trivia Isn't Trivial

While driving to school the other day, I heard a trivia contest on the Christian radio station. The question was, "On any given day, one quarter of us use the phone for this purpose. What is it?" I was out of the car by the time they gave the correct answer; so, I'll never know what it is. However, I did get to hear the first two guesses. The first was a woman who said, "To make a doctor's appointment." The second was another lady who suggested, "To make a call about a sick family member."

I couldn't believe my ears – the first thing that came to mind for these Christian believers was that one fourth of telephone conversations have to do with sickness. The experience makes me wonder why we are so obsessed with illness – especially, if we are believers. The answer is simple – we aren't really believers; instead, we are just as carnal and unbelieving as the rest of the world. If we were really believers who knew, understood, and genuinely believed in the goodness of God, the thought of sickness would be at the bottom of the list rather than at the top. Real believers should have the covenant of healing as much in focus as we do our salvation covenant.

> *Beloved, I wish above all things that thou mayest prosper and be in health, even as thy soul prospereth.* (III John 2)
>
> *I am the Lord that healeth thee.* (Exodus 15:26)
>
> *Bless the Lord, O my soul, and forget not all his benefits: Who forgiveth all thine iniquities; who healeth all thy diseases.* (Psalm 103:2-3)
>
> *Who his own self bare our sins in his own body on the tree...by whose stripes ye were healed.* (I Peter 2:24)

January 13

Predestination and Foreknowledge

Predestination and foreknowledge is like telling a teenage boy with a new driver's license not to speed. God knows the end from the beginning, and He tries to warn us – but He won't stop us.

We see a great example of this principle in the story of the selection of the first king in Israel. After generations of divine guidance through God-ordained prophets and patriarchs, the people of Israel had dug in their heels as they laid out their demands before Samuel. They had drawn the line in the sand as they insisted that he appoint a king to rule over them just like all the other nations that surrounded them. Although Samuel had insisted that they not force his hand, he came to an impasse as the people's insistence grew stronger and stronger and their logic – that he was too old to continue in the role of leadership and that his sons were unworthy candidates to replace him – seemed incontestable. After hearing from God that he was not to take any offense at the people's request because the problem was not a personal affront to his leadership but a rejection of the very governance of God Himself, Samuel returned to the people with one last negotiation – to warn them of all the evil that would come through their monarch. (I Samuel 8:11-18)

No matter how clearly God was able to predict the future of the people, the decision was still in their hands. Of course, the reverse is just as equally true – no matter how explicitly God intends to bless us, we still hold the key to our own destiny. Jeremiah 29:11 assures us that God is making great plans for our future, but Jesus made it clear in Matthew 23:37 that the final decision for our destiny lies in our own free will.

January 14
Passing on the Torch
In I Kings 19:15, God directed Elijah to ordain three men as the leaders of the next generation: Hazael as king of Syria, Jehu as king of Israel, and Elisha as the prophet to take the place of Elijah after his ascension. However, Elijah only fulfilled one of these three commands. He did anoint Elisha as his successor in the role of the prophet of God. We all remember the epic story of how Elisha received a double portion of Elijah's anointing by catching his mantle upon his departure from Planet Earth. However, it may come as a surprise that it was Elisha – not Elijah himself – who anointed Hazael as king of Syria and prophesied that he would bring much death and suffering upon the people of Israel. (II Kings 8:7-13) Even more amazing is the fact that it was an unnamed disciple of Elisha who anointed Jehu to his position as king of Israel. (II Kings 9:1-10) Just as Paul taught Timothy that what he received from the Apostle was to be advanced into further generations (II Timothy 2:2), so the prophetic anointing on Elijah was so tangibly transferable that God considered the actions two generations later to be the works of the prophet himself.

In the history of the modern missions movement, we often find stories of missionaries who say that missions was on the hearts of their mothers or grandmothers but they never got to go overseas to minister. These missionaries all confess that they believe that their work is the literal fulfillment of the call that God originally placed on the hearts of their mothers and grandmothers. Dr. Lester Sumrall often said that he went to Hong Kong and later to mainland China because of the call that the Lord had given his mother years before.

Martin Luther King Jr. Day

Prejudice vs. Progress

Prejudice shows itself in many different forms:

Social status or occupation – Genesis 46:34 records Joseph's warning to his father and brothers that they not refer to themselves as shepherds since shepherds were considered an abomination in Egypt.

Race or skin color – Miriam criticized Moses for marrying a black woman. (Numbers 12:1)

Geographical origin – Nathanael questioned if any good thing could possibly come out of Nazareth. (John 1:46)

Family heritage – Jephthah was a social outcast because his mother was a prostitute. (Judges 11:1-6)

Progress occurs when all men and women are given equal opportunities regardless of their origin.

Just look at these examples of progress made by Afro-Americans: Jan Matzeliger invented the automatic shoe lasting machine, Charles Brooks invented the street sweeper, Fredrick Jones invented the refrigeration system for trucks, Garrett Morgan invented the traffic signal and the gas mask, Henrietta Bradberry invented torpedoes, Madame CJ Walker became the first woman millionaire through developing a line of cosmetic products, Charles Drew developed blood banks, Daniel Williams performed the first open heart surgery, Lewis Latimer assisted Thomas Edison in developing the light bulb and Alexander Bell in developing the telephone, Andrew Beard invented the automatic railroad car coupler, and Elijah McCoy invented the automatic lubrication system for locomotives – a product so good that railway engineers insisted on having his product rather than a substitute, giving rise to our common expression, "the real McCoy."

January 16
It's Not My Fault
One of the most perplexing verses in the Bible is II Kings 6:31 in which the king of Israel declared that he wanted to execute Elisha when the city of Samaria was in starvation mode during the siege by the Syrian army. The thing that makes the king's action so intriguing is that prior to this point, he had held the prophet in respect and their relationship had been very beneficial to the monarch's reign. Elisha had prophesied a supernatural victory over the armies of Moab. He apparently gained unlimited access to the king in that he offered to arrange an audience for the Shunammite woman. The prophet was taken into the king's circle of advisors and was able to supernaturally advise him of the strategies of the Syrian army. The fact that the communication was apparently two-way is revealed in the encounter in which the prophet was advised of the king's dilemma when the Syrian king sent Naaman to Israel to be healed. When Elisha brought the blinded Syrian troops to the king, he referred to the prophet as his father – revealing a high level of respect. Later, the king asked Elisha's servant to reminisce with him about the prophet's life – again showing the place of honor that Elisha held in the king's heart. The only logical reason that the king could have had for wanting to kill Elisha during the siege of Samaria would be that the prophet had talked the king out of executing the army when they were at his palace after being blinded. Perhaps the king felt that the present situation would not have occurred had he followed his own instincts.

However, the bottom line is that he – like all humans – simply didn't want to take the blame. In the garden of Eden, Adam felt that it was Eve's fault – and even God's fault for making the woman. (Genesis 3:12)

January 17
Points to Ponder
Be cautious about whom you invest your life in. It took Jesus all night to pick the twelve disciples.

It's easier to build strong children than to repair broken men.

Focus on all that you do have rather than the few things that you don't have. Eve was focused on the fruit of the one tree that she was not allowed to have rather than all the fruits and vegetables in the garden that she could have.

Power will intoxicate the best hearts as wine will intoxicate the strongest minds.

To say that someone is hopeless is to say that God is hopeless

The Christian life is an adventure too thrilling to miss.

Promote what you live; live what you promote.

Love is what's left when being in love is over.

Live in the moment – not through it.

Are you willing to change your life to change other people's lives?

The problem with being a lukewarm Christian is that you don't fit in anywhere. You are too holy for the old crowd and not holy enough for the new one.

Our internal capital builds our eternal securities – our conscience, our heart, our passion, our ideas, our divine calling, our will power, our character, our personality, and our spiritual giftings.

Our external capital builds our temporal careers – body, gender, technical skills, networks, time, etc.

If your presence were removed, what would be missing from this community?

"Good" is "God" with an "O" added. "Evil" is the "devil" with the "D" being taken.

January 18
More Points to Ponder
Ego is <u>e</u>dging <u>G</u>od <u>o</u>ut.

Matthew only mentioned himself two times. Once he called himself the tax collector, and when he gave the list of the apostles, his name was in eighth place. John's name does not appear in his gospel. Paul referred to himself as a fool, the least of the apostles, less than the least of saints, and the chief of sinners. David wrote a psalm about his failure with Bathsheba but never said anything about his felling a giant.

The pain of staying the same exceeds the pain of changing.

Failure is an event – not a person. We're all failures – at least, the best of us are. The only way to avoid failure is to do nothing. Failure simply means that you haven't succeeded yet. Norman Vincent Peale's wife had to salvage <u>The Power of Positive Thinking</u> out of his trashcan, and <u>The Living Bible</u> was rejected on its first submission.

Show me a thoroughly satisfied man, and I'll show you a failure. – Thomas Edison

You can make excuses or you can make progress, but not both.

Resting before you are tired is laziness

A trapeze artist once said, "Once you learn that the net below you will catch you, you stop worrying about falling. The only way to learn that the net will catch you is by falling. Therefore, the more you fall, the better trapeze artist you become. At that point, you learn to focus on the trapeze, not the net."

Our greatest fear should not be of failure but of succeeding at things in life that don't really matter. – Francis Chan

January 19

American Hippos

I recently uncovered some information about an intriguing chapter in American history – the story of hippopotamus ranching! In 1910, the US Congress proposed a plan that would simultaneously solve two pressing problems – a national meat shortage and a growing ecological crisis caused by the invasive water hyacinth that was killing fish and choking waterways. The plan was to import hippos from Africa and raise them in the bayous of Louisiana to produce "lake cow bacon." Since swamp land was not productive for grazing cattle, the proposal seemed like an ideal solution to the meat shortage that had resulted from the current flood of immigrants. The idea seemed like a perfect solution with the side benefit of solving the problem of the noxious hyacinth. Although one Agriculture Department official insisted, "I hope to live long enough to see herds of these broad-backed beasts wallowing in the Southern marshes and rivers, fattening on the millions of tons of food which awaits their arrival; to see great droves of white rhinos…roaming over the semiarid desert wastes, fattening on the sparse herbage which these lands offer; to see herds of the delicate giraffe, the flesh of which is the purest and sweetest of any known animal, browsing on the buds and shoots of young trees in preparation for the butcher block," the Department eventually decided against the proposition and planned to turn the marshes into grassy pastures and raise cattle on the reclaimed land. The reason: beef is a normal meat.

Although I've never eaten hippo, I can testify that other African meats – zebra and ostrich, for instance – are delicious. We should never settle for the way things are just because that's the way things are.

January 20
Excess
Just eight men, from Bill Gates to Michael Bloomberg, own as much wealth as more than three and a half billion of their fellow citizens on Planet Earth. That's right – the top eight wealthiest humans own as much of the total wealth of the human family as do the bottom half of the population combined! One in ten members of the human race survive on less than two dollars a day, while the wealthiest individual has a net worth of some seventy-five billion dollars. Interestingly enough, the gap continues to grow more exaggerated in that only a year earlier it took the wealth of the sixty-two richest people on the planet to equal the resources of the bottom half.

Concerned over the potential that public anger against this kind of inequality could lead to seismic political changes, many have suggested radical changes in taxation that would strip the wealthy of their funds and distribute them more evenly among the needy. Such concerns over an eventual public backlash are certainly justifiable. In fact, we see an example in scripture in the story of Solomon – who, by the way, had wealth that exceeded the holdings of the eight individuals in today's lesson. At his death, the kingdom of Israel was divided due to the inequitable distribution of wealth, with ten tribes suffering greatly to support the extravagant lifestyle of the king and his courtiers from the other two tribes. However, the concept of a communistic or socialistic state is not the solution. The only answer is a voluntary distribution of resources as we see modeled by Nehemiah when he refused to take from the people and instead funded his own campaign. (Nehemiah 5:17) Charity cannot be legislated; it must be voluntary.

January 21

Keys

When I was growing up, I would occasionally accompany my dad on little runs to the factory where he worked. In his supervisory position, he had access to almost every part of the plant – meaning that he had a huge keyring full of keys. Over the years, things have gotten a lot simpler as various forms of keyless access have been introduced. I remember when I saw my first automatic garage door opener. During my time as a seminary student, a family asked me to housesit for them as they traveled out of the country. I was actually surprised when they left me a remote control for the garage door rather than an actual key. Since that time, we have seen the development of keyless entry pads that require a series of numbers instead of a key. Currently, key cards are a very common method of unlocking entryways. With one little credit-card-like piece of plastic, I can get into as many doors on the campus where I teach as my father could access with his huge ring of keys. Of course, the simple pass card is not nearly as impressive as that bulky, rattling ring of keys on the long chain that hung from my dad's belt!

Let's draw a little spiritual parallel from the keyring and the pass card. We have all heard sermons like "Five Keys to Prosperity," "Ten Keys to Health," and "Twelve Keys to a Happy Home." In fact, I've actually preached these exact messages. At any rate, this approach leaves us with the mentality of the huge keyring that my dad used to carry. On the other hand, Jesus made life much simpler when he said that the total message of faith could be summed up in one commandment – to love God and our fellowman. This is the simple key card that opens every door to prosperity, health, and relationships.

January 22
Every Nation Has an Inheritance
*When the Most High divided to the nations
their inheritance...he set the bounds of the
people according to the number...of Israel.*
(Deuteronomy 32:8)

When the Lord divided the original land mass into continents during the time of Peleg (Genesis 10:25, I Chronicles 1:19), He actually set boundaries for each nation (Acts 17:26). However, this passage tells us that the allocation of those inheritances is predicated upon the nation of Israel.

History has confirmed this principle over and over again as empires have expanded their borders only to implode upon themselves because of their relationship with the Jewish race. Egypt collapsed from being the greatest empire in the world to a barely subsistent country when Pharaoh refused to grant Moses and his people their freedom. Babylon, the golden head of nations, died the night that they mocked the Jewish people and their God by drinking from the golden cups that belonged in the Jerusalem temple. The Persian Empire that once spread over one hundred twenty-seven provinces from India to Ethiopia shriveled up to essentially nothing after the attempted ethnic cleansing of God's people. Once she abandoned her responsibility to help the Jews rebuild a homeland in Palestine, Great Britain lost her global holdings upon which the sun never set and became simply Britain. Germany was on its way to dominating Europe but adopted a policy of genocide against the Jews.

The nations may force their way beyond their pre-ordained boundaries, but they will soon fall back if they don't honor the God-given inheritance of Israel.

January 23
Should God Send Himself to Hell?

Wow! What a question! But I have a legitimate reason for asking it. In Matthew 5:22, Jesus said that anyone who calls his brother a fool is in danger of hell fire. However, Jesus and God repeatedly called people fools. In Matthew 23:17 and 19, Jesus called the scribes and Pharisees fools because they honored the gold in the temple more than the temple itself – and ultimately more than God Himself. In Luke 11:40, He called the Pharisees fools because they put their religious rituals above true devotion to God. In the parable about the rich man who wanted to store up his abundant harvest for himself, God the Father called the man a fool. (Luke 12:20) The resurrected Jesus called the men with whom He walked on the road to Emmaus fools because they didn't comprehend the words of the prophets concerning the suffering that the messiah was to endure. (Luke 24:25) Therefore, we have half a dozen occasions on which God has made Himself liable to His own ruling concerning judgment in hell fire.

Unless we are to assume that God is above His own law – which would be totally out of line with His nature – we have to ask if there is a logical reason for this seeming discrepancy. Let's begin by looking at Jeremiah 17:11, *Those who gain riches by unjust means…in the end they will prove to be fools.* This passage precisely describes the man in the parable in Luke chapter twelve and helps us to understand that God was not making an accusation against the man; rather, He was simply showing him that he had qualified himself for the judgment of a fool. All the other occasions in which Jesus called individuals fools were identical – He was pointing out their own faults, not cursing, judging, or ridiculing them.

January 24
Bathsheba

When you hear the name Bathsheba, what is the immediate image that comes to mind? The tryst with King David, of course. However, there may be more to the story that we should realize – implications that we might not immediately recognize.

The message that I have in mind today is the story of God's grace and justification. To see it, we have to take a step back from the actual story and look at the composition of the Old Testament. Just as we have four presentations of the life of Jesus in the New Testament, we have two presentations of the lives of the Jewish kings in the Old. The account given in the books of Samuel and Kings lay out the historical outline of the events; however, the books of Chronicles give a different perspective on the same events. The main emphasis in this second recounting of history is to record how God saw David as the fountainhead of a covenant between God and His people. David is repeatedly referred to as the standard by which all the other kings are evaluated and as the source of God's mercy when the rulers and people deserved God's judgment. In essence, the Samuel-Kings account is man's perspective on history; whereas, Chronicles is history from God's viewpoint.

So what does this have to do with Bathsheba? Simply that Chronicles never mentions her! Because of David's sincere repentance, the Lord justified him and looked at his life as if the whole thing had never happened! It is as if He totally forgot the event – actually, He did, *He will turn again, he will have compassion upon us; he will subdue our iniquities; and thou wilt cast all their sins into the depths of the sea.* (Micah 7:19)

State of the Union Day

Congressman, Did You Use a Proper Toilet Today?

In India, some regions require that political candidates prove that they use toilets rather than open defecation. Don't laugh, the people are excreting a sincere effort to bring their nation to a new standard – and, in a nation where there are more cell phones than toilets, public sanitation is a major issue.

But let's look back at the original constitutions of the states that comprised our founding union including requirements that seem totally foreign to us today. In Delaware, any individual who was to serve in public office had to make a public declaration that he believed in the Bible and the Trinity. In Massachusetts, only professing Christians were eligible for elected positions. Other state constitutions required belief in one God and the Bible, and some stated that anyone who denied the faith would be disqualified. To many modern thinkers, these regulations may seem as antiquated as the bathroom laws in India certainly will in a few generations. However, just because there will come a time when the toilet requirements will be outdated, the practice of proper sanitation will not be. By the same token – even though some may feel that it is discriminatory to say that only practicing Christians can serve in political office in a country that welcomes members of any faith – that does not mean moral and godly principles are outdated. On the contrary, the very fact that we do have a diverse citizenry necessitates that we need men and women of principle and faith in office more today than at any time in the past. Since the populace has such divergent worldviews, we desperately need more leaders with clarity of where we are to go and discernment on how to get there.

January 26

Shouting for the Battle

In the story of David's fight with Goliath as recorded in I Samuel chapter seventeen, there is a reference to the fact that the Israelite army shouted for the battle as if they were going out to fight. (verse 20) The part of the story leaves me with a major question, "Why were they shouting since they knew that they weren't going to fight?" After all, this was the fortieth day that they had heard the challenge from Goliath (verse 16), and they had uniformly responded with fear and dismay (panic) every time (verse 11). So, why did they continue day after day to show up and scream like they were such brave warriors when they knew in their hearts – and had publicly proven – that they were cowards who would not go out to battle?

Of course, this is not such a conundrum after all. In fact, all we have to do is look at our own lives and we will see the same scenario played out on a weekly basis. We go to church every Sunday and sing songs about putting the devil under our feet and about treading on serpents – but then we go out the front door of the sanctuary and live the next six and a half days under all the pressures that the enemy imposed upon us rather than putting the pressure on him. We see all the injustices that Satan has perpetrated upon society and mumble and complain about the problems – but never actually take any proactive steps toward destroying the works of the enemy all around us.

This is essentially just spiritual fantasizing – getting all excited but not resulting in anything that produces life. Let's stop being shouters and start actually running into the battle.

January 27

Eradicating Egyptians

In yesterday's meditation, we talked about the need to actually take action rather than to simply shout about how brave and victorious we are. Today, I'd like for us to follow up on that idea from the perspective of the necessity of making sure that we are taking the proper action.

Again, I need to reference my friend Dr. Tunde Bakare, "Moses wanted to kill the Egyptians one at a time; God wanted to bury the whole army at once." I'm sure that we all remember the story of how Moses killed an Egyptian in his attempt to rescue a Hebrew slave from abuse. The result was that he lost his position of influence in the kingdom and had to spend the next forty years living in the desert as a fugitive. However, when he finally got back in alignment with God's directives, Moses was able to rescue, not just one Hebrew slave, but the whole race plus other slaves and to eliminate, not a single Egyptian abuser, but the entire nation of oppressors.

Too many of us – possibly inspired by the Nike ad to "Just do it" – seem to live by the motto, "Do something – even if it is wrong." Now, that is not at all what I am suggesting when I say that we need to stop shouting and start running to the battle. No, if we are going to wage successful warfare, we need to make sure that we are operating under the direction of the leadership of the Holy Spirit. When Moses <u>released</u> the excitement of the battle shout, he wound up getting himself exiled for the next *four decades*. But when he learned to <u>harness</u> the excitement of the battle shout and channel it strategically, he was able to break *four centuries* of bondage.

January 28

Did God Sent Sickness?

A few days ago, a couple students came to me with the question about statements in the Bible in which God is attributed with having sent plagues, sickness, and even evil spirits upon people. They were perplexed by the fact that God is a good God who gives good gifts. If we also see Him as being the perpetrator of these evil things, then either He is schizophrenic in His character or we are schizophrenic in our interpretation of Him. Of course, they also challenged the standard answer of the Old versus the New Testament view of God with the fact that He is the same yesterday, today, and forever – the God who never changes.

My answer was in the form of a couple questions for them, "Is gravity good? Who invented gravity?" Of course, gravity is good. Without it, we would float around and never be able to function profitably on earth. Secondly, it is obvious that God is the author of this wonderful gift of gravity. I then told them about my time as a chaplain in Yosemite National Park and described the many times I had seen people deliberately climb over the guard rails and venture past the "Do not go beyond this point" signs. The end result in many of these cases was injury or even death. The good thing that God created – gravity – proved destructive and deadly when the cautionary perimeters were ignored. Then I asked them to show me any place in the Bible where a plague, sickness, or demonic activity came upon anyone who was not previously warned not to pass the point of no return.

From this perspective, we can see how God is ultimately behind any evil thing that happens. However, His direct gift was totally good. It is only man's abuse after God's warnings that results in any harmful effects.

January 29

Tongues and Ears of the Learned

The Lord God hath given me the tongue of the learned, that I should know how to speak a word in season to him that is weary: he wakeneth morning by morning, he wakeneth mine ear to hear as the learned. (Isaiah 50:4)

In a conversation about a young man who had been in an accident, the medical doctor I was talking with mentioned that the boy had lost two digits. Anyone else would have said that he had lost two fingers, but the doctor's words echoed with the tone of his education. In another discussion with another doctor, I was evaluating the possibility of replacing a piece of equipment when he said that we could get another instrument that would have the same footprint as the old one but would have much more efficient output. Of course, everyone else would have said that we could replace the appliance with one of the same size that would do more work. Neither of these doctors was trying to be ostentatious or pretentious – that's just the way they talk because they think in a totally different vocabulary from other people.

The same is true with men and women of other professional backgrounds in terms of how they hear things. An attorney or police officer will hear incriminating evidence in what everyone else would consider simple conversation.

Isaiah said that his tongue and his ears were educated by the Lord – not by his schooling. What a wonderful goal in life – to be able to express ourselves and to understand everything that we hear not from an ordinary human perspective, but from God's viewpoint!

January 30

It's the Adam and Eve Thing All Over Again

It was another of those "women aren't as smart as men" conversations in which Eve was getting blamed for all man's problems when a lady injected, "Have you ever noticed how all of women's problems start with men: <u>men</u>tal illness, <u>men</u>strual cramps, <u>men</u>tal breakdown, <u>men</u>opause, <u>gyn</u>ecological issues? And when we have real trouble, it's a <u>hys</u>terectomy!"

Actually, she may not have been too far off base if we consider the biblical passage, *By one man sin entered into the world.* (Romans 5:12) Notice that this verse blames Adam – not Eve – for the sin and, therefore, all the other problems in the world. In another letter, Paul seems to explain how it was that Adam was at fault, *And Adam was not deceived, but the woman being deceived was in the transgression.* (I Timothy 2:14) The problem was not who was the first to eat of the forbidden fruit; rather, the issue was who was the one who <u>knowingly</u> ate. Notice, in the Genesis account of the event, that Eve was not even created at the time of the directive about not eating of the Tree of the Knowledge of Good and Evil. The commandment came in verses sixteen and seventeen of chapter two, and Eve was created in verses twenty-one and twenty-two. The implication is that anything that Eve knew about the tree was told to her by Adam; therefore, it seems that she was able to be deceived because Adam did not do such a good job of educating her. Additionally, it appears that Adam was present during the temptation in that Genesis 3:6 says that he was with her. In this case, Adam failed in his responsibility to protect her.

Yes, it is possible that all women's problems do start with men!

January 31

True Lies

A little less than a quarter century ago, Arnold Schwarzenegger starred in a Hollywood blockbuster entitled True Lies. The plot of the movie centered around a man who kept from his wife the secret of his true identity as an international spy. When she got involved with a man who pretended to be a spy as a way of impressing her with the intrigue of adventure, the real spy had to respond by actually pulling his wife into his adventurous life as an international agent.

I often think of that movie when I hear people prophesy because they often are speaking the truth but are actually lying in the process because God has not actually told them to deliver the message. Therefore, even if the message is true, it is a lie in that the messenger is pretending when he says that it was given to him by God. The humorous illustration is, "The Lord spoke to me and told me that you breathe oxygen." Yes, it is true that the person does breathe oxygen, but it didn't take God to reveal that.

In fact, we have biblical proof that the true test of prophecy is not accuracy. Remember that Jonah prophesied that Nineveh would be destroyed within forty days; however, God had mercy on the city and allowed it to survive for a hundred and fifty years. On the other hand, Balaam had a rebellious heart in that he actually taught Balak how to seduce the people of Israel into bringing God's judgment upon themselves. (II Peter 2:15, Jude 1:11, Revelation 2:14) All the while, the words that he spoke were true and came to pass.

The bottom line here is that we shouldn't just automatically accept a prophetic word – even if it is true – without knowing the heart and motivation of the prophet.

February 1
Jesus in 3D

I believe that it was Dick Eastman, president of Every Home for Christ, who coined the expression, "Jesus in 3D." The idea is based on the phrase, "Disciples Discipling Disciples" – the biblical concept of multiplication of ministry through active involvement of every member of the Body of Christ rather than expecting a few people in full-time ministry to do the work. The principle was clearly spelled out by the Apostle Paul in his instructions to his disciple Timothy, *And the things that thou hast heard of me among many witnesses, the same commit thou to faithful men, who shall be able to teach others also.* (II Timothy 2:2)

Paul poured his heart and soul into his young protégé but realized that his investment shouldn't stop there – no matter how authoritative and anointed Timothy's ministry might be. Instead, Paul insisted that Timothy should find others who were just as eager to learn as he was. Timothy was to be as diligent about infusing these new believers with all that Paul had downloaded into him. But even that was not enough – these men were to funnel everything that they received on to another tier of believers as well, creating a continuous pipeline from generation to generation and beyond.

We need to ask ourselves if we are living 3D lives or are we allowing the gospel that has been poured into us to become a reservoir in our lives rather than a pipeline through it. The only way that we can fulfill the task of changing our generation with the gospel is to deliberately invest in disciples – not just share an occasional word of encouragement, but purposely train up a new generation of apostles, pastors, and leaders.

Since Groundhog Day is a Big Joke Anyway...

In the middle of the long, hard winter, it's always good to have a little levity to get our minds off the cold. Therefore, let's laugh a little.

My favorite workout at the gym is the "walk out."

Interviewer: Why are you applying for the position? Man being Interviewed: My wife wants me to get a job.

Teacher: Use "etiquette" in a sentence. Student: I don't know what "etiquette" means.

Teacher: What state is a peninsula? Student: Peninsulvania.

Warning label on bicycle bell: Cycling can be dangerous. Failure to heed this warning may result in serious injury or death.

Warning label on baby stroller: Remove child before folding.

Warning label on bike-helmet decal: Decoration only and will not prevent any bodily harm or injury.

Customer in restaurant: I'd like to try the chickenpox pie.

Veterinarian: The only way a Chihuahua could hurt a Rottweiler would be to get stuck in its throat.

Student who couldn't answer a question in class: But, Ma'am, I'm not a rock scientist.

Pastor during baptism service: I baptize you in the name of the Father, Son, and hold your nose.

Letter to M&M company: The bag of M&Ms I purchased is defective. Half are labeled "W&W."

This one is for real – Newspaper headline: Autopsies Ordered for Six Dead Teens. (As if we might do autopsies on living teens!)

Only Jesus and Saint Peter are allowed in our community pool. The sign that normally reads, "No running" was replaced with, "Walk please."

February 3
What a Friend We Have in Jesus

I'm certain that we can all quote the familiar biblical passage about friends, *A man that hath friends must shew himself friendly: and there is a friend that sticketh closer than a brother.* (Proverbs 18:24) However, it often comes as a surprise when we look at the passage in other translations. For instance, the American Standard Version renders this same verse in a way that makes it unrecognizable when compared to the King James Version, *He that maketh many friends doeth it to his own destruction; But there is a friend that sticketh closer than a brother.* Other translations say that having friends will bring us to ruin. Of course, the difference comes from the fact that the various translations are based on different ancient texts – a topic that is far beyond the limits of the one page I have available for today's discussion.

However, assuming that the more contemporary translations are correct, we can learn something very important from this verse. Of course, we know that the friend who sticks closer than a brother is a prophetic reference to Jesus. And, certainly, Jesus' life validated the modern rendering of the verse. As He knelt down to wash Judas' feet at the Last Supper, He knew that those same feet were on their way to betray Him. As he reached out to embrace Him in the Garden of Gethsemane, He knew that the lips that kissed Him were the same ones that had told the officers where to find Him. Even though He knew that befriending Judas would lead to His arrest, trial, and execution, Jesus spared nothing in being a friend to the betrayer.

In exactly the same way, Jesus knows that every one of us will disappoint and hurt Him, but He eagerly embraces us as His friends unconditionally.

February 4
Shout Among...the Nations (Jeremiah 31:7)

When Clarence Wesley Jones graduated from Moody Bible Institute in 1921, he served under evangelist Paul Rader and was part of the founding staff of the Chicago Gospel Tabernacle where he assisted with Rader's weekly radio ministry. He was so impressed by the impact of Christian radio that he felt called to establish a missionary radio ministry in Latin America. As a result, he traveled to Venezuela, Colombia, Panama, and Cuba in 1928 to look for a suitable location for his envisioned radio station. Unable to obtain the necessary government permits, Jones returned to Chicago where he spent the next two years until the Lord crossed his path with that of missionaries from Ecuador who convinced him to consider Ecuador as the location for his envisioned missionary radio station. In 1930, the government of Ecuador granted him the permits for the endeavor, and the station – HCJV, the Voice of the Andes – began broadcasting on Christmas Day of the following year.

Today, Reach Beyond (the ministry that grew out of that single station) operates over five hundred radio stations worldwide – many in areas where traditional evangelism is impossible. One example of their effectiveness is the fact that, in North Africa, over two million Muslims listen in each week. Many of them are open to the gospel simply because they feel unthreatened by the message since it comes from a messenger that they invite into their homes every day.

But here's the reason I chose to tell the story. When Clarence Jones went on the radio that first day, there were only six receivers in the whole of Ecuador! He had a vision that far outran logic. If you have a dream or vision from God, never let it be deterred.

February 5
I Can Feel It in My Bones
Why was there a specific instruction that none of the bones of the Passover lamb were to be broken? (Exodus 12:46) The easy answer is that it was prophetic of Jesus, the ultimate Passover Lamb. Even though all His bones were pulled out of joint during the crucifixion (Psalm 22:14), not one bone was to be broken (Psalm 34:20, John 19:36). But there is also a deeper significance to the prophecy.

Just think of what David said about his bones during the time of his guilt over the affair with Bathsheba and the murder of Uriah. "There is no soundness in my flesh because of thine anger; neither is there any rest in my bones because of my sin. (Psalm 38:3) *When I kept silence, my bones waxed old through my roaring all the day long.* (Psalm 32:3) His prayer for restoration after that transgression included a specific mention of his broken bones, *Make me to hear joy and gladness; that the bones which thou hast broken may rejoice.* (Psalm 51:8) David's literal bones were not injured or broken; however, the innermost part of his spiritual man was disturbed by his sin.

Although Jesus became sin for us (II Corinthians 5:21), He did not participate in sin (Hebrews 4:15); therefore, His inner man was free from guilt – a truth that was symbolically portrayed by ensuring that no bone was broken!

The story of how a dead man was thrown into the grave of Elisha and was raised from the dead by simply touching the prophet's bones (II Kings 13:21) takes the symbolism one step further. Jesus not only became sin for us; He also gave us new life through His sinless nature that is demonstrated in the unbroken bones!

February 6
Progression
The Christian life is marked with progression. We are to constantly be developing from one position in grace to another. This development is expressed in terms of movement – moving from some negative things and toward other positive things. Just look at the partial list of negative qualities that we are to walk away from and positive attributes that we are to walk into:

Romans 6:4 – in newness of life.

Romans 8:1 – after the Spirit, not after the flesh

Romans 13:13 – honesty

Romans 14:15 – charitably

1 Corinthians 3:3 – not as carnal men

2 Corinthians 4:2 – not in craftiness

2 Corinthians 5:7 – by faith, not by sight

Galatians 2:14 – uprightly according to the truth

Ephesians 2:2 – not according to the course of this world and the prince of the power of the air

Ephesians 2:10 – in good works

Ephesians 4:1 – worthy of your vocation

Ephesians 4:17 – not in the vanity of the mind

Ephesians 5:2 – in love

Ephesians 5:8 – as children of light

Ephesians 5:15 – circumspectly

Colossians 1:10 – worthy of the Lord

Colossians 4:5 – in wisdom

I Thessalonians 4:12 – honestly

II Thessalonians 3:6 – not disorderly busybodies

I Peter 4:3 – not in lasciviousness and such

II Peter 3:3 – not after lusts

1 John 1:6 – not in darkness

1 John 1:7 – in the light

II John 1:4 – in truth

II John 1:6 – after his commandments

February 7

Passing It On – Part I

We all know that the most powerful leader of the early church was the Apostle Paul; however, his story wouldn't even exist without the man who invested in him and the ones who carried on his ministry. After his conversion, Saul of Tarsus found acceptance among the believers in Jerusalem impossible since they feared that his conversion was only a ploy to get inside information that would lead to raids, arrests, trials, and executions. Fortunately, one person believed him and helped him gain acceptance – Barnabas. Before long, the situation in the city grew so hostile that Saul had to escape in order to save his own life. He resorted to Caesarea and then to his hometown of Tarsus. Later, when some Greeks in the Syrian city of Antioch accepted the gospel and were in need of someone to disciple them, Barnabas stepped to the forefront and traveled to Tarsus to recruit Saul to come to Antioch and mentor these gentile believers.

Years later, Paul found a young man in whom he saw exceptional leadership potential. Now, Paul stepped forward in the same way that Barnabas had done for him and – taking this young disciple under his wing – transformed Timothy into one of the most significant movers and shakers of the second generation of Christianity. In essence, Paul promoted Timothy the same way Barnabas had promoted him.

We all know the principle of reaping what we have sown, but the lesson we can learn from this story about Barnabas, Paul, and Timothy is to sow into the lives of others what we have reaped from the care and concern of those who invested in us when we were young believers. We must continue to re-develop discipleship in every generation.

February 8
Passing It On – Part II

In the one page I have allotted for the daily meditation, I cannot address the full parallel between the two epistles of Ephesians and Colossians; however, if you were to take the time to read through the two letters side-by-side, you would soon realize that they essentially follow the same outline. However, there are two significant differences between them. In the first chapter of Colossians, Paul incorporated "The Christ Hymn" (Colossians 1:14-20), a section of scripture that epitomizes the revelation of the Risen Christ. Paul does not incorporate a similar section in Ephesians. On the other hand, he gives a strong teaching on putting on the armor of God in order to stand against the attacks of the enemy in the concluding chapter of Ephesians – a teaching that is omitted in Colossians.

In Colossians 2:15, Paul summarizes his teaching on spiritual warfare by boldly proclaiming that the victory has already been won, *Having spoiled principalities and powers, he made a shew of them openly, triumphing over them in it.* In this context, it seems clear that a truly spiritual believer should not have to be taught how to struggle since our real position is one of authority over the forces of the enemy. Of course, this teaching is not omitted in Ephesians. After all, it is in this letter that we are taught that we are seated with Christ far above all spiritual powers and that we are in a position of standing unwaveringly when confronted by them. The lack of specific reference to the spiritual armor seems to be an encouragement to always view the battle as already settled. And how are we to come to that conclusion? Through highly exalting the victorious Risen Christ! In essence, we dethrone the enemy by simply enthroning Christ!

February 9
Suddenly
I remember doing various laboratory procedures when I was a chemist that required a certain amount of time for the reaction to take place. It was always amazing to me that the chemicals could sit in the Pyrex beaker for a period of time with seemingly no results until – all of a sudden – everything would change. The consistency would morph, the color would be altered, and there might even be a release of heat. You've probably also seen the same sort of thing happen in your kitchen. When mixing the ingredients for a cake, it takes a certain number of stokes with the beater before the mixture suddenly takes on the nature of batter and can be baked into a delicacy.

The same is true in the spiritual world. There is a set time when all the necessary ingredients for supernatural reactions suddenly combine to bring about incredible change. The Living Bible translation of II Chronicles 20:22 records that God set ambushments against the enemy at the moment that the people of Israel began to sing and praise Him. Haggai reports that it was on the very day that the people returned to the repairs on the temple that their cycle of poverty was broken. (Haggai 2:18-19) When all the proper spiritual ingredients are properly blended together under the correct conditions, something miraculous happens – everything changes in an instant. The prayers, the witnessing, and the loving and nurturing that all seem so unrelated suddenly congeal in the salvation of the loved one that has seemed so resistant. The faith, the giving, and the anticipation seem to instantly precipitate in the miraculous financial supply. God has a set time for our miracle to come suddenly. We just have to keep on mixing the ingredients until that time comes.

February 10

In Whom I'm Well Pleased

On two different occasions in the life of Jesus, the Father spoke audibly from heaven saying that He was the beloved Son in whom the Father was well pleased – at His baptism (Matthew 3:17) and at the Transfiguration (Matthew 17:5). Although Jesus was well into His earthly ministry at the time of the Transfiguration, He hadn't even begun to do any ministry at the time of the baptism. Yet, He was just as loved and was just as well pleasing to the Father at the first of His ministry as He was after He had been teaching, preaching, cleansing lepers, restoring sight to the blind, healing the sick, and casting out devils. Of course, it could be argued that Jesus had earned the Father's love through the act of willfully surrendering His position in heaven in order to come to earth to redeem the human race. It seems to me that the message we should read from this gospel story is that Jesus was God's beloved Son and well pleasing to the Father even before He did anything to earn any credits.

In exactly the same way that we love our babies from the second that they are born, God loved Jesus without His having to do anything to earn that love. In like manner, He loves us extravagantly without our having to earn His favor. As radical as that statement may seem in a society that equates acceptance with earned or deserved merit, it is actually a huge understatement. Romans 5:8-10 teaches us that God loved us and that Jesus sacrificed His life for us while we were still His declared enemies! Okay, so God loves without our having to earn it; but, is He well pleased without our efforts. Let's think back about our babies – yes, we are pleased with them, even when we may not be pleased with their actions!

February 11

Gatekeepers

My missionary work takes me out of the country several times each year, and I have to deal with a number of different inspections every time I travel –TSA officers at the security screening point, passport officials at every border, and customs officers before I'm allowed out of the airport. Each of these individuals serves an important role in ensuring the safety of the people of their country by guarding the influences that are allowed to pass their checkpoints.

In the Bible, the gates of a city are symbolic of authority because that is where the elders and decision makers of the city gathered to hold their court and council. (Genesis 19:1; Deuteronomy 16:18, 22:15, 25:7; Ruth 4:11; II Samuel 19:8; Esther 2:21; Proverbs 24:7, 31:23) Those men who sat at the gates as gatekeepers were like the TSA agents, customs officers, and passport control officials of today. Since the gates they guarded were interfaces between their city and the society outside of the city, the city elders and leaders were positioned there to filter out any influence that they did not want to enter their society. The gates were open so that commerce and trade could occur, but the gatekeepers made sure that undesirable men with dangerous philosophies or contraband didn't take advantage of the open door policy to get inside and damage their society.

Dr. Lester Sumrall often referred to the believers in a city as gatekeepers in that they are responsible to defend the city from detrimental influences – through spiritual warfare, through political action, through educating the general populace in righteousness, through raising up godly families, and through nurturing the Body of Christ into holiness.

February 12

Puns For Educated Minds

The fattest knight at King Arthur's round table was Sir Cumference. He   acquired his size from too much pi.

I thought I saw an eye doctor on an Alaskan island, but it turned out to be an optical Aleutian.

She was a whiskey maker, but he loved her still.

A rubber band pistol was confiscated from algebra class, because it was a weapon of math disruption.

No matter how much you push the envelope, it'll still be stationery.

A dog gave birth to puppies near the road and was cited for littering.

A grenade thrown into a kitchen in France would result in Linoleum Blownapart.

Two silk worms had a race. They ended in a tie.

A hole has been found in the nudist camp wall. The police are looking into it.

Time flies like an arrow. Fruit flies like a banana.

Atheism is a non-prophet organization.

Two hats were hanging on a hat rack in the hallway. One hat said to the other: You stay here; I'll go on a head.

I wondered why the baseball kept getting bigger. Then it hit me.

A sign on the lawn at a drug rehab center said: Keep off the Grass.

The midget fortune-teller who escaped from prison was a small medium at large.

The soldier who survived mustard gas and pepper spray is now a seasoned veteran.

A backward poet writes inverse.

February 13

Prayers of Paul

Paul recorded four of his specific prayers for the believers in the churches. Interestingly enough, a key element in each of these prayers was knowledge. In Ephesians 1:15, he prayed that they might have the spirit of wisdom and revelation in the knowledge of Him. Later in the same letter, he interceded for the believers that they might know the love of Christ, which passes knowledge. (Ephesians 3:19) His prayer for the Philippians was that they would abound even more and more in knowledge. (Philippians 1:9) His constant request for the Colossian church was that they would be filled with the knowledge of God's will in all wisdom and spiritual understanding. (Colossians 1:9-13)

Seeing this emphasis on godly knowledge, it is easy to understand why he insisted that our distinction from the world is that we have renewed our minds. (Romans 12:2) Realizing the principle so aptly proclaimed by King Solomon – as a man thinks in his heart, so is he (Proverbs 23:7) – Paul knew that the only way to advance the church was to get them to change their thinking and educate themselves in the things of God.

Notice how he defined the influences that can destroy our spiritual health, *Casting down imaginations, and every high thing that exalteth itself against the knowledge of God, and bringing into captivity every thought to the obedience of Christ.* (II Corinthians 10:5) Our spiritual maturity and victory are determined by what we know and how we focus our thoughts. If we don't concentrate on different truths from those of our unsaved friends, we will never be able to live with any more victory or authority than they do. As soon as we change our mental focus, we change our destiny.

Valentine's Day

Love Stories

In Berlin, Germany, an eighty-two-year-old gentleman picked a carrot that was wearing his wedding band that he lost while gardening – just after his fiftieth wedding anniversary.

Ian Johnstone missed his girlfriend so much that he flew back to Britain from Australia to propose to her. She had the same idea and flew to Australia. Johnstone and Amy Dolly missed each other as they sat in the same airport lounge in Singapore at the same time waiting for connecting flights. But they did find a way to make the story end happily ever after.

Of course, the greatest love story in all of eternity is recorded by the Apostle John – the one whom Jesus loved.

> *For God so loved the world, that he gave his only begotten Son, that whosoever believeth in him should not perish, but have everlasting life. For God sent not his Son into the world to condemn the world; but that the world through him might be saved...In this was manifested the love of God toward us, because that God sent his only begotten Son into the world, that we might live through him. Herein is love, not that we loved God, but that he loved us, and sent his Son to be the propitiation for our sins...We love him, because he first loved us.* (John 3:16-17, I John 4:9-19)

As you express your love to your husband, wife, girlfriend, or boyfriend today, be sure to remember the greatest Lover you have ever known.

Presidents Day
Quotes from Our Former Presidents

George Washington: It is the duty of all nations to acknowledge the providence of Almighty God, to obey His will, to be grateful for His benefits, and humbly to implore His protection and favor.

John Adams: We have no government armed with power capable of contending with human passions unbridled by morality and religion. Our Constitution was made only for a moral and religious people. It is wholly inadequate to the government of any other.

James Madison: Before any man can he considered as a member of civil society, he must be considered as a subject of the Governor of the Universe.

Thomas Jefferson: And can the liberties of a nation be thought secure when we have removed their only firm basis, a conviction in the minds of the people that these liberties are the gift of God? That they are not to be violated but with His wrath? Indeed, I tremble for my country when I reflect that God is just; that His justice cannot sleep forever.

John Quincy Adams: Is it not that in the chain of human events, the birthday of the nation is indissolubly linked with the birthday of the Savior? That it forms a leading event in the progress of the Gospel dispensation? Is it not that the Declaration of Independence first organized the social compact on the foundation of the Redeemer's mission upon earth? That it laid the cornerstone of human government upon the first precepts of Christianity?

February 16
Where Have All the Christians Gone?

Christianity (Catholics and Protestants) is the world's largest religion, with almost two and a half billion adherents – about a third of the world's population. In 2010, there were just less than five hundred sixty million Christians in Europe, more than five hundred thirty million in Latin America, almost five hundred twenty million in Sub-Sahara Africa, close to two hundred ninety million in Asia and the Pacific, over two hundred sixty million in North America, and twelve million in the Middle East and North Africa.

The world population of Christians is in a state of shift today. For example, Christianity was the main religion in Egypt between the fourth and sixth centuries; today Egypt is a Muslim stronghold. Just a couple hundred years ago, England was the major evangelical force that was spreading the gospel around the world; today, only about four percent of the country's population claim to be born again. In 2010, one and a half percent of the world's evangelical Christians were in Sub-Sahara Africa; today, almost a quarter of the world's evangelical population is in the region – over sixty percent of the local population. By 2050, there will be more than a billion Christians (thirty-eight percent of the world's Christians) in this part of Africa. You will probably be amazed to hear that sixteen thousand African Muslims convert to Christianity every day and that Christianity is the fastest growing religion in Iran. With the current rate of growth in some regions and decline in others, two-thirds of Christians will live in Africa, Asia, and Latin America by 2025. By 2050, only one fifth of the world's Christians will be non-Hispanic whites.

February 17
Words of Wisdom

We are too young to realize that certain things are impossible...
So we will do them anyway. — William Wilberforce

A wise man should have money in his head, but not in his
heart. – Jonathan Swift

Muhammad Ali refused to put on a seatbelt by telling the
stewardess, "Superman didn't need a seatbelt." She
replied, "He didn't need an airplane either."

Man does not live by words alone – despite the fact that he
sometimes has to eat them. – Adlai Stevenson

The man who keeps on going will either get there himself or
make it possible for a later man to reach the goal. – LBJ

Never let the fear of striking out get in your way. – Babe Ruth

In making Oriental rugs, errors are craftfully woven into the
pattern. We need to do the same in life. – Norman
Vincent Peale

Incompetent people never ruin an organization. They never get
to the position to do so. The problem is successful
people who get into position and rest on their
achievements, forever clogging things up. – Henry Ford

The best way out is through. – Robert Frost

If you are going to think anyway, why not thing big? – Donald
Trump

Rodney Dangerfield took the universal experience of being
miserable and made something funny out of it.

Charlton Heston said that you never get it right, but your goal
can always be to get it right one time.

A winner is someone who recognizes his God-given talents,
works his tail off to develop them into skills, and uses
those skills to accomplish his goals. – Larry Bird

February 18
Who Has All Power – Jesus or the Devil?

According to Matthew, Jesus is the one with all power; however, II Thessalonians makes it sound as if the devil is the one with all power. I honestly doubt if any of us would – ideologically – really think that there is actually a contest. Our immediate response would be that, without a doubt, it is Jesus who is the all-powerful one. However – in practice – we often act like it is the devil who has the upper hand. It just so happens that these two verses may actually help us to understand why we react this way. Although the two verses seem to say the same thing in English, they bear distinctly different messages in the Greek text. In Matthew, Jesus announced that He has all *exousia* (authority); in II Thessalonians, Paul confirms that Satan has all *dunamis* (physical strength).

To get an image of what these two words communicate, let's envision that an armed bandit has broken into your house. Of course, your first response would be one of fear because of the loaded gun in the hand of a criminal who has aggressively barged into your home. At this point, the intruder is the one with all strength since you don't have any weapon with which to defend yourself. Fortunately, your house is wired with a burglar alarm system that notifies the local police precinct when the system has been violated. Before the invader can do any harm, you hear the sound of sirens and see red and blue lights flashing outside the front window of your house. Upon realizing that the police are on the scene, the thief rushes for the backdoor in an attempt to escape. Immediately, your anxieties begin to fade – even though the police have not yet entered the house and you haven't seen their drawn firearms.

Who Has All Power – Part II

The scenario I described in yesterday's meditation contrasts *dunamis* and *exousia* perfectly in that the thief had physical strength in the form of his loaded gun and the police demonstrated authority in their lights and siren. Of course, their authority was backed up by physical force with their arsenal of weapons; however, the thief fled before even seeing what kinds of firearms they were wielding. Authority overruled physical strength.

The wonderful promise from our Lord is that He has given us both physical strength and spiritual authority. Thus, we can live in assurance and confidence no matter what conditions we are forced to confront. In reality, the answer to the question of who has all power is, "We do!"

> *When he had called unto him his twelve disciples, he gave them power against unclean spirits, to cast them out, and to heal all manner of sickness and all manner of disease.* (Matthew 10:1)
>
> *He ordained twelve, that they should be with him, and that he might send them forth to preach, And to have power to heal sicknesses, and to cast out devils.* (Mark 3:14-15)
>
> *He called unto him the twelve, and began to send them forth by two and two; and gave them power over unclean spirits.* (Mark 6:7)
>
> *Then he called his twelve disciples together, and gave them power and authority over all devils, and to cure diseases.* (Luke 9:1)
>
> *Behold, I give unto you power to tread on serpents and scorpions, and over all the power of the enemy: and nothing shall by any means hurt you.* (Luke 10:19)

February 20
Roaring Lions – Part I
In Ezekiel 22:25, the prophet is addressing the backsliding and rebelliousness of the people of Israel and of Jerusalem in specific, *There is a conspiracy of her prophets in the midst thereof, like a roaring lion ravening the prey; they have devoured souls; they have taken the treasure and precious things; they have made her many widows in the midst thereof.* In doing so, he "leaves no stone unturned" – addressing every level of society, including the common people, the royalty, the clergy, and the prophets. Concerning the prophets, who were supposed to be the voice of God to bring guidance and correction to those in all the other strata of society, he says that they have formed a conspiracy. This means that the error was not the act of any one individual prophet or even the acts of several or all the prophets acting randomly and independently of one another. On the contrary, they have all coordinated together to perpetrate one united plot against the people. This conspiracy he likens to the attack of a roaring lion. Looking back at this passage from a New Testament perspective, we immediately recognize the underlying message that this is the work of the devil himself in that Peter has alerted us to the fact that the devil is indeed a roaring lion seeking whom he may devour.

With this insight, we can see the epitome of the enemy's craftiness in that he perverted the very messengers whose purpose it was to correct and guide. Now, instead of directing the people into godliness, they were actually devouring and robbing them. Furthermore, the conspiracy of the prophets is an orchestrated and organized plan.

February 21
Roaring Lions – Part II
The tragic reality is that the devil is still using the same approach from Ezekiel 22:25 today – and we haven't yet caught on to his ploy.

In my own lifetime, I have had the vantage point to watch this same scenario played out through the modern-day counterpart of the prophetic ministry. Back in the 1970s when I was in seminary, there was a strong emphasis on the message of love. Yes, God loves everyone and calls us to also love everyone. However, the simple deviation from the true course of biblical truth was the idea that love negated judging. In other words, if I loved you I would not hold you accountable. Once that idea was fairly widely accepted, the specific issue of homosexuality began to be discussed in light of this new mindset – and I don't need to tell you where things went from there.

The conspiracy started among the theologians who were then able to infiltrate the thinking of the pastors who in turn were able to influence the mentality of their congregations – including leaders in business, education, and government. Before long, the minds of a whole generation – many of whom had no direct connection with the church – had been poisoned. It was the work of a roaring lion seeking whom he could devour.

Praise God, there is another lion who is not in a conspiracy to devour – the Lion of the Tribe of Judah!

> *One of the elders saith unto me, Weep not: behold, the Lion of the tribe of Judah, the Root of David, hath prevailed.* (Revelation 5:5)

February 22
The World was God's Plan All Along
Part I

And the scripture, foreseeing that God would justify the heathen through faith, preached before the gospel unto Abraham, saying, In thee shall all nations be blessed. (Galatians 3:8)

It is interesting to me that so many Christians are not aware that God's plan to save the world didn't begin with the Great Commission. In fact, it would be more realistic to say that the Great Commission was more like His last word on the topic rather than His initiation. Actually, from before creation, God's plan was that the whole human race would be redeemed. (Ephesians 4:1) But let's leave that point for another day since the verse that we are looking at today starts with the time of Abraham.

When God first called Abraham, He gave him a superlative covenant that heaped blessings upon him and his seed. However, these covenant promises were concluded with the criterion that, in Abraham and his seed, all the families of the earth would be blessed. In all actuality, the blessings that God promised to Abraham and the Jewish nation that would be birthed through him were essentially advertisements to the rest of the world. The basic idea was that God intended to make the Jewish people so prosperous that they would catch the attention of everyone else – and, in doing so, make them jealous enough to know what the secret behind their prosperity was. (Deuteronomy 4:7)

The World was God's Plan All Along
Part II

Please pardon the analogy, but hopefully it will communicate the point. I've met several top-rung members of multi-level marketing companies, and they were all millionaires – by design! The point is that the companies structured their programs so that they could make a few people very wealthy, very quickly. Then, they promoted the stories of these successful individuals as a means for recruiting more people to join the scheme with hopes of recreating the same wealth for themselves. Now, I know that that is a very poor analogy since there was no greed or manipulation involved in what God did with Abraham. The thing I wanted to illustrate is that the multi-level marketing companies were not as interested in making their selected "poster boys" rich as they were in being able to use their success as a way to recruit new associates into their programs.

Yes, God did want to bless Abraham specifically and does continue to want to purposely bless the Jews; however, His vision was far bigger than that – He wanted to use the Jews as a catalyst to reach the nations. On this side of the cross, His heart is still the same. Yes, He wants to bless you and me individually – but His real heart is that those blessings flow through us, not just to us. Jesus gives us health, wealth, and spiritual anointing so we can fulfill the commission that He verbalized just before His ascension back to the Father, "Go into all the world and be my witnesses!"

February 24
Acceleration – Part I

I first learned computer data entry and programming in the days of Fourtran – the pioneer computer system that operated on punch cards. Back then, it would take whole trays of cards to enter the necessary commands to get the computer to do even the simplest of tasks. Additionally, the hardware of the computer system had to be housed in a full-size building rather than on a desktop or even in a handheld portable devise. In those days, we had to book a time to submit our trays of cards and then wait hours – or even days – for the results to come back. You could only pity the person who made one punch error and had to repeat the whole process – possibly delaying his project for several days.

Then came the advancements in technology that did away with the punch card and brought the "brain" of the computer right into our own homes. Next came the introduction of the information highway that we know of today as the Internet. However, the only way we had to access this wonderful new tool was through our telephone line – meaning that we had to either have a second line installed or disconnect our phone in order to take a ride on the information highway. Those were the days of dial-up, a process that seems unimaginably laborious according to today's standards even though it was miraculous to us at the time.

Please be patient until tomorrow so that I can apply this idea to our spiritual lives.

February 25

Acceleration – Part II

Well, to the point of the lesson. Now that we live in the fiber optic world, it is almost impossible to imagine how we ever survived in the days of dial-up, much less Fourtran! In fact, my son was using my internet service the other day and mumbled the whole time because it was so slow. I tried to contain myself as I thought about what he would have said had he been given a dial-up system. Of course, he had my service upgraded – but that's beside the point.

Today, I want to remind us that we live in an age when not only the computer systems are accelerating – so is the true work of God. It took the Gideon's ninety-seven years to distribute their first billion Bibles, the second billion were passed out in only fourteen years. When I try to get a grasp on how rapidly people are being won to the Lord through the ministry of Every Home for Christ, I want to throw my hands in the air – both in celebration and in frustration. I celebrate how many new converts are coming to the Lord on a daily basis, but I just can't keep up with the acceleration. By the time I get one statistic recorded, it is already out of date.

We live in a world of acceleration, but my question would be whether we, as individuals, are stagnant or are we moving forward with God's increased pace. Let go of Fourtran and dial-up and get on board with God's latest and fastest.

February 26

Ambassadors – Part I

In my travels around the world, I've had the privilege of meeting several ambassadors – and even staying in one's home. The interesting thing about them was how ordinary they were – well, at least to me. That is because they (except for the one in whose home I was a house guest) were Americans and I am an American. However, I'm sure that the average citizens of the country where they were serving would not have thought of them as ordinary people.

Since the scripture defines us as ambassadors from heaven to this present world (II Corinthians 5:20), it would be appropriate for us to draw a parallel between these ambassadors that I've met around the world in order to understand our intended role in the world. I've already said that the ambassadors were quite ordinary men and women to me. This was because they lived like Americans – a lifestyle that I was totally accustomed to. In the spiritual realm, we – as ambassadors of heaven – should live exactly in accordance with the standards of heaven's lifestyle. Just as I have never seen an American ambassador living in a mud hut even though the people of the nation where he was serving did so, ambassadors of heaven are not expected to adapt to the standard of the world where they are assigned. No, we won't have mansions lining golden streets, but we can have homes filled with righteousness, peace, and joy – the spiritual substance of heaven. (Romans 14:17)

Ambassadors – Part II

All the ambassadors I've ever met spoke fluent English even though they lived in countries where only an elite minority could understand English. Oh yes, many of them had learned the local language for communication purposes, but their standard was always English. Likewise, the ambassadors of heaven need to be fluent in the language of the country they represent. It is good that we can understand the language of the people whom we serve so that we can understand their needs and situation; however, we must never be trapped into speaking like they do – with negativism, deception, and ridicule. (John 17:15)

Additionally, ambassadors follow the laws of the local country out of respect for the people and the government they are serving; however, they are actually only subject to the legal system of the United States. Likewise, ambassadors of the kingdom of heaven must abide by the transcendent laws of the kingdom while following the legal requirements of the present temporal system.

In the life of Paul, we see several examples where he exercised his rights as a Roman citizen to protect him from unwarranted beatings and imprisonments – and he wasn't even an ambassador of the imperial force. Imagine how much more authority his words would have carried had be been able to say that he was more than just a citizen – that he was an ambassador. Although he wasn't able to make that claim in the natural, he did have that right in the spiritual realm – and by exerting that authority, he made the demons tremble and back down!

Busybodies

But let none of you suffer as a murderer, or
as a thief, or as an evildoer, or as a busybody
in other men's matters. (I Peter 4:15)

Hold the bus! There's something here that needs our attention! Being a busybody is listed in the same category with being a murderer or a thief. Now, that requires an explanation. It may seem a bit out of kilter from the immediate surface reading; however, it actually makes logical sense once we stop to think about it. When a person intrudes into another person's affairs, he is essentially doing the same thing that a thief does. Whereas a thief steals an individual's physical property, a busybody steals his emotional and intellectual property – the essence of what is known today as an invasion of privacy. When we intrude into other people's private lives, we steal from them their dignity and rob them of their dreams and aspirations by exposing their private lives before their plans and visions have come to full maturity. In such cases, we also murder the potential for those dreams and visions to become realities – and, therefore, derail, destroy, delay, deter, or detour the person's future. In other words, we murder him while he is still living in that we don't take his physical life but we destroy his hopes and plans for the future.

Now, this does not mean that we are not to involve ourselves in the lives of others – we just don't barge in uninvited or stalk them against their will. The biblical approach to investing in the lives of others is known as edifying them. *Let us therefore follow after the things which make for peace, and things wherewith one may edify another.* (Romans 14:19)

February 29

Interpretation

First Corinthians 4:5 warns us that we should never judge anything until the Lord comes to clarify everything and remove all misrepresentations and erroneous assumptions. I'm certain that Paul had an apocalyptic, futuristic time of judgment in mind when he spoke of the Lord's coming. But I suspect that it is not out of line to apply this verse to the "aha" moments when we suddenly get enlightenment on a situation.

For a case in point, let me share about a situation that I encountered in Nigeria. While still in the US, I was reading reports of a new law that was poised to attack the religious freedom of the Christians in Kaduna State in the country. The result was that a strong prayer movement was interceding for the persecuted believers and the oppressive government in that state. However, when I got to Nigeria, I had the privilege of meeting the very man who had initiated the whole plan. He was a very strong Christian and an incredibly likable gentleman. Rather than intending to oppress believers, his whole intent was to protect and bless them. He knew that the Christian pastors had nothing to hide from the general public; therefore, there was nothing offensive about asking for copies of their sermons. On the other hand, he wanted to expose everything that was being said in the Muslim mosques.

The irony of the situation was that Christians all over the world were "binding and loosing" something that was actually intended to bless rather than curse Christians.

The point of the lesson is that God is the only one who has the right to interpret dreams, visions, and circumstances. Let's stop jumping to conclusions and allow Him to have the last word!

March 1

Voice Activated

Voice activation is very interesting and helpful. We can speak to Siri and get all sorts of helpful information, phone numbers, weather forecasts, and directions to our destinations. My son can turn on the lights in his house, adjust the temperature, and do all sorts of other amazing feats. Other people I know can select the type of music that they want to hear on their radios and even get a specific song on demand. It's mind-boggling what this modern technology can do.

But the fact is that voice activation is not new technology at all. In fact, it was actually the first technology that was ever developed. In the very creation process, the universe came into being as a result of God's voice activated technology. Furthermore, that same technology of voice activation has been available to each of us since the days of Jesus. He gave us power to speak to our problems and see them respond.

> *For verily I say unto you, That whosoever shall say unto this mountain, Be thou removed, and be thou cast into the sea; and shall not doubt in his heart, but shall believe that those things which he saith shall come to pass; he shall have whatsoever he saith.*
> (Mark 11:23)

Let's not waste this God-given ability on simply getting directions, turning on lights, and selecting the music we want to hear. Let's use it for its original purpose – manifesting the authority of God in a world that has fallen subject to much lesser powers.

March 2
Loving Others as Ourselves – Part I
Have you ever wondered about the contradiction of terms in our Christian vocabulary? We are taught that selfishness is a sin and that we should be self-sacrificing and selfless. (Luke 9:23) Then, on the other hand, we are taught that the second greatest commandment is to love others as ourselves. (Mark 12:30-31) If we are to be so self-abasing and so oriented to others rather than ourselves, how can we know how to love others since we are denying ourselves rather than loving ourselves?

The whole issue is that we have erroneously developed an either-or mentality when the kingdom of God actually operates on the both-and value system. You see, we think that there is just so much of any particular commodity available; therefore, for you to have more, I must have less. On the contrary, the God we serve is El Shaddai – the God of More than Enough. (Genesis 17:1) Therefore, there is plenty to go around so that no one has to suffer in order for others to be blessed. Let's begin with some non-physical things to make the point easier to grasp. Let's take smiles for instance. If I share a smile, it in no way diminishes the quantity of smiles I have access to. The same goes with words of encouragement, joy, good wishes – and the list can go on and on. Actually, the same is true with the physical necessities in the world as well. I don't have to deny myself breath so you can breathe. I don't have to stop enjoying the sunrise so that you can appreciate it. I don't have to get out of the sunshine in order to allow you to experience its warmth.

Tomorrow, we will explore how this principle applies to material blessings as well.

March 3
Loving Others as Ourselves – Part II

If you were to research the statistics, you'd find that there is plenty of food so that every human can eat full, healthy meals, enough water for everyone to have a sufficient supply, enough gold and silver so that no human needs to live on a substandard wage. It is literally impossible to find anything that is lacking on our planet.

The only problem is that humans don't think like God. (Romans 12:2) He thinks that He loves us to the point where He wants to give us more than we could ever imagine or dare to think about asking for. Why? Because He knows that there is more than enough. On the other, our mentality is that there is barely enough – or maybe even a shortage – therefore, we feel that we have to make a choice in whether we want to love and bless others or ourselves. Wishing that others are blessed is the remedy for covetousness. You can have what you want as long as you don't wish for others to suffer so you can get it.

The other dimension to which we need to apply this concept is the spiritual dimension. We obviously know that there is no shortage to the love and grace of God; however, we live as if we feel that it is actually on ration. Oftentimes, we act as if there isn't even enough for ourselves – much less, enough to share with others. Just think about all the times when you have wondered if God had enough healing to take care of your ailment or enough forgiveness to handle your shortcoming. Now, remember all the times when you questioned if He had sufficient healing for your terminally ill friend or family member or adequate grace to deal with a homeless person's addiction. Let me assure you that He does – and even more!

March 4
March Forth – Part I
I've always felt that today should be declared International Missions Day. After all, the very name of the day proclaims the whole purpose of missions. Therefore, I'd like to dedicate our meditation today and the next few days to some great missions quotations.

As long as there are millions destitute of the Word of God and knowledge of Jesus Christ, it will be impossible for me to devote time and energy to those who have both. – J. L. Ewen

The command has been to "go," but we have stayed – in body, gifts, prayer and influence. He has asked us to be witnesses unto the uttermost parts of the earth...but 99% of Christians have kept puttering around in the homeland. – Robert Savage, Latin American Mission

People who do not know the Lord ask why in the world we waste our lives as missionaries. They forget that they too are expending their lives...and when the bubble has burst, they will have nothing of eternal significance to show for the years they have wasted. – Nate Saint, missionary martyr

We must be global Christians with a global vision because our God is a global God. – John Stott

Believers who have the gospel keep mumbling it over and over to themselves. Meanwhile, millions who have never heard it once fall into the flames of eternal hell without ever hearing the salvation story. – K.P. Yohannan, founder of Gospel for Asia Bible Society

Tell the students to give up their small ambitions and come eastward to preach the gospel of Christ. – Francis Xavier, missionary to India, the Philippines, and Japan

March 5

March Forth – Part II

The mark of a great church is not its seating capacity, but its sending capacity. – Mike Stachura

"Not called!" did you say? "Not heard the call," I think you should say. – William Booth, founder of the Salvation Army

It is not in our choice to spread the gospel or not. It is our death if we do not. – Peter Taylor Forsyth

If God's love is for anybody anywhere, it's for everybody everywhere. – Edward Lawlor, Nazarene General Superintendent

Never pity missionaries; envy them. They are where the real action is – where life and death, sin and grace, Heaven and Hell converge. – Robert C. Shannon

People who don't believe in missions have not read the New Testament. Right from the beginning Jesus said the field is the world. The early church took Him at His word and went East, West, North and South. – J. Howard Edington

In no other way can the believer become as fully involved with God's work, especially the work of world evangelism, as in intercessory prayer. – Dick Eastman, president of Every Home for Christ

What's your dream and to what corner of the missions world will it take you? – Eleanor Roat, missions mobilizer

We can reach our world, if we will. The greatest lack today is not people or funds. The greatest need is prayer. – Wesley Duewel, head of OMS International

Love is the root of missions; sacrifice is the fruit of missions. – Roderick Davis

March Forth – Part III
Missionary zeal does not grow out of intellectual beliefs, nor out of theological arguments, but out of love. – Roland Allen

I have but one passion: It is He, it is He alone. The world is the field and the field is the world; and henceforth that country shall be my home where I can be most used in winning souls for Christ. – Count Nicolaus Ludwig von Zinzendorf

If you take missions out of the Bible, you won't have anything left but the covers. – Nina Gunter

If the Church is in Christ, she is involved in missions. Her whole existence then has a missionary character. Her conduct as well as her words will convince the unbelievers and put their ignorance and stupidity to silence. – David Bosch

Missions is not the "ministry of choice" for a few hyperactive Christians in the church. Missions is the purpose of the church. – Unknown

The average pastor views his church as a local church with a missions program; while he ought to realize that if he is in fact pastoring a church, it is to be a global church with a missions purpose. – Unknown

The will of God – nothing less, nothing more, nothing else. – F. E. Marsh

The history of missions is the history of answered prayer. – Samuel Zwemer

Prayer is the mighty engine that is to move the missionary work. – A.B. Simpson

"Go ye" is as much a part of Christ's Gospel as "Come unto Me." You are not even a Christian until you have honestly faced your responsibility in regard to the carrying of the Gospel to the ends of the earth. – J. Stuart Holden

March Forth – Part IV

If the Great Commission is true, our plans are not too big; they are too small. – Pat Morley

A congregation that is not deeply and earnestly involved in the worldwide proclamation of the gospel does not understand the nature of salvation. – Ted Engstrom, World Vision

To stay here and disobey God – I can't afford to take the consequence. I would rather go and obey God than to stay here and know that I disobeyed. – Amanda Berry Smith

I believe that in each generation God has called enough men and wo men to evangelize all the yet unreached tribes of the earth. It is not God who does not call. It is man who will not respond! – Isobel Kuhn, missionary to China and Thailand

God is a God of missions. He wills missions. He commands missions. He demands missions. He made missions possible through His Son. He made missions actual in sending the Holy Spirit. – George W. Peters

The Church must send or the church will end. – Mendell Taylor

I have but one candle of life to burn, and I would rather burn it out in a land filled with darkness than in a land flooded with light. – John Keith Falconer

God's work done in God's way will never lack God's supply. – Hudson Taylor

God isn't looking for people of great faith, but for individuals ready to follow Him. – Hudson Taylor

The Great Commission is not an option to be considered; it is a command to be obeyed. – Hudson Taylor

If I had a thousand lives, I'd give them all for China. – Hudson Taylor

March Forth – Part V

God uses men who are weak and feeble enough to lean on Him. – Hudson Taylor

Expect great things from God; attempt great things for God. – William Carey

To know the will of God, we need an open Bible and an open map. – William Carey

Is not the commission of our Lord still binding upon us? Can we not do more than now we are doing? – William Carey

The spirit of Christ is the spirit of missions. The nearer we get to Him, the more intensely missionary we become. – Henry Martyn, missionary to India and Persia

He is no fool who gives up what he cannot keep to gain that which he cannot lose. – Jim Elliot, missionary martyr who lost his life in the late 1950's trying to reach the Auca Indians of Ecuador

We are debtors to every man to give him the gospel in the same measure in which we have received it. – P.F. Bresee, founder of the Church of the Nazarene

In the vast plain to the north I have sometimes seen, in the morning sun, the smoke of a thousand villages where no missionary has ever been. – Robert Moffat, who inspired David Livingstone

If a commission by an earthly king is considered an honor, how can a commission by a Heavenly King be considered a sacrifice? – David Livingstone

Sympathy is no substitute for action.– David Livingstone

Can't you do just a little bit more? – J.G. Morrison pleading with Nazarenes in the 1930's Great Depression to support their missionaries

March Forth – Part VI

Lost people matter to God, and so they must matter to us. – Keith Wright

The Bible is not the basis of missions; missions is the basis of the Bible. – Ralph Winter, missiologist

God cannot lead you on the basis of information you do not have. – Ralph Winter, missiologist on the importance of mission education

Some wish to live within the sound of a chapel bell; I wish to run a rescue mission within a yard of hell. – C.T. Studd

If Jesus Christ be God and died for me, then no sacrifice can be too great for me to make for Him. – C.T. Studd

Christ wants not nibblers of the possible, but grabbers of the impossible. – C.T. Studd

No one has the right to hear the gospel twice, while there remains someone who has not heard it once. – Oswald J. Smith

Any church that is not seriously involved in helping fulfill the Great Commission has forfeited its biblical right to exist. – Oswald J. Smith
The mission of the church is missions. – Oswald J. Smith

We talk of the Second Coming; half the world has never heard of the first. – Oswald J. Smith

This generation of Christians is responsible for this generation of souls on the earth! – Keith Green

There is nothing in the world or the Church – except the church's disobedience – to render the evangelization of the world in this generation an impossibility. – Robert Speer, leader in Student Volunteer Movement

March 10
March Forth – Part VII
If God calls you to be a missionary, don't stoop to be a king. – Charles Haddon Spurgeon

If you found a cure for cancer, wouldn't it be inconceivable to hide it from the rest of mankind? How much more inconceivable to keep silent the cure from the eternal wages of death. – Dave Davidson

World missions was on God's mind from the beginning.– Dave Davidson

In our lifetime, wouldn't it be sad if we spent more time washing dishes or swatting flies or mowing the yard or watching television than praying for world missions? – Dave Davidson

Let my heart be broken with the things that break God's heart. – Bob Pierce, World Vision founder

No reserves. No retreats. No regrets – William Borden

If ten men are carrying a log – nine of them on the little end and one at the heavy end – and you want to help, which end will you lift on? – William Borden, as he reflected on the numbers of Christian workers in the US as compared to those among unreached peoples in China

The reason some folks don't believe in missions is that the brand of religion they have isn't worth propagating. – Unknown

When James Calvert went out as a missionary to the cannibals of the Fiji Islands, the ship captain tried to turn him back, saying, "You will lose your life and the lives of those with you if you go among such savages." To that, Calvert replied, "We died before we came here."

March 11

March Forth – Part VIII

Someone asked, "Will the heathen who have never heard the Gospel be saved?" It is more a question with me whether we – who have the Gospel and fail to give it to those who have not – can be saved. – Charles Spurgeon

The gospel is only good news if it gets there in time. – Carl F. H. Henry

Our God of Grace often gives us a second chance, but there is no second chance to harvest a ripe crop. – Kurt von Schleicher

Missions is the overflow of our delight in God because missions is the overflow of God's delight in being God. – John Piper

To belong to Jesus is to embrace the nations with Him. – John Piper

God is pursuing with omnipotent passion a worldwide purpose of gathering joyful worshipers for Himself from every tribe and tongue and people and nation. He has an inexhaustible enthusiasm for the supremacy of His name among the nations. Therefore, let us bring our affections into line with His, and, for the sake of His name, let us renounce the quest for worldly comforts and join His global purpose. – John Piper

Go, send, or disobey. – John Piper

You can give without loving. But you cannot love without giving. – Amy Carmichael, missionary to India

Only as the church fulfills her missionary obligation does she justify her existence. – Unknown

March Forth – Part IX

The concern for world evangelization is not something tacked on to a man's personal Christianity, which he may take or leave as he chooses. It is rooted in the character of the God who has come to us in Christ Jesus. Thus, it can never be the province of a few enthusiasts, a sideline or a specialty of those who happen to have a bent that way. It is the distinctive mark of being a Christian. – James S. Stewart

The Christian is not obedient unless he is doing all in his power to send the Gospel to the heathen world. – A. B. Simpson

If missions languish, it is because the whole life of godliness is feeble. The command to go everywhere and preach to everybody is not obeyed until the will is lost by self-surrender in the will of God. Living, praying, giving and going will always be found together. – Arthur T. Pierson

The best remedy for a sick church is to put it on a missionary diet. – Unknown

I esteem it the crowning mercy of my life that not only the chief ends I contemplated on becoming a missionary are attained, but I am allowed to see competent, faithful, and affectionate successors actively engaged in the work. – Adoniram Judson

The man who will not act until he knows all will never act at all. – Jim Elliott

God always gives His best to those who leave the choice with him. – Jim Elliott

When it comes time to die, make sure all you got to do is die. – Jim Elliott

March 13

We Are in Christ and Christ is in Us – Part I

The New Testament apostles present a very interesting paradox concerning our relationship with Jesus. The Apostle John says that we are in Christ while at the same time He is in us. (I John 3:24) He then goes on to say that we can be sure that this is actually true in that the Holy Spirit confirms this reality. It would seem that this is the same confirmation that the Apostle Paul was speaking of in Romans 8:15-16 and Galatians 4:6 where he said that the Holy Spirit would bear witness with our human spirits by declaring that we have an intimate father-son relationship with God that allows us to address Him as "Abba" (Daddy).

In considering what the significant difference between being in Christ and having Him in us, our first thought should be that being in Christ means that we are totally new creatures from who we were before we were reborn in Him. (II Corinthians 5:17) The scriptures state this point as a determined fact, not a negotiable or optional element. On the other hand, having Christ in us is described with somewhat more leeway. In Galatians 6:12, Paul stated that he was in travail until the time when Christ would be formed in the believers. Obviously, they were in Christ – a done deal! However, it seemed that "the jury was still out" concerning the fact that Christ was in them, and Paul was taking serious responsibility to make the fact conclusive. In Ephesians 3:17, he prayed earnestly that Christ would dwell in the hearts of the believers – who, by the way, were addressed as saints and faithful ones in the opening verse of the letter. Certainly, they were in Christ, or he could not have addressed them with such definitive words; however, there was still an issue with exactly how much Christ was in them.

March 14

We Are in Christ and Christ is in Us – Part II

Perhaps, Paul gives us some insight into this question in Romans 8:9-10.

But ye are not in the flesh, but in the Spirit, if so be that the Spirit of God dwell in you. Now if any man have not the Spirit of Christ, he is none of his. And if Christ be in you, the body is dead because of sin; but the Spirit is life because of righteousness.

In this verse, he seems to suggest that we actually have some responsibility in relationship to allowing Christ to live in us through our decisions regarding following the flesh or following the spirit. There is likely an error in the way it is translated in the King James version. When Paul wrote this letter, the Greek language did not incorporate the use of capital letters as we do today. Therefore, it is likely that he was trying to say that we are in the spirit – meaning our human spirit rather than the Holy Spirit – as a contrast to being in our fleshly carnal nature. The follow-up statement is that, through having the Spirit of Christ in us, we can escape the flesh's control and become controlled by our spiritual nature.

This is why Paul travailed and interceded over the saints that they would allow Jesus to fully be in them. In what would seem to be his concluding summation on the topic, he told the Colossians that the fact that Christ was in them was their hope of glory. (verse 1:27) Allowing Jesus into our lives to the point where we are actually dead to the old carnal self and alive to the new spiritual man does indeed give us a glorious hope – in this present life as well as in the one to come! In Christ.

Palm Sunday

Why Did Jesus Ride a Donkey?

Jesus was a walker, not a rider. We never read of His ever riding on any form of transportation except an occasional boat ride – and, even then, He sometimes simply opted to walk on the water! But He had to ride this day so that He could prove His meekness and lowliness, *Rejoice greatly, O daughter of Zion; shout, O daughter of Jerusalem: behold, thy King cometh unto thee: he is just, and having salvation; lowly, and riding upon an ass, and upon a colt the foal of an ass.* (Zechariah 9:9)

The only other time we read of Jesus' riding an animal is in Revelation 19:11-16 when He will come on a white horse to judge and make war against the Antichrist and his forces. At this point, He is no longer meek and lowly; He is no longer meeting wrath with a soft answer; He is no longer is weeping for the rebel; He is no longer granting us a warning of impending judgment. Now He comes on His white steed with the full fury of God's judgment upon those who have not accepted Him when He was on His humble donkey; now He comes with a sword in His mouth to decimate those who would not heed the tearful warning He uttered from Olivet.

The choice is ours, will we cry out to Him joyful "Hosanna"s today or will we cry out in horror at His Second Coming? Over the next few days, we'll look at the events that were part of the story that played out between Palm Sunday and Good Friday. As we do, this will be an opportunity to re-evaluate our own lives and determine exactly where we would find ourselves in the crowd. This is not just history – it is His story. And we all fit into it in one role or another.

March 16

The Temple Plots

Immediately after His Triumphal Entry on Palm Sunday, Jesus went into the temple and caused a rather significant uproar. Yes, He overturned the tables of the money changers and disrupted the sale of sacrifice animals, but there was a lot more disturbance going on in the spiritual realm than in the physical. It is significant that we understand that all this merchandizing occurred in the plaza in front of the temple rather than in the building itself. This area was called the Court of the Gentiles, and the Jews didn't consider it to actually be part of the temple itself – much like we would not think of the parking lot as part of the church. However, Jesus insisted that it was also part of His Father's house which was supposed to be a house of prayer for all nations – not just for the Jews. In other words, Jesus was expanding the kingdom to all humanity, not just limiting it to the Jewish race. This act would certainly "ruffle some feathers" among the Jewish elite.

As He actually entered the temple proper, Jesus was confronted by representatives of every strata of Jewish leadership. The Pharisees and the Herodians – political and theological archrivals – team up to try to trick Him with the question about the coin. They thought that they could trick Jesus because He would have to answer in a way that would please one side of the debate and incriminate Him on the other side. Instead, He incriminated both of their parties. The Sadducees tested Him with the question about the resurrection – a theological concept that they actually denied. Then a lawyer attempted to trap Him with a question about the greatest of the commandments, thinking that any answer could be used against Him.

March 17

The Olivet Prayer

All the gospels record that, after the Triumphal Entry and the confrontation by the Jewish leaders, Jesus and His disciples went to the Mount of Olives where Jesus showed remorse over the city, the people, and their leadership, *Jerusalem, Jerusalem, how oft I would have gathered you under my wings but you would not...If only you had known the day of your visitation...Now, destruction will have to come upon you; not one stone will be left on top of another.* Rather than blasting the ones who tried to trap Him, He gave them a kind answer and allowed them yet another chance to face up to their sins. Even to the Cross, He was crying out, *Father, forgive them for they know not what they are doing.*

In the Olivet discourse, Jesus warned that destruction would come; He then outlined the signs to watch for concerning this impending doom. But notice how much grace He extended in the middle of the predictions of judgment. He repeatedly gave them opportunity to avoid the coming devastation. Notice these admonitions from Matthew's account in chapter twenty-four: Verse four, *Take heed that no man deceive you*; verse six, *See that ye be not troubled*; verse sixteen through twenty, *Flee*, verse twenty-two, *For the elect's sake those days shall be shortened*; verse twenty-three and twenty-six, *Believe it not...for...they shall deceive the very elect*, verse thirty-three, *Know that* [the end] *is near*; verse forty-two, *Watch*; verse forty-three, *Know*, and verse forty-four; *Be ye also ready: for in such an hour as ye think not the Son of man cometh.*

March 18
The Hallel Hymns

As we have seen, the leaders of the Jewish people were plotting against Jesus. When the trap that the Pharisees and Herodians had laid failed, the Sadducees stepped in with their equally unsuccessful attempt, followed by another foiled plot by the lawyer. With no more approaches to get Jesus to directly incriminate Himself, they had to turn to subterfuge in their scheme to eliminate Jesus. They hired one of Jesus' own followers to betray Him, they recruited false witnesses to fabricate indictments against Him, they pressured the Roman official into acting against his own better judgment, but – worst of all – they manipulated the emotions of the entire populace to denounce Him.

At this point, we need to remember a couple of statements from the Palm Sunday account as it is recorded in John's gospel. The reason for the Palm Sunday excitement was the banquet in honor of Lazarus' having been raised from the dead. The beloved disciple also notes that the majority of the people were there to see Lazarus, not Jesus. In their exhilaration, the people sang praises to Jesus – but it was that same excitable nature that caused them to be able to be aroused into the "Crucify Him! Crucify Him!" frenzy just a few days later.

Of course, none of this came as a surprise to God. In fact, He had already recorded history in advance – and had even incorporated it into the very Passover liturgy in that the Hallel Hymns (Psalm 118:25-26) sung during the time of the slaying of the Passover lambs actually included the prophecy about the stone that the builders rejected – the message of Jesus' denunciation and execution.

March 19
Between Good Friday and Easter Sunday

I've often wondered what was going on in the minds and hearts of the disciples on the Saturday between Good Friday and Easter Sunday.

Obviously, they were all terrified after what had just happened. If their leader had been so brutally murdered, certainly they must also be on the radar of the Pharisees and the Romans. After all, they were integral parts of Jesus' movement. Additionally, they were filled with remorse for having run away when the arresting army invaded the garden. Even Peter, who tried to bravely defend his master and friend, concluded the evening by denying Him three different times. There is no question that they were full of grief over the loss of their dear friend – the one they had abandoned houses, land, and families to be with. But there was more than just grief; there was an intensely bitter grief for the fact that He had not been taken from them in a simple passing away from natural causes – but a horrifying and torturous slaughter. Furthermore, there was dismay at the fact that they had believed without a doubt that He was to be the liberator of their nation and possibly of the entire human race. They had no question that Jesus' mission was to overturn the Roman Empire's control over the people of Israel, and it is arguable that they could have also anticipated that this revolution might have resulted in a worldwide liberation. After all, the entire world that they knew of was under the heels of the Romans.

My question is if they even had a glimmer of hope based on all that He had said about His coming death and resurrection. As we go through trials in our own lives, we can relate with all their emotions; but, we must cling to hope because resurrection is coming!

Good Friday
Three Crosses
On Passover Eve, 33 AD, at least three crosses were planted atop Golgotha's Hill. Of course, we always focus on the one in the middle; however, today, I'd like for us to take a minute to reflect on all three of them. On one cross was a thief who ridiculed Jesus – an amazing hostility considering the horrible agony he was enduring. It is unthinkable that a person going through such torture would want to invest his precious breath in mocking another crucifixion victim. On another of the crosses hung the thief who begged for Jesus' mercy – again an unthinkable response considering that the man he was praying to was being executed as a criminal just like he was, or even more brutally since we have no record that the thieves were flogged prior to their crucifixion as Jesus had been. And, of course, on the cross in our main focus hung Jesus who – even though He was totally innocent – was being mercilessly executed as if He were the most wicked of criminals.

These three crosses represent three divine options. The first thief died <u>in</u> his sin – a terrible option, but one that the majority of people choose in spite of the fact that they are graciously offered pardon through the simple act of accepting salvation through Jesus. The second thief died <u>to</u> his sin – a divine choice since salvation in Christ required of him, and us, only that he accept the free gift of eternal life. The cross that made the difference between the eternal destinies of the other two crucifixion victims bore Jesus Christ who died <u>for</u> sin – not His own sins, but for the sin of the whole world, including the thief who accepted His forgiveness, the thief who rejected His offer, you, and me!

March 21

Welcome to Spring

Today, as we celebrate the spring solstice and welcome the first day of spring, I'd like to draw on some of history's master wordsmiths to describe the feeling of new life that the season brings:

Spring is Nature's way of saying, "Let's party." – Robin Williams

When spring came, even the false spring, there were no problems except where to be happiest. The only thing that could spoil a day was people and if you could keep from making engagements, each day had no limits. People were always the limiters of happiness except for the very few that were as good as spring itself. — Ernest Hemingway

She turned to the sunlight and shook her yellow head, and whispered to her neighbor, "Winter is dead." — A.A. Milne

It is spring again. The earth is like a child that knows poems by heart. — Rainer Maria Rilke

If people did not love one another, I really don't see what use there would be in having any spring. — Victor Hugo

Spring shows what God can do with a drab and dirty world. — Victor Kraft

Behold, my friends, the spring is come; the earth has gladly received the embraces of the sun, and we shall soon see the results of their love! – Sitting Bull

The beautiful spring came; and when Nature resumes her loveliness, the human soul is apt to revive also. – Harriet Ann Jacobs

Every spring is the only spring, a perpetual astonishment. – Ellis Peters

The Resurrection

The New Testament is filled with references to the fact that Jesus was raised from the dead on Easter. (Acts 2:24, 2:32, 3:15, 3:26, 4:10, 5:30, 10:40, 13:30, 13:33, 13:34, 13:37, 17:31; Romans 4:24, 4:25, 6:4, 6:9, 7:4, 8:11, 10:9; I Corinthians 6:14, 15:15, 15:16, 15:17; II Corinthians 4:14; Galatians 1:1; Ephesians 1:20; Colossians 2:12; I Thessalonians 1:10; II Timothy 2:8; I Peter 1:21) Most of the passages state that God raised Him. At least one reference indicates that it was the Holy Spirit who raised Jesus from the dead, and several simply state that He was raised without attributing the act to any specific entity. However, there are also a number of references that state that Jesus rose from the dead (Acts 10:41; Romans 14:9; I Corinthians 15:4, 15:12; II Corinthians 5:15; I Thessalonians 4:14) rather than saying that He was raised. In this case, it seems as if Jesus brought Himself back to life. Granted, the question of whether Jesus was raised or if He rose on His own may seem like a petty issue and a question of wording; however, it seems that it may also be a window into a great revelation. In John 10:17-18, Jesus said that no one could take His life from Him but that He had the power to lay it down and pick it up again. The description of His death on the cross confirmed that He volitionally yielded up His spirit rather than being killed. (Mark 15:37, 15:39; Luke 23:46; John 19:30) In like manner in which He had authority over His own life to end it volitionally, He apparently had the authority over His death and could terminate it at will.

The point of the Easter message is that Jesus is actually God in that it could be said that God raised Him even though Jesus raised Himself!

March 23

All at Once

Joshua 10:42 says that Joshua took on all the kings of the Canaanites "at one time." The immediate impression that this statement gives is that all the armies of all the city-states in the Promised Land were lined up in one great mass against Joshua's forces. Actually, a better translation is that he fought them "one at a time" – in sequence rather than simultaneously. In fact, a number of translations suggest this reading by saying that he fought them in one campaign. In other words, he went from one victory to the next without pausing to lose momentum.

In the New Testament, we are promised the same kind of compounding victory when Paul wrote in II Corinthians 3:18 that we are changed into the same image of Jesus <u>from glory to glory</u> by the Spirit of the Lord. Just as Joshua knew that he could not stop to rest on his laurels after just one victory but that he had to press on to the next enemy and the next one after that, we understand that no matter what state we have achieved in Christ – it is not our ultimate achievement. Paul testified from his own experience that, even when he was near the end of his life and ministry, he had not yet attained (Philippians 3:12) but was continuing to press toward the goal before him (Philippians 3:14).

Unfortunately, there are those in the Body of Christ who feel that they "got it all" when they were saved. They feel that they dealt with all their issues at one time as it seems on the surface that Joshua did. Hopefully, they will read a little deeper and figure out that they have to face their challenges one at a time as Joshua really did.

Keep pressing for the high mark, a step at a time.

Becoming a Son of God – Part I

But as many as received him, to them gave he power to become the sons of God, even to them that believe on his name. (John 1:12)

Become the sons of God – very interesting wording. After all, aren't we sons of God from the moment we are born again? If so, why does John say that we will become His sons? A similar discussion erupted in one of my classes when I made mention of spiritually maturing. One of my students challenged me with the argument that our spirit man is totally like Jesus from the moment of our salvation. The only way I could get him to listen long enough to hear what I was saying was to point him to the biblical concept of a man child. (Genesis 17:10) How can we be men and children at the same time? Even though this may seem like a contradiction of terms, it is actually a clear description of the principle that is at play here. From the moment of conception, the new life has in it all the parental DNA that it will ever have. However, if you look at the pictures of the baby as it develops through the stages of zygote, embryo, and fetus in a biology book, you'll wonder if it is even a human in some of the early stages. Then, as it matures over the gestation period, it will become more and more obvious that it is a human – but you would never be able to identify the baby during its fetal stage as being the offspring of any specific parents. When the baby is eventually born, the first thing that people will do is begin to say, "Oh, he's got his father's eyes," and so on. One of my college classmates had very fat, stubby fingers. When his children were born, they all had those same signature fingers. There was no mistake who their father was!

Becoming a Son of God – Part II

But the ideas we covered in yesterday's lesson are just the beginning of the story. As a child grows into adulthood and then into his senior years, more and more of his father's characteristics will develop. I remember visiting with one of my cousins after not having seen him for several years. When he walked into the room, I was taken aback because he looked exactly like my deceased uncle. Then, as we talked, it became even more and more uncanny in that his facial expressions were exactly like his father, his voice was his father's, his semi-stuttering manner of speech was totally like his father's, and his sense of humor with the habit of chuckling at his own jokes were nothing other than his father's. Of course, there's also the fact that I often scare myself when I take that first peek in the mirror each morning and wonder why my dad is looking back at me.

We all have the full DNA of our parents from the moment we are conceived, but it takes a while for it to become obvious. In the same manner, we are born a man child – with the full man of Christ inside us that is manifested as a child that still needs to mature to become the sons of God.

After all, even Jesus Himself went through this maturing process during His life here on earth, *And Jesus increased in wisdom and stature, and in favour with God and man.* (Luke 2:52)

Actually, the whole purpose of the church is *For the perfecting of the saints...Till we all come in the unity of the faith, and of the knowledge of the Son of God, unto a perfect man, unto the measure of the stature of the fulness of Christ.* (Ephesians 4:12-13)

Irony

Have you ever noticed that the devil is the one who talks you into sinning and then is the one who condemns you for doing what he just convinced you to do? To me, this is one of the great ironies of life.

We should never listen to him in the first place. But, when we listen to him and allow him to talk us into sinning, we should see where it got us and decide not to go even further by listening to him as he wants to add insult to injury by dragging us further down under guilt and condemnation for our failures. Of course, the reason that many fall into the second tier of the devil's trap is that they think that the voice they hear after their sin is the voice of God rather than the voice of the devil. However, it only takes a quick look into the pages of the Bible to dispel that concept. In the story of the woman caught in the act of adultery, the condemnation and accusation came from the self-righteous religious leaders whose only concern was to prove a point – even if it cost the woman her life to do so. Jesus simply said that He didn't condemn her and allowed her to go free with the admonishment that she sin no more. Notice that He did not simply ignore her sin; instead, He dealt with it in a non-condemning way. In the story of the prodigal son, the father did not condemn the boy for his error; he welcomed him home and immediately restored him to his position. He never accused the boy of wrongdoing, but he didn't stop the boy from confessing his faults. In other words, he did acknowledge the boy's sin, but he refused to condemn him for it. This is the same way our Heavenly Father deals with our errors, failures, and rebellion; He expects that they be properly dealt with, but He never condemns us in the process.

March 27

Telling Time – Part I

I began working with Dr. Lester Sumrall when he was sixty-seven years old – the time when most people are thinking of retirement. However, that word simply wasn't part of his vocabulary; he was determined to continue to minister until the day he dropped dead. And that is exactly what he did. He was still traveling all over the world right up until the last month of his life and preaching in his local church until the week leading up to his death at age eighty-three. That gave me the opportunity of working closely with him for sixteen years – a privilege that I actually considered to be a divine assignment. However, the desire to reach the nations for Jesus was burning in my heart the whole time, and I always assumed that as soon as Dr. Sumrall passed away, I would be released to launch that missions endeavor. However, when Dr. Sumrall did go on to be with the Lord, I felt a strong direction from the Lord that I was not to resign from his ministry but that I should stay and help his son Steve through the transition in the ministry. So, I stayed on in my position at the Bible college, but I was surprised that I was never given any responsibility in helping make the transition that occurred within the ministry after Dr. Sumrall's death. Days turned to weeks, weeks to months, months to year – nine years to be exact! All the while, I knew that I had heard God's direction but was totally puzzled that nothing worked out as I had anticipated. Then came the day that Steve decided to move out of his father's ministry and start his own – and he asked me to work with him to make it happen. It was only then that I knew what the Lord's direction was all about.

March 28
Telling Time – Part II

After spending a year and a half helping Steve through that transition, I felt released to make my move to Colorado Springs to initiate our mission work. The amazing thing is that there were doors that opened for me the same week that I made the move – doors that would not have been open had I tried to make the move nine years earlier. The director of the Bible school where I now teach left the same week that I moved to town – leaving a vacancy that I walked right into. Also, I had the opportunity to meet Dick Eastman, president of Every Home for Christ, exactly when he was looking for someone with my skills to assist with their ministry's new discipleship department. The lesson here is that since we simply don't know how to tell time, it's best to just let God be in control of the hands on the clock.

I remember having a dream when I was in college – I was preaching before crowds of black faces that mysteriously turned brown. The interpretation that I took from that dream was that I would be ministering to people in various nations and of different ethnic backgrounds. When I didn't start traveling around the world within the next few months, I began to question that the dream was really a prophetic message. Yes, it took years to come to pass, but, today, I make multiple trips every year to Africa, Asia, and Latin America – where the faces in my audience morph from black to brown and every hue in between. The lesson here was recorded in the book of Habakkuk 2:3,

> *For the vision is yet for an appointed time,*
> *but at the end it shall speak, and not lie:*
> *though it tarry, wait for it; because it will*
> *surely come, it will not tarry.*

March 29

Telling Time – Part III

Just because we don't see the where, when, or how of God's plan doesn't mean that He doesn't have one. As I was facing graduation from college, I sat across the cafeteria table from one of my classmates discussing our futures. Since neither one of us knew exactly what was coming up next, we ended the conversation with, "Well, the Rapture will probably come the day after graduation." That was close to half a century ago, and the Rapture hasn't occurred yet, but lots of other exciting things have unfolded in my life and ministry during those years. The point of the story is – live each day as God gives it to you and let Him take care of the ultimate timetable.

> *But, beloved, be not ignorant of this one thing, that one day is with the Lord as a thousand years, and a thousand years as one day. The Lord is not slack concerning his promise, as some men count slackness; but is longsuffering to us-ward, not willing that any should perish, but that all should come to repentance.* (II Peter 3:8-9)

Ephesians 5:16 admonishes us to redeem the time for the days are evil; however, James 4:13-15 defines our correct position in that we don't just make up our minds on our own as to how to utilize our time – we must submit our plans to God for His approval and direction.

March 30
Specks and Logs – Part I

I'd be a rich man if I had a nickel for every time I've heard someone say, "I'd be a rich man if I had a nickel for every time...." And here's one of those things that could have made us all rich if we just had the nickels: "Don't judge the speck in your brother's eye when you've got a log in your own." Sure, that is a true principle directly from the words of Jesus. However, the problem is that everyone stops short of what Jesus was actually saying. The statement is recorded twice – Matthew 7:3-5 and Luke 6:41-42. The wording is almost identical in both versions and the message is definitely the same in each – once you deal with the log in your eye, you can see clearly to deal with the speck in the other person's eye.

> *And why beholdest thou the mote that is in thy brother's eye, but considerest not the beam that is in thine own eye? Or how wilt thou say to thy brother, Let me pull out the mote out of thine eye; and, behold, a beam is in thine own eye? Thou hypocrite, first cast out the beam out of thine own eye; and then shalt thou see clearly to cast out the mote out of thy brother's eye.* (Matthew 7:3-5)

Jesus' objective was not to leave the church powerless to deal with people's errors by forcing us to keep our mouths shut due to fear that we don't have the right to correct others because of some sort of guilt complex over our own faults. Let's explore the real intent of His statement tomorrow.

March 31

Specks and Logs – Part II

On the contrary, He directly told us that we needed to take responsibility for dealing with our logs so that we would not be subject to the guilt and uncertainty associated with them. *If we confess our sins, he is faithful and just to forgive us our sins, and to cleanse us from all unrighteousness.* (I John 1:9) Once we have passed that hurdle, we have the responsibility – notice that it is not just a right; it is a responsibility – to deal with others' errors.

It's funny how the introduction of the idea of a log somehow makes us lose focus on the real issue – the speck. Even a tiny speck is very painful and dangerous, with the potential of leading to permanent damage or even blindness. I recently experienced an irritation in one of my eyes that was so uncomfortable that I had to stop wearing my contacts. When the irritation persisted for several days without any relief, I eventually had to make a visit to the optometrist, who found an injury that had been made by a bit of foreign matter so tiny that I was not even aware when I got it in my eye. I'm not sure how to describe my gratefulness to the eye doctor for washing out the alien matter and helping me on my way to recovery.

That's our ministry – rescuing others from every injury that the enemy wants to perpetrate against them. Of course, we have to make sure that we have first been through the major surgery that has removed our old carnality and transplanted the new Christ-like man in its place.

April Fool's Day
April Fool Jokes that Worked

The Chinese government is trying to do away with April Fool's Day as a Western element that doesn't fit into their culture. However, the day's shenanigans have become a favorite part of our Western culture.

The first documented April Fool's prank was a 1698 invitation to see the lions being washed at the Tower of London.

In 1905, the Germans published an article saying that all the gold and silver had been stolen from the US Treasury. The story was picked up and spread as news in papers throughout Europe.

In 1957, the British Broadcasting Network reported a bountiful harvest of spaghetti in Italy.

The Chicago Tribune ran an article about Russian scientists retro-breeding wooly mammoths in 1984.

Richard Nixon caught the nation off-guard in 1992 when he said that he was going to run for the presidency again.

In 1994, PC Magazine ran an article stating that Congress was considering a bill to ban drinking while on the internet. After all, why should you drink on the information superhighway?

In 1998, USA Today ran a Burger King ad for left-handed diners. I actually remember seeing this joke and wrote the company that the joke was on them since it takes two hands to handle a Whopper.

In 2000 The Daily Mail advertised FatSox that suck fat out of sweating feet

The Swiss Tourism Board announced in 2009 that the Swiss Association of Mountain Cleaners climb the mountains every morning and polish them so they will look fresh and clean each day.

April 2
Why Baptism?

In Ethiopia, grooms-to-be take part in a ritual before they are permitted to marry. Participants must successfully jump over a castrated bull four times while naked, symbolizing the childhood they are leaving behind them. In Vanuatu, young boys come of age by jumping off of a ninety-eight-foot-tall tower with a vine tied to their ankles, just barely preventing them from hitting the ground. Unlike a bungee cord, the vine lacks elasticity; therefore, even a slight miscalculation in vine length could lead to broken bones or even death.

I never jumped over a bull or off a high tower – although I'd love to try – but I was baptized as a young boy, simply because that was what a new believer should do. Actually, I never gave it a thought as to why in the world it was necessary to go through the process of being dunked under water.

Today, I want to begin a short study on the Christian practice of water baptism. My intent is to give some clarification as to the meaning of this ceremony and to help us understand that it is more than just a ritual – it is an actual spiritual experience that adds value and victory to our Christian lives.

Over the next several days, I'd like to explore several reasons for baptism:
1) Because Christmas is More Popular than Easter
2) Because Paul Wasn't in Rome or Colosse
3) Because Catholics Have Crucifixes with Jesus on Them
4) Because Hurricanes Make for Stormy Seas
5) Because the Shroud of Turin is Probably a Fake
6) Because the Ringling Brothers Circus Doesn't Stop for Snow

April 3
Because Christmas is More Popular than Easter

Have you ever noticed that Christmas is never mentioned in the Bible? Yes, the nativity story is told a couple times, but the word "Christmas" itself never appears in the scripture. Easter, on the other hand, is specifically mentioned in Acts 12:4. Of course, to be honest, I do have to admit that the Greek text actually speaks of Passover rather than Easter in this verse. But – be that as it may – it is true that the early Christians began to celebrate or commemorate the death and resurrection of Jesus long before they began to recognize His birth as a holiday. However, the notoriety of Christmas has essentially eclipsed the observation of Easter. This is, of course, obvious here in the United States where we begin weeks in advance in preparation for Christmas and spend millions of dollars decorating for the Christmas season, celebrating the holiday with extravagant parties and lavish meals, sending cards – or at least email greetings – to every relative, friend, and business associate we can think of, and buying gifts for everyone we love and even for people we don't care for but want to be careful not to offend. Easter, however, can come and go with only minimal recognition – a special service at church and maybe a family dinner at the most. However, if you were to travel around the world as I have the privilege of doing, you'd see that Christmas is a favorite holiday in countries that don't even espouse the Christian faith. Of course, who could resist all the colored lights and joyous festivities? Not to mention the merchants who can't resist the profit margin they can make off of the holiday!

But what does all this have to do with baptism? We'll start finding out tomorrow.

April 4
Christmas, Easter, and Baptism

The simple answer as to what the popularity of Christmas and Easter has to do with baptism is that baptism is our way of identifying with the death, burial, and resurrection of Christ – the message of Easter. *For if we have been planted together in the likeness of his death, we shall be also in the likeness of his resurrection.* (Romans 6:5)

All religions celebrate the birth of their leader, but only we Christians can celebrate the resurrection of our Savior. In Sri Lanka – a predominately Buddhist country – I've witnessed the magnificent celebration of the birth, enlightenment, and death of Siddhartha Gautama (the founder of the faith). Fortunately, all three significant events occurred on the same day of the calendar; so, they can combine all the celebrations into one. I've also been present for the elaborate Perahera festival when Buddha's tooth is paraded through the streets of the city of Kandy on the back of a massive male elephant. I've visited the shrines where various parts of Buddha's body are enshrined – a tooth here, a shoulder bone there, and three strands of hair elsewhere. For us Christians, we have no relics – only an empty tomb and two holidays – one for the birth of Jesus and one for the day He abandoned that tomb nearly two millennia ago.

Unfortunately, we have fallen into the subtle trap of the enemy of preferring Christmas over Easter and, therefore, degrading our faith to the level of all the other world religions. In His infinite wisdom, God mandated this ritual of baptism so we can identify with something greater than any other creed or doctrine – the miraculously unique nature of our faith – the death and resurrection of Jesus.

April 5
Because Paul Wasn't in Rome or Colosse
Of course, Paul was in Rome. In fact, he spent a number of years in the city – and likely was executed there. But what I am referring to here is that he had not been in Rome at the time that he wrote the book of Romans. This church was not one he had founded and, as I just said, it was not one he had even visited. Since he was not involved in their lives like he was in the other churches, he could not speak to them in the corrective tone with which he addressed the other churches. In writing to the Romans, Paul made reference to his desire to visit them and impart a gift to them so that they would be established. (Romans 1:11) After consideration of all the possibilities of what it could have been that he planned to give to these fellow believers, the most apparent possibility is that he wanted to leave them with a clear understanding of the doctrine of Christ. This is exactly what his epistle to the Romans is – a full, systematic treatise on the theology of salvation, explaining that all men are sinners, that God has made a plan for salvation and complete restoration of man, that the Holy Spirit is the power of the Christian life, and that certain responses are required on man's part. In this, the book of Romans stands apart from Paul's other writings. Since he was not correcting their behavior or theology, he took the opportunity to write to them about the comprehension he had of what was essential to the gospel. To the Romans, he imparted his spiritual gift of teaching in a more methodical manner by laying out a systematic explanation of the theology of salvation. And, in fact, it is likely that the most significant time when Paul did put quill to parchment in a theological statement was when he penned the epistle to the Romans.

April 6

Paul and Colosse

Although we do know that Paul ministered in the region near to Colosse (Acts 16:6, 18:23) and he mentioned his plans to visit the city (Philemon 22), there is no biblical or historical proof that he actually ever set foot in the city itself. In fact, his statement in Colossians 2:1 seems to indicate that he had not, *For I want you to know what a great conflict I have for you and those in Laodicea, and for as many as have not seen my face in the flesh.* We can also add the fact that there are no personal greetings to members of the church at Colosse (whereas his other letters generally make reference to the people he knew in the city) as an argument that he was not personally associated with the church there. As in the case with Romans, Paul's letter to the Colossians is more doctrinally oriented than his other epistles – a result of his lack of direct relationship with the Colossians.

Many Bible scholars have noted that there is a very close parallel between the letter to the Colossians and the one to the Ephesians. Furthermore, many Bible teachers speculate that the letter to the Ephesians was not actually directed to the Ephesian church specifically; rather, they suggest that it is more likely to have been a circular letter that was intended to be read by all the churches in Asia Minor, which is modern-day Turkey. The very earliest copies of the letter to the Ephesians did not bear this title; they simply were not addressed to anyone at all. This lack of a title, along with the general terminology used throughout the book has led many students of the Bible to conclude that Paul had intended it for a much wider audience than just one church.

April 7
The Letter to the Ephesians
When compared to the way most of his letters give point-blank advice to specific issues in the churches, it is readily observable that the Ephesian letter has a rather generalized tone. It is likely that the copies that do say "Ephesians" were from the copy of the circular letter that was actually sent to that specific city while other copies went to other churches in the same general area, perhaps the seven churches of Asia Minor mentioned in the second and third chapters of Revelation.

Even a cursory overview of the letters to the Colossians and the Ephesians reveals that the two are very similar. This similarity has led Bible students to surmise that it is likely that the two were written at about the same time and may have even been based on the same outline – at least the same mental outline, if not the same physical outline. Based on references in Colossians about another letter that had been sent to the Laodicean church, some scholars have gone so far as to suggest that Colossians was also a circular letter that was to be passed between the two churches of Colosse and Laodicea, if not all the churches in Asia Minor. It is an intriguing idea to consider that this "Laodicean letter" may have even been the untitled version of the letter we now know as Ephesians. If these letters were indeed circular letters, there is a certain richness to them that will not be found in the more where-the-rubber-meets-the-road letters where Paul offered more practical counsel concerning specific issues. In these letters, the apostle was not addressing any specific issues; therefore, he was able to give in-depth revelation concerning the issue – who Christ is in us and who we are in Him!

April 8

The Theology of Baptism

Now, back to our question, "Why baptism?" It is in these three epistles – Romans, Colossians, and Ephesians – that we find the defining statements about the essence of the sacrament of baptism. In fact, all the other mentions that we find in the gospels, Acts, and the other epistles are little more than historical references to the fact that the early Christians saw significance in the practice of this ritual. It is only in these three epistles that we begin to understand why.

In the book of Romans, Paul takes the first three chapters to prove that everyone is guilty of sin and needs a savior. He then turns to the hopeful message of the gospel that human sinfulness has been overcome through the gracious gift of forgiveness that is not dependent upon human achievement but upon God's free gift through faith in Jesus. He then introduces such theological concepts as justification, reconciliation, and atonement to explain the salvation process. In chapter six, Paul centers the discussion around the sacrament of baptism as a physical object lesson of the transformation that occurs in the salvation experience. In the seventh chapter, he deals with the dilemma of the Christian who knows that his life should be characterized by victory over sin and failure but is still dealing with guilt and defeat. In chapter eight, the apostle turns to the explanation that it is through a life empowered by the Holy Spirit that the theoretical victory becomes a practical experience.

In the next few lessons, we'll see why Paul considered baptism so pivotal that he dedicated a whole chapter of Romans and other significant references in Colossians and Ephesians to the topic.

April 9

Because Catholics Have
Crucifixes with Jesus on Them

Have you ever noticed that Catholic crucifixes have Jesus still hanging on the cross whereas Protestant jewelry always displays an empty cross? The truth is that the Catholic orientation to the passion of Christ is far more focused on the crucifixion than on the resurrection. In fact, in many traditionally Catholic countries, it is Good Friday that is the focal point of the week and Easter is essentially marginalized and minimalized in comparison. In many places, pilgrims and devotees actually try to emulate Jesus' sufferings by going through various forms of torture. In Rome, I witnessed pilgrims on their knees climbing the Scala Sancta (the Holy Stairs that led up to the praetorium of Pontius Pilate in Jerusalem on which Jesus Christ stepped on his way to trial during His Passion). In Latin America, I've also visited pilgrimage sites where devotees crawl for miles on stony roads as penitence for their sins. Additionally, I've seen Dr. Lester Sumrall's old sixteen-millimeter films of the flagellants in the Philippines who beat themselves with whips to simulate the scourging of Jesus and even have themselves nailed to crosses on Good Friday. The sad reality is that these acts of seeming devotion are nothing different from the depraved practices that I've witnessed among the pagans of the world – Buddhists crawling and rolling on the ground before their stupas, and Hindus impaling themselves with meat hooks before their idols.

Yes, we are moved with respect for those who are so dedicated in their devotion that they are willing to identify with the suffering of Jesus, but there is an important element missing in this formula.

April 10
Let's Not Be Too Hard on the Catholics

But here's the tragic reality, Protestants live exactly the same way. Oh, maybe they don't crawl up stairs, but they focus most of their teaching and preaching on dying to self – the spiritual counterpart to physical self-debasement. From the moment of our salvation, we are taught in the "sinner's prayer" to acknowledge the need to be freed from sin; however, all too little emphasis is given to the power of the new life we have in the resurrection.

That's why we have baptism – because we have to come back up after we are dunked. If all we did was submerge our baptism candidates, it wouldn't be long until there would be no more Christians. The power of baptism is that we bring them back up after we immerse them. Baptism is about resurrection as much as it is about crucifixion. This is where the teaching in Paul's letter to the Ephesians comes in. When believers were baptized in the first century church, they did not just go into the water and come back up out of the water. There was another step they followed that we don't use today. The new believers would wear their old dirty coats to the baptismal waters. Many times, their coats were stained and tattered. When they would go into the water, they would take their old coats off and throw them back to the shore. When they came up out of the water, there would be somebody standing there ready to put new coats on them. These new garments would be perfectly white, sparkling clean robes. In addition to symbolizing the burial and resurrection, baptism also demonstrated the taking off of the old man and the putting on of the new man. They came to the river looking like normal people, but they walked out of the water looking like saints.

April 11
New Clothes – And a New Mentality
When Paul used the illustration of taking off the old and putting on the new in Ephesians 4:21-25, every believer who had ever seen a baptism understood perfectly what he was saying. There was a process to putting on the new coat during baptism. The new coats didn't automatically just come upon them; there was a conscious effort to place one arm in a sleeve, then to put the other arm into the other sleeve, and then to pull the coat into proper place. The same thing is the case with our new nature in Christ. When we get born again, we do become new creatures automatically. However, there must also be an effort on our part to pull off the old ways and let them drop away. We have to be conscious to the fact that there are things we don't want in our lives – attitudes, characteristics, and personality traits. At the same time, we have to consciously put on the new garment. Now, before we get misdirected here and turn this teaching into an expose on religious "do"s and "don't"s, notice that Paul tells us that this change comes through the renewing in the spirit of our mind. (Ephesians 4:23)

At first reading, this passage seems to say that there is a spirit of the mind – something separate from our human spirit. A more accurate way of translating this passage would emphasize "in or through the spirit." Here's the key – our job isn't to earn merit by doing good deeds or to accumulate credit by refusing to do bad deeds; our task is to renew our minds through the spirit and then let that renewed mentality manifest itself in righteous actions as opposed to our faulty old human nature. This is the message of Romans chapters seven and eight – our failure to live up to God's standard versus the Holy Spirit's empowerment to hit the mark.

April 12
Having our Minds Renewed through the Spirit

In another of his letters, Paul wrote, *But as it is written, Eye hath not seen, nor ear heard, neither have entered into the heart of man, the things which God hath prepared for them that love him. But God hath revealed them unto us by his Spirit: for the Spirit searcheth all things, yea, the deep things of God.* (I Corinthians 2:9-10) It is the Spirit of God (who understands God, His characteristics, and what He is doing) who comes to us and reveals to us what is the mind of God and what are the hidden things that God has in store for us. It is through our spirit man, in tune with the Holy Spirit, that our minds are renewed.

In Romans 8:6, Paul wrote, *For to be carnally minded is death; but to be spiritually minded is life and peace.* His point was that our spiritual life is all about taking off and putting on. It is a matter of our actually making a change. He didn't tell us to have Jesus take it off and let Jesus put it on. He said for <u>us</u> to take off and for <u>us</u> to put on. Just as our clothes do not jump onto our bodies each morning and then back into the closet each evening, our thoughts, actions, and attitudes will not automatically change themselves without an effort on our part. We have to take the responsibilities in disciplining ourselves. Perhaps it would be easy to have somebody pray for us, pour oil on us, and knock us to the floor so that we could get up as saints, but the Bible doesn't say that this is the way to become renewed; it tells us that we are to take off the old man and that we are to put on the new man.

Remember that this change is taking place by the way we think, not by changing our actions – and it is often harder to change our minds than our deeds. Thank God, we have the Holy Spirit to empower us!

April 13

Going Under and Coming Back Up

Becoming a saint in Christ requires that we put in some discipline. The Bible tells us that our key to becoming the saints Jesus wants us to be is that we put some effort into taking off and putting on as we deliberately renew our own minds through the revelation of the Holy Spirit.

In yesterday's lesson, we noted Paul's observation in Romans 8:6, *For to be carnally minded is death; but to be spiritually minded is life and peace.* Here, he brings into play the totality of our personality – the body, soul, and spirit. Although most English Bibles translate the term "mind" here, the words that flowed from the Apostle's pen were "spiritually souled" and "carnally souled." In other words, Paul was expressing to us that we can have our soul linked either to our spirit or to our flesh. I often envision this verse as depicting a light switch that can either be in the "up" position to illuminate the room or in the "down" position allowing the room to be invaded by darkness. Just as there is no neutral position for the light switch, there is no neutrality for the soul; it must either link with the spirit and produce life and peace or it will link with the flesh resulting in death.

However, the glory of the baptism symbol is that the same minister who puts us under the water is also the same one who pulls us back out of it! It is only through the power of the Holy Spirit that we can subdue our flesh, and it is through that same power that we can be raised to a new victorious life through the renewing of our minds. Again, we come back to the significance of the outline Paul used in Romans – with the chapters on human frustration and the Holy Spirit's empowerment following the baptism chapter.

April 14
Because Hurricanes Make for Stormy Seas

Over the years of my ministry, I've had the privilege of baptizing hundreds of believers in almost every possible venue: official church baptisteries, swimming pools, creeks, rivers, the Caribbean Sea, and – who could ever forget – the Jordan River. For one memorable baptism, we trekked far up a creek in Nepal to ensure that there was no possibility that anyone would see me baptize a high-ranking Brahman convert – else everyone present could have wound up in jail. But the most unforgettable baptism I've ever done was in the Atlantic Ocean while a hurricane lingered just off shore. As we baptized the group of college students, the waves swelled taller than any of us and we had to battle to keep our footing as they crashed over us. One four-foot-five co-ed, after she was pulled out of the surf, remarked, "I feel like I was just baptized in a washing machine!" – a comment that reminded me of the words of Ananias as he encouraged Saul of Tarsus to be baptized, *And now why tarriest thou? arise, and be baptized, and wash away thy sins, calling on the name of the Lord.* (Acts 22:16) Of course, baptism does not actually wash away our sins like tossing clothes into a washing machine. On that note, I will always remember the words of the old Pentecostal pastor who spoke of some people as going down dry sinners and coming back up wet ones. On the other hand, the real power of baptism was described by the Apostle Peter when he penned the words, *The like figure whereunto even baptism doth also now save us (not the putting away of the filth of the flesh, but the answer of a good conscience toward God) by the resurrection of Jesus Christ.* (I Peter 3:21)

April 15

A Washed Conscience

Herein is the mystery of the sacrament – it changes our consciousness from a sin, guilt, and shame consciousness to a consciousness of righteousness, victory, and authority. We don't have to come up wet sinners; we can come up believers with a renewed awareness of Christ in us and ourselves in Him. This brings us to the message about baptism that Paul recorded in the book of Romans chapter six. Paul begins with the explanation that we don't have to live in sin any longer, with the explanation that we have been associated with Jesus' death to the power of the enemy through baptism and that we have been raised up from that death by the glory of the Father so that we can now have the authority to walk out that new life. *Knowing this, that our old man is crucified with him, that the body of sin might be destroyed, that henceforth we should not serve sin...Now if we be dead with Christ, we believe that we shall also live with him: Knowing that Christ being raised from the dead dieth no more; death hath no more dominion over him. For in that he died, he died unto sin once: but in that he liveth, he liveth unto God.* (verses 6-13) He then tells us that the process requires us to "reckon" ourselves to be dead to sin and alive to God through His grace. Our job is to reckon – make the mental decision to believe – that this thing really worked!

Wow! What a liberating realization – we are no longer subject to a sinner's mentality; we are free to think victorious, overcoming thoughts and to live on the resurrection level, benefiting from the gift of eternal life in Christ! The filth of the flesh has been washed away just as if we were baptized in a washing machine!

April 16
Because the Shroud of Turin
is Probably a Fake

I've always been in the corner of the scientists who have subjected the Shroud of Turin to scientific scrutiny in an attempt to validate that it is the authentic burial cloth of Jesus. And as much as I have rooted for them every time that they have presented even a shred (pun intended) of positive evidence and objected every time the other side presented convincing evidence, I've recently had to rethink my stance. The prevailing theory as to how the image was made on the cloth is that it was etched there similarly to the way an image is burned onto photographic paper. The idea is that the energy released at the resurrection must have radiated into the cloth to produce a picture of the Lord. If that is the case, then the image that would be emblazoned on the fabric would be one of the Lord at His resurrection, not at the crucifixion. Yes, there would be bloodstains from the body from when it was wrapped in the cloth. They would definitely indicate the wounds, lashes, and piercings in the body; however, the "photographic" image would have only the nail prints in the hands and the spear hole in the side. In none of the post-resurrection appearances of the Lord was there any indication that He still bore any other disfigurement. If His visage were still marred beyond recognition as described in Isaiah 52:14, there would be no way Mary Magdalene would have mistaken Him for a gardener, the men on the road to Emmaus could have walked for even a yard – much less miles – without knowing that He was not just another traveler, or that Thomas would have needed to see His hands and side in order to acknowledge Him.

April 17

No More Scars

But my thoughts today are not really about the Shroud of Turin; rather, they are about the menacing lies of the devil that shroud our understanding concerning who we are as the resurrection church. When Jesus was resurrected, His body was totally restored except for the scars that He retained as proof of the sacrifice that He made for us. So it is with us – we have that same resurrection power working in us to totally restore us. (Romans 8:11) We can live free of all our emotional, spiritual, and physical scars! I know that Paul's statement in I Corinthians 15:42-43 about the resurrection of the dead is in the context of the physical resurrection at the end of this present dispensation, but I can't help but believe that the principles also apply to the spiritual resurrection that we symbolize – and actually experience – in baptism, *It is sown in corruption; it is raised in incorruption: It is sown in dishonour; it is raised in glory: it is sown in weakness; it is raised in power.* After all, Jesus was delivered for our offences, and was raised again for our justification (Romans 4:25) and through baptism we have put on Christ (Galatians 3:27); therefore, in baptism, we receive the right to live as totally justified and righteous new creatures freed from all the dishonor, corruption, and weakness of the old life. The Apostle Paul testified to how this principle worked in his own life, *I am crucified with Christ: nevertheless I live; yet not I, but Christ liveth in me: and the life which I now live in the flesh I live by the faith of the Son of God, who loved me, and gave himself for me.* (Galatians 2:20)

April 18

Because the Ringling Brothers
Circus Doesn't Stop for Snow

While I was studying for my doctorate degree, I worked as a technician in a chemistry lab. One winter day, a snow storm closed the local school where the wife of one of my co-workers taught. It just so happened that her class had passes to the Ringling Brothers Barnum and Bailey Circus that was performing in town that day. Since the school was closed, the tickets were going to be wasted; so, she stopped by the lab and asked if we could take off to see the show. As it turned out, four of us wound up accepting the tickets and showed up at the matinee performance in place of the two hundred school children that were expected. I can only imagine all the disappointment in the hearts of the hundreds of children who missed that trip to the circus. I'm sure that there were buckets of tears and myriads of pouty faces on the kids who missed the special treat.

But the interesting thing about that afternoon was that the show went on as scheduled, the clowns went through all their jokes, the acrobats went through all their acts, and the animal trainers put the elephants and big cats through all their routines in spite of the thin crowd. There were hundreds of empty seats in the arena that day – seats that represented admission tickets that had been paid for and issued to school groups that didn't come because of the snow storm. But the fact that no one cashed in the tickets didn't stop the circus from going on. Every performer gave his or her all with no concern for who was missing in the audience.

April 19

Our Admission Ticket

The memory of that day at the circus came to mind recently when I was meditating on Romans 5:2 which says, *By whom also we have access by faith into this grace wherein we stand, and rejoice in hope of the glory of God,* using the Greek word that speaks of an admission ticket to denote "access." In essence, Paul is telling us that faith is our admission ticket to God's grace. The truth that gripped me when I thought about that day at the circus was that God's grace is never diminished dependent upon the fact that people don't have the faith to accept it. We all hold the admission ticket necessary to experience the grace of God (Romans 12:3), but it is up to us if we are actually going to step up to the turnstile and cash in the faith for entrance into that grace. God is always forgiving, but we have to exert our faith to experience it. God is always empowering, but, if we don't apply our faith, we'll not receive it. God is always blessing, but we'll miss it if we don't accept it by faith.

Psalm 78:41 says that the people of Israel limited the Holy One of Israel by not remembering how He had delivered them from Egypt. If we want to think about God properly, we must always be careful to magnify (Psalm 69:30) rather than to minimize Him and His love for His children. When we put a specimen under a microscope or examine it with a magnifying glass, we don't actually change its size; all we do is alter our ability to see it. Magnifying has nothing to do with the reality; it only has to do with correcting our inability to see what already exists. When we magnify the Lord, all we are doing is adjusting our view of God. We access God's grace by getting rid of limiting thoughts and allowing only magnifying thoughts.

April 20

Raised by Faith

Now, back to the topic at hand – baptism. We have learned that baptism is our opportunity to participate in the death and resurrection of Christ to the point where we die to our old nature and are resurrected to a new life that is totally free from the corruption of the old nature. However, I can personally testify that this does not automatically happen. If you will remember from my opening remarks, I was baptized as a young boy and did so just because it was the thing that was expected of me. It wasn't until years later that I realized what the whole thing was about. When I did come to that understanding, I actually considered being re-baptized since the ritual now made sense. But it was at that point that I realized a most important truth from the book of Colossians – remember, this is one of the places where Paul presents his systematic theology. In Colossians 2:12, he spoke of being *Buried with him in baptism, wherein also ye are risen with him through the faith of the operation of God, who hath raised him from the dead.* When I saw the words, *risen with him through the faith of the operation of God*, I understood that I could release my faith at any time – not just at the baptism service – to activate the power of the baptism and experience this victorious resurrection. At that point, I decided to look back to my baptism day and declare that it was a tombstone marking the burial of the old corruption, dishonor, and weakness in my life. I also can look back to that same time and, through faith in the operation of God, remember how I gasped a lungful of air after coming back out from under the water and know that God Himself breathed new life without corruption, dishonor, or weakness into me at that instant.

April 21
Activate Your Baptism

My closing encouragement – whether you are yet to be baptized or were baptized many years ago – is to remember that the circus goes on even if you don't turn in your admission ticket. God's grace that frees you from the old man and resurrects you to a new victorious life is always operative, even if you don't take advantage of it. Your faith in the operation of God is your admission to the new victorious life that is yours through baptism. Cash in your ticket!

Baptism is your ticket to a mentality that is no longer victim to the old mentality of failure and defeat to a new victor mentality of freedom and triumph. Baptism is your entrance to a life directed by the spirit rather than dictated by the flesh. Baptism is your voucher to experience God's grace and edification rather than the devil's guilt and condemnation. Baptism is your doorway to peace and tranquility instead of turmoil and confusion. Baptism is your admission to loving acceptance rather than judgmental scrutiny.

Even Jesus experienced a great blessing by being baptized – empowerment from the Spirit and approval from the Father. *And Jesus, when he was baptized, went up straightway out of the water: and, lo, the heavens were opened unto him, and he saw the Spirit of God descending like a dove, and lighting upon him: And lo a voice from heaven, saying, This is my beloved Son, in whom I am well pleased.* (Matthew 3:16-17)

Baptism is far more than just a ritualistic requirement of the church. It is an actual transforming experience. And – best of all – it has nothing to do with jumping over bulls or off of hundred-foot towers!

April 22

Ten-Second Sermons

Mercy is not getting what you do deserve; grace is getting what you don't deserve.

When we judge others, we do not define them; we define yourselves.

If you are born again, you're born to win.

Attitude determines altitude. Looking up takes you up. Looking down takes you down.

Nothing can stop the man with the right mental attitude from achieving his goal; nothing on earth can help the man with the wrong mental attitude. – Thomas Jefferson

The rich see life as a purpose. The average see life as making a living. The poor see life as victim.

A thousand-mile journey begins with one step. That's not so bad; it's the millions that follow that can be a problem.

Need a little pick-me-up? Don't let it be six pallbearers.

You're only limited by your own imagination – and money, talent, other people, your gene pool…

Problems are only opportunities in work clothes. – Henry Kaiser

The key to a successful marriage is two great forgivers. – Billy Graham

Confession is what you do on your way down to your knees; repentance is what you do on your way back up to your feet. – Dick Eastman

"I can forgive, but I can't forget" is another way of saying, "I won't forgive." – Henry Ward Beecher

Communism had its day. Nazism and Fascism had their days. The Roman persecution and the Japanese extermination of Christians had their day. But Jesus is the Daystar!

April 23

Twenty-Second Sermons

Some people take their cars in for regular maintenance; others wait until they have to be towed to the garage. Be like the first group when it comes to your spiritual life.

Take the Word of God like medicine – by prescription, not just in random dosages.

Just like a criminal who has served his time – because we are pardoned from our offenses against God's Law, the Law is on our side, not against us. We are not in opposition to the Law.

The difference between what happened to Christ and what happened in Him is like the difference between a photograph and an x-ray. In the gospels, we get the external picture of the crucifixion; in the epistles, we see the inside story of how He took our sins to the cross and dealt with our guilt and shame.

God never said that the journey would be easy, but He did say that the arrival would be worthwhile. – Max Lucado

We have a God who delights in impossibilities. – Billy Sunday

God does not give us everything we want, but He does fulfill His promises – leading us along the best and straightest paths to Himself. – Dietrich Bonhoeffer

I used to ask God to help me. Then I asked if I might help Him. I ended up by asking God to do His work through me. – Hudson Taylor

We are called to have soft hearts and hard feet, not hard hearts and soft feet.

The man who does not read has no advantage over the man who cannot read. – Mark Twain

Jesus exposed the Samaritan woman in a way that left her no longer ashamed or feeling rejected.

Fruits of Righteousness

There seems to have been a lot of emphasis on imputed righteousness lately. Based on the teaching in Romans 4:11-24 and James 2:23, the concept is that God sees us as righteous because His grace covers our sinful nature. This is a totally accurate concept in that no one is able in his own strength to earn salvation or merit with God. Unless God credits us with undeserved righteousness, none of us would be worthy of His acceptance. However, it seems that most of the teaching falls short of the full biblical concept in that there is little or no emphasis on the principle of the fruit of our righteousness. The scriptures repeatedly reference the fact that this imputed righteousness will bear fruit in our lives. (II Corinthians 9:10, Philippians 1:11, Hebrews 12:11, James 3:18)

The unfortunate result of the way that many people interpret the concept of imputed righteousness is that they feel that they don't have to live holy lives because God has credited them with righteousness. This imputed righteousness overrules their sinful nature and allows them to continue in unrighteous actions while still being seen by God as righteous. However, if we complete the teaching with the concept of the fruit of righteousness, we readily understand that we are expected to manifest righteousness in our lives as an outworking of the inward work of grace in our lives.

In fact, Jesus had a lot to say about judging a tree by its fruit and even added that any tree that doesn't produce good fruit should be eliminated. (Matthew 3:10, 7:17-19, 12:33; Luke 6:9, 6:43, 13:6-7)

Let's allow the righteousness that God has imputed to us begin to blossom and bear fruit!

April 25
Our Wedding Dress
In describing the bride of Christ, Revelation 19:8 says that her wedding dress is the righteousness of the saints. However, as we look through the various translations of this passage, we find some inconsistencies in how the imagery is rendered. The King James focuses on righteousness where other translations clearly identify the garment as righteous deeds. <u>The Amplified Version</u> speaks of righteous acts and goes on to define them as the ethical conduct, personal integrity, moral courage, and godly character of believers; whereas, <u>The Classic Amplified Version</u> speaks of righteousness with the definition as the upright, just, and godly living, deeds, and conduct, and right standing with God. In essence, it seems that what the verse was intended to say is that being in a right relationship with God will manifest itself in right actions.

Perhaps we can get a clearer understanding by looking at the Old Testament background to the imagery used in this passage. Isaiah 61:10 specifically speaks of righteousness as a wedding garment and makes reference to the fact that God is the one who put this robe of righteousness upon the prophet – an apparent reference to the fact that God imputes righteousness to the believer. However, Job 29:14 uses the image of a robe of righteousness with the explanation that Job himself took responsibility for donning the garment – apparently referring to the need for believers to do righteous actions. Of course, we can't ignore Isaiah's statement that all our righteousness is nothing more than filthy rags. (Isaiah 64:6) So, what can we conclude from these passages? A righteous life will produce righteous living, but righteous living may not necessarily produce a righteous life.

April 26

The Kingdom of God

For the kingdom of God is not meat and
drink; but righteousness, and peace, and joy
in the Holy Ghost. (Romans 14:17)

In the second chapter of his second epistle, Peter addressed corruption and falsehood in the church. He point-blankly declared that God had judged and will continue to judge those who pervert the faith while pretending to be godly people – and even angels. However, in the midst of this commentary on judgment, he mentions two men who escaped the wrath of God – Noah and Lot. The interesting thing about the description that the Apostle gave in relation to these two men is that they both were associated with righteousness. Noah was defined as a preacher of righteousness, and Lot was acclaimed a righteous man who dwelt among the corrupt, *in seeing and hearing, vexed his righteous soul from day to day with their unlawful deeds.*

In applying the idea of righteousness as being the determining factor between judgment and blessing, I'd like to make one simple suggestion that might help to explain why we sometimes have unpleasant experiences even when we know that we have received imputed righteousness through Christ. The kingdom of God consists of much more than just righteousness. In fact, it is actually defined as peace and joy in addition to righteousness. Thus, we can surmise that even if we are the righteousness of God in Christ through imputed righteousness, we won't automatically have peace and joy with sin in our lives if we live in ways that rob us of those qualities.

April 27
Time to Lighten Up a Bit

A burglar broke into the Five Guys restaurant in Washington, DC, and decided to cook himself a meal before leaving the premises. The culinary episode was caught on surveillance footage. I wonder if it will be broadcast on the food channel.

When a thief "liked" his photo on the Crime Stoppers' Facebook page, he was easily arrested.

A job applicant claimed to have worked at a prison. In reality, he served time there.

Another applicant claimed to be the former CEO of the company to which he was applying.

A customer claimed that his pizza arrived with no toppings, but he eventually realized that he had opened the box upside down.

The sum of all the numbers on the roulette is six hundred sixty-six.

"Tofu" is short for "trying to fool you."

Have you ever heard of a stay-at-home mom who works out of the house.

One of the athletes in our high school thought that he was going to go down in history. He did, but he also went down in math and science.

A penitent young man confessed to me that he intended to stop wine, women, and song. My response was that he first needed to stop lying.

What does a bishop do? He moves diagonally.

A proud mom said that her son was "in a class all his own." It was true; he's home-schooled.

What do Holiness women call the pink foam rubber curlers that they put in their hair every night? Holy rollers.

April 28

A Little More Levity

With all the concern lately of whether the US Constitution was intended to include trans-genders, have you ever stopped to think that it was written by men in high heels and wigs?

A friend accidentally went to an Alcoholics Synonymous meeting where he met a wino, a drinker, a boozer, a slut, and a lush.

A customer at the diner complained about the coffee being cold before it was served to him. When the waitress asked how he could tell, he pointed out that her thumb was in it.

When an employee was fired for lack of punctuality, he responded with, "Well, I'm not a grammar Nazi or anything!"
When the doctor asked his patient if he had experienced any traumas, his reply was, "Well, I have been married twice."

When the husband asked his wife to sell all his stuff after his death, she asked why and he responded, "If you remarry, I don't want some other jerk using all my stuff." Her retort was, "Don't worry. I'd never marry another jerk."

Psychic to frog: "You will meet a beautiful girl who will want to know everything about you?" Frog: "Where?" Psychic: "In biology class."

What do you call a person who annoys others by talking on the phone? Cellfish

Advice to televangelists: Don't put all your begs in one ask it.

What is a psychologist? A person who pulls habits out of rats.

Just a Few More Jokes

Tom Swift is often attributed with clever adverbial puns such as: "I think the lobotomy went well," Tom said absentmindedly and "I really hate this weather," said Tom anticlimactically.

I believe that it was Winston Churchill who questioned Lady Astor, "Would you rather be treated like a lady or an equal?"

Mae West once said, "Between two evils, I always pick the one I've not tried before."

When Abraham Lincoln was accused of being two-faced, he replied with, "If that were the case, do you think that I'd be using this one?"

In a democracy, it's your vote that counts. In feudalism, it's your count that votes.

Did you hear about the Buddhist who refused Novocain during a root canal? His goal was transcend dental medication. If you jumped off the bridge in Paris, you'd be in Seine.

When a vulture boarded an airplane carrying two dead raccoons, the stewardess stopped him, "I'm sorry, sir, only one carrion allowed per passenger."

When two fish swam into a concrete wall, one turns to the other and said, "Dam!"

Two Eskimos sitting in a kayak were chilly, so they lit a fire in the craft. Unsurprisingly, it sank, proving once again that you can't have your kayak and heat it too.

When two hydrogen atoms met, one said, "I've lost my electron." The other asked, "Are you sure?" The first replies, "Yes, I'm positive."

April 30
If You Can Take it, Here are a Few More

It is a historical fact that the treadmill was used as punishment in English prisons for nearly one hundred years and was banished at the beginning of the Twentieth Century as cruel and unusual punishment.

When a very fit woman went into a coma, her brain died, but her body was too healthy to go.

One mother commented, "I tell my children that it is important to stay in school, but they come home every afternoon anyway."

The mother and older sisters always told the other girl that they all walked on water on their twenty-first birthday; so, when she turned twenty-one, she tried it too. When she came home drenching wet from her failed attempt, her mother and siblings explained that they – unlike her who was born in July – had all had birthdays in February when the lake was frozen.

This one is a true story. As the director of a Bible college that my wife and I were visiting was driving us to dinner, he was telling us about how some of his students had come up with very creative ways to support themselves while in school. We were shocked to hear him tell about one student who had opened and escort service. He then explained that it worked out perfectly well since he worked at night and had his days free for school. Just before we died of shock, he pointed out a little car with a yellow flashing light driving in front of a large truck with an oversized load and commented, "In fact, I think that might him right there"!

When people who know that I travel all over the world ask if I know a number of languages, I reply, "Of course. In fact, I'm try-lingual."

National Day of Prayer
Counsel from a Real Prayer Warrior
Vicky R. Benson, Director of Prayer Mobilization for World Missionary Press, shares with us the following thoughts about God's Word:

Time spent with God is so special. Acknowledging the truth of His loving presence, our hearts are warmed. Praying scripture, which is much more than just reading it, brings the Word of God alive.

Personalize God's Word
I read His Word as a message from Him to me personally. I receive it as food for my soul. (Habakkuk 2:1, Job 23:12, Matthew 4:4)

Ponder God's Word
When a verse stands out to me, catching my attention, I stop to ponder what God is saying to me – for my own life or concerning those I am praying for. I often read more of the context of the passage. I sense that God is doing something very special, and I am in awe and deeply thankful. (Psalm 119:47, 119:97, 119:129-133, 119:162)

Pray God's Word
I respond in what becomes a two-way conversation with God. When I pray these life-changing words and God later reminds me of them, incredible things happen. (Psalm 5:3)

Practice God's Word
God's Word is powerful and life-changing. I let it work deeply in me. I depend on Him to empower me to obey it. (Philippians 2:13) How relevant God's Word is for every situation of life! It pierces our hearts, convicts, and warns, but it also consoles, strengthens, heals, and delights.

May 2

Ambushed

Wherefore seeing we also are compassed about with so great a cloud of witnesses, let us lay aside every weight, and the sin which doth so easily beset us, and let us run with patience the race that is set before us.
(Hebrews 12:1)

In the passage that we are looking at today, we are told that sin and weights can beset us. In fact, the wording is even more emphatic in that it says that these things can <u>easily</u> beset us. Well, actually, it is even more dramatic in that we are told that they can <u>so</u> <u>easily</u> beset us. With such a purposeful warning, we should take cautious heed to the warning. However, there is actually more to this warning than we might think in that we can actually translate the word "beset" with an even more traumatic reading than we would normally consider. On the surface, we think of beset as annoy, harass, or torment. Now, that is a serious enough issue and certainly a valid reason to rid ourselves of weights and sins. After all, who wants unnecessary trouble in his or her life? However, when we consider that the Greek word for "beset" can also mean ambush, the whole discussion elevates to a totally new level. The story of the Good Samaritan tells of a man who was ambushed as he journeyed from Jerusalem to Jericho. The result was that he was left on the side of the road to die. The Old Testament recounts several stories of armies that ambushed their opponents. Again, the result was their death.

The bottom line is that weights and sins can do much more than just trouble us. They can actually kill us by surprise attack – and they can do it with ease!

Present Yourself to God

I beseech you therefore, brethren, by the mercies of God, that ye present your bodies a living sacrifice, holy, acceptable unto God, which is your reasonable service. (Romans 12:1)

Today, let's consider an acrostic to help us understand what it is that we are expected to present to God as a reasonable service for His kingdom.

School and intelligence: When Jesus was tempted by Satan during the forty-day fast at the initiation of His ministry, He responded to each challenge with the Word of God – something that He could not have done had He not schooled Himself in the scriptures.

Energy: Jesus went about doing good. He did not spend His time here on earth just sitting around watching television.

Life and time: Jesus' life was characterized by rising early – even a great while before daylight – to spend time in prayer and fellowship with His Heavenly Father.

Valuables: Jesus taught that we should render unto God what is His.

Emotional personality: In the Garden of Gethsemane, Jesus wept so intensely that His perspiration actually exuded drops of blood.

Spiritual gifts: Jesus' ministry was distinctly marked by manifestations of the work of the Holy Spirit through healings, deliverances, and miracles.

If Jesus presented Himself acceptable in all these ways, then we can take His life as a pattern for knowing what is the reasonable lifestyle that we should pursue.

First-century Evangelism – Part I

For I am not ashamed of the gospel of Christ: for it is the power of God unto salvation to every one that believeth; to the Jew first, and also to the Greek. (Romans 1:17)

The first-century Christians were persuaded that the Gospel was the answer to everyone's problems and issues. Because they were so convinced that this message was the only solution to man's issues, they were not reluctant to share it. Additionally, they were unquestionably certain that sharing this message was not optional – it was mandated by God. The end result was that nothing – hardships, financial restraints, governmental disapproval, rejection, persecution, or simple weariness – stood in their way of taking the gospel to every man everywhere.

Through mighty signs and wonders, by the power of the Spirit of God; so that <u>from Jerusalem, and round about unto Illyricum, I have fully preached the gospel of Christ</u>. (Romans 15:19)

If ye continue in the faith grounded and settled, and be not moved away from the hope of the gospel, which ye have heard, and <u>which was preached to every creature which is under heaven</u>; whereof I Paul am made a minister. (Colossians 1:23)

If we get the same revelation that they had, we can have the same impact that they did! God has not changed. His gospel has not changed. The only thing that has changed is our motivation. The result is that our world has not been changed!

Twenty-first-century Evangelism – Part II

In yesterday's meditation, we considered the motivational force in first-century evangelization. Today, let's fast-forward two millennia. But first, let's make a stopover in the thirteenth century.

In 1271, after Marco Polo's visit, Kublai Khan wrote to the pope requesting one hundred teachers of Christianity for his empire; however, the pope was distracted by political fighting in Europe and dispatched only a few illiterate monks. At the same time, the khan invited in Buddhist lamas, and the nation became predominantly Buddhist. Today – a leading Buddhist monk in Mongolia read the gospel of Luke, renounced Buddhism, and burned more than a thousand idols. He began a church next door to the Buddhist temple and soon brought so many converts to Christ that the temple now stands vacant while the church is continually packed with worshipers. The same motivation that propelled the gospel in the first century is propelling it in many parts of the world today; however, the same distractions that hampered the advancement of the gospel in the thirteenth century are afoot today as well.

Let's also consider the advancement of Islam in the twenty-first century in order to get a perspective on the need to return to first-century evangelism motivation and methods. The global population will grow by thirty-five percent between 2010 and 2050; however, the Muslim population will grow by seventy-three percent during that same time period. For the gospel to fully penetrate the growing human population, we must return to the same spirit that propelled it in the first century – the concrete conviction that the gospel of Jesus Christ is the only hope for every man.

May 6

When Things Get Really Bad

Have you ever noticed that God often waits until things get really bad before He makes His move?

He gave the prophet Ezekiel a vision about a valley filled with dried up, scattered out bones and commanded him to bring them back to life. It would have been a big enough challenge to expect the prophet to minister to some freshly dead corpses – but, no, He wanted Ezekiel to bring life to an army of men who had been dead for years and whose bodies were not only decayed but parched in the sun and scattered so that not one bone was still connected to its associated parts. Even though He could have gone to Lazarus while he was still sick, Jesus waited until his friend was dead, buried, and decaying to go and raise him from the dead. The Lord waited until Pharaoh had repeatedly refused to let the Israelites go before He lead His people out of Egypt. Then He waited until they were trapped between the devil and the deep blue sea to open the waters of the Red Sea. Of course, He could have lead them along another route with no water hazards, but that's just not the way He does things. Even though Jesus responded immediately to Jairus' request to come heal his daughter, He stopped long enough to heal the woman with the issue of blood – who, by the way was not a simple case, but had suffered for many years and had tried every possible treatment. The result of the delay was that He had to raise the girl from the dead rather than to simply heal her.

The bottom line is that God loves being the God of the impossible. He likes to wait until the situation needs more than mediocre intervention. He thrives in desperate situations. When it looks like things are really bad, that's the time to expect Him to show up!

The Key to Success

Beware that thou forget not the Lord thy God...Lest...thine heart be lifted up, and thou forget the Lord thy God...And thou say in thine heart, My power and the might of mine hand hath gotten me this wealth. But thou shalt remember the Lord thy God: for it is he that giveth thee power to get wealth, that he may establish his covenant.
(Deuteronomy 8:11-18)

In observing the way so many evangelists and Christian workers tried to raise money to support their ministries (not to mention their lavish lifestyles), Dr. Lester Sumrall once turned to me and said, "If you can heal the sick, you can get the money." On the surface, this statement may have sounded rather cynical – as did a lot of what came out of the mouth of that great evangelical statesman. However, once you consider the words for a few minutes, it becomes evident that he was only confirming the message of the scripture we are looking at today. When we feel that we have to use our skills or cleverness to accomplish our tasks, we have forgotten that it is only the blessing of God that can cause us to prosper. Since it is obvious that none of us has the ability to heal the sick on our own, we have no problem acknowledging that such miracles are the work of God.

If we can only bring that same mentality into everything that we set our hands to we will prosper in all other areas as well. The original verse was in the setting of our daily lives – our homes, our employment, and our families. In all these areas, we prosper only because God puts His blessing on us.

Mother's Day
World Changers
Men want to revolutionize the world, but mothers want to transform their families. That's a much bigger task.

In reality, it is the transformed family that revolutionizes the world. I've heard so many stories of men who became world changers, and there is a common theme that runs through the majority of those testimonies – their mothers' prayers. Dr. Lester Sumrall used to tell of the times he would come in from a night of running with the gang only to find his mother kneeling over his bed, soaking his pillow with her tears, as she interceded for her son's soul. But his story is just one of a myriad of such tales that I've heard over the years – confirming that it was the influence of their mothers that made these men into the world changers that they became. But the world would have never been changed had not the hearts of those men been changed first – and that change would never have come about had it not been for the determination of their mothers to transform their families.

We certainly appreciate women who have stepped forward to impact society directly, but we must never overlook the influence that mothers have through the families they raise.

Today, as we take time to honor our mothers, let's stop to imagine what kind of individuals we would have become had we not had the influence of our mothers to shape us. Then, let's imagine what our world would be like if we had not passed that influence on through our lives. I'm sure that, before long, we'll find ourselves amazed at the catalytic influence our mothers have had on society as a whole by simply investing themselves in their families.

Watch and Pray

Take ye heed, watch and pray; for ye know
not when the time is. (Mark 13:33)

How many times have you heard people say that they don't watch the evening news because it is all bad and they just don't want to fill their hearts and minds with the media's negativism? I'm sure that we've all heard it more times than we care to try to count. In fact, I've even heard this message preached from the pulpit. But, as spiritual as these comments may sound, they simply aren't biblical or spiritual.

Jesus taught us to be vigilant in our prayers – to watch and pray. The reality is that we would have no idea what to pray for if we isolated ourselves from the problems that the world is facing. Therefore, I suggest that we do watch the news broadcasts – but change our perspective as to why we would tune in. Let's turn these news reports into prayer requests and intercession motivators.

Dr. Lester Sumrall heard the radio newscast about a young female inmate in the local jail who was being bitten by demons. He turned that information into a prayer item and then into an action agenda. Before long, this news report became the catalyst of a revival that saw more than one hundred and fifty thousand souls come into the kingdom in a six-week period! David Wilkerson watched a news report about street gangs in New York City and took the matter to prayer. Eventually, he found himself in the ghettos of the Big Apple bringing these young men to the Lord. The end result was the initiation of Teen Challenge – a ministry that has saved innumerable lives around the world!

Pentecost

The Day of Pentecost

It is amazing to me that Pentecost is not even on most calendars – yet it commemorates one of the most significant events in all history. Jesus repeatedly told the disciples that they were to go out and preach the gospel around the world; yet, He suddenly jerked them back from that task by telling them that they could not do so until they had received the promise of the Father – a promise that was fulfilled on the Day of Pentecost. (Luke 24:49, Act 1:4) If this Pentecostal promise was so important that it hindered the initiation of the Great Commission, it certainly is significant enough for us to commemorate the day it was fulfilled.

John the Baptist had promised that Jesus would baptize the disciples in the Holy Spirit. (Matthew 3:11, Mark 1:8, Luke 3:16, John 1:33, Acts 1:5) As these faithful followers traveled through the Holy Land with Jesus, they witnessed many incredible things – turning water into wine, healing the sick, cleansing lepers, casting out demons, feeding multitudes, raising the dead, and many other outstanding miracles – yet the day when their Master would baptize them in the Holy Spirit never came. After His resurrection, Jesus renewed this promise and guaranteed them that it would empower them to take the gospel to the very ends of the earth. (Acts 1:8)

The miracle of Pentecost was not simply that there were supernatural manifestations of wind, fire, and tongues (Acts 2:2-4), that on one day the gospel was preached to men from every nation under heaven (Acts 2:5), or that three thousand responded to the message (Acts 2:41). It was that men were emboldened and empowered to stand up and preach the gospel. (Acts 2:14)

May 11
The Power of Pentecost
Because of the power that the disciples received when they were filled with the Holy Spirit on the Day of Pentecost, the number of believers multiplied from one hundred twenty to three thousand in a single day – a twenty-five hundred percent increase! (Acts 1:15, Acts 2:41) As phenomenal as that may seem, the report of what happened when the Spirit was poured out in Ephesus is even more earthshaking – the church grew from just twelve believers until it had spread throughtout all of Asia in just two years. (Acts 19:7-10) Saul of Tarsus was transformed into the Apostle Paul when he had a life-changing encounter on the road to Damascus and was filled with the Holy Spirit a few days later. (Acts 9:17) The result of this spiritual infilling was that he was able to fully preach the gospel from Jerusalem all the way to Central Greece (Romans 15:19) and to attest that there was no more place that had not been penetrated with his ministry (Romans 15:23). Additionally, he had such a powerful ministry in the Turkish city of Ephesus that the temple of Diana (one of the Seven Wonders of the Ancient World that drew devotees from all around the world) almost went into bankruptcy due to the loss of worshipers. (Acts 19:26)

Matthew 24:14 promises that, in the last days, the gospel of the kingdom will be preached in all the nations of the world. A parallel promise concerning the end time is that the Holy Spirit will be poured out upon all flesh. (Joel 2:28, Acts 2:17) And – as they say – it shouldn't take a rocket scientist to see the connection. For the gospel to penetrate the nations today as it did in the days of the early church, the contemporary church needs the same power that those first-century believers had – the power of Pentecost.

Tongues

But I thought that this Pentecostal thing was all about speaking in tongues! Well, yes and no. If you analyze the events in the book of acts in which people received the infilling of the Holy Spirit, you'll see that there is an overwhelming correlation between being filled with the Holy Spirit and speaking in tongues. On the Day of Pentecost, they all spoke in tongues. (Acts 2:4) In Samaria, something so unusual happened that a magician was willing to pay to get the ability to have the same power. (Acts 8:19) Even liberal Bible scholars surmise that the phenomenon that inspired this reaction was speaking in tongues. Even though it is not indicated that Paul spoke in tongues when he received the Holy Spirit, we know that did during his Christina life. (Acts 9:17, I Corinthians 14:18) When the household of Cornelius was filled with the Holy Spirit, they all spoke in tongues (Acts 10:46) as did the disciples at Ephesus (Acts 19:6).

However, there is one other incident recorded in Acts chapter four in which the believers received the infilling of the Holy Spirit – and this account reports that the Holy Spirit gave them the power to speak the word of God with boldness. (Acts 4:31) This story does not say that the believers spoke in tongues, but they did receive an empowered ability to speak in their own language – the element that followed the speaking in tongues on the Day of Pentecost. After the apostles experienced glossolalia (Acts 2:7-11), they then stood up boldly and proclaimed the gospel in their own language (Acts 2:14). The significance of speaking in tongues is that it gets the believer into the proper position to speak boldly and effectively in his own language. Jude verse twenty, says that it builds us up in our faith – faith that will result in effective witnessing.

May 13

Speaking in Tongues Renews Our Minds

The weapons of our warfare are not carnal, but mighty through God to the pulling down of strong holds; Casting down imaginations...and bringing into captivity every thought to the obedience of Christ. (II Corinthians 10:4-5)

In this passage, the Apostle Paul taught us that we have weapons that are mighty through God that enable us to subdue our carnal minds. Certainly, there are many aspects to the spiritual forces that we can use in this conquest of our rebellious thoughts; however, speaking in tongues is unquestionably one of them. After all, Paul's definition of these weapons is that they are not carnal, or related to anything that could be mustered up by our natural abilities – a perfect definition of the supernatural gift of speaking in a language that we have not learned through our own human intellectual abilities.

Paul further explained that these weapons result in the dislodging of our erroneous human way of thinking and they establish our thoughts under the authority of Christ. In I Corinthians 14:14, he explained that praying in tongues is prayer from our spiritual man that supersedes anything that goes on in our human intellect. It does exactly what we expect of the mighty weapons of God – it brings the spiritual man into dominance and the carnal man into a submissive state. No matter how determined we may be, we can never renew our minds in our own efforts; yet, as we practice this spiritual exercise, we'll find that it becomes easier and easier to have a Christ-like mentality.

Another Reason to Speak in Tongues

I often have people challenge me about speaking in tongues with arguments that it doesn't do anything useful. They say that the Bible says that it is better to prophesy because it blesses other people whereas speaking in tongues doesn't help others. Of course, their point is well founded in I Corinthians chapter fourteen.

> *He that speaketh in an unknown tongue edifieth himself; but he that prophesieth edifieth the church.* (I Corinthians 14:4)
> *For thou verily givest thanks well, but the other is not edified.* (I Corinthians 14:17)

However, it is pertinent that we understand that, in this chapter, Paul was correcting the excessive use of tongues in public meetings. Indeed, he went so far in verse twenty-three to say that the way they were operating in the gift actually made them look like crazy people. But the thing that we have to realize here is that Paul never minimized the gift itself, only the way that the members of the church in Corinth were implementing it. In fact, Paul validated the gift by saying that it was a vital part of his own life. (I Corinthians 14:18)

So, what is the bottom line on this issue? Speaking in tongues may not encourage and strengthen the congregation like prophesying does; however, it does strengthen the individual believer in his personal faith. (I Corinthians 14:4, Romans 8:26-28, Jude 20) And it takes strong Christians to be able to bless and encourage others. Therefore, speaking in tongues does bless the church – howbeit, indirectly.

Living Water

Many times, there is confusion as to the difference between the baptism in the Holy Spirit and the fact that we received the Holy Spirit when we were born again. During His conversation with the disciples over the Last Supper, Jesus made it perfectly clear that at salvation the entire Trinity – Father, Son, and Holy Spirit – would take up residence in the lives of all believers. (John 14:23) Therefore, the Holy Spirit has been part of each of our lives since the instant that we punctuated "the sinner's prayer" with the closing "Amen." However, there is a difference – not in the presence of the Holy Spirit in our lives – but in the quantity and direction of His operation in us when we are baptized in the Holy Spirit.

Speaking of our salvation, Paul described the Holy Spirit's presence as taking a drink. (I Corinthians 12:13) Notice that the movement is inward and the quantity is limited to as much as we can consume. On the other hand, Jesus described the baptism in the Holy Spirit as rivers of living water flowing out of us. (John 7:38-39) Here, the movement is outward and the quantity is unlimited – think of the raging Colorado, the flowing Nile, the flooding Mississippi, the gushing Amazon, the roaring Columbia, and the surging Niagara, and the flowing Danube all combined. The important thing to understand here is that the baptism of the Holy Spirit is God's way of releasing what He put in us at salvation. Like the seed that goes into the ground as a single kernel and comes back out of the ground thirty, sixty, or a hundred times more abundant (John 12:24, Mark 4:8), the Holy Spirit is released to do a more abundant outward work to bless others after He has done His internal work to bless our lives.

Receiving the Spirit

The Bible gives us some significant instruction as to how we can release this wonderful gift in our lives.

A common external practice in the Bible was that the gift was released through the laying on of hands by other believers (Acts 8:17, 19:6; I Timothy 4:14; II Timothy 1:6); however, not every occurrence required this external act – for example, the household of Cornelius received simply by hearing the preaching of the Word of God (Acts 10:44).

We are also encouraged to have an internal desire and determination for this manifestation. Paul actually used rather strong wording by saying that we should literally covet the Holy Spirit's working in our lives. (I Corinthians 12:31, 14:1, 14:39) He also directed his protégé Timothy to not passively neglect the gifts of the Holy Spirit (I Timothy 4:14) but, instead, to actively stir them up in his life and ministry (II Timothy 1:6). The Apostle also used his own experience to illustrate the necessity to aggressively pursue and activate the Holy Spirit's manifestation when he said that he willed (or determined) to pray in the spirit on the same level that he disciplined himself to pray in his natural language. (I Corinthians 14:15) Additionally, he encouraged believers not to settle for just an occasional experience with just one manifestation of the Holy Spirit's operation but to seek for multiple expressions of these gifts. (I Corinthians 12:11)

It is God's desire to give us the Holy Spirit, but the biblical pattern seems to be that He releases the manifestations of His Spirit in direct response to our earnestness to have them.

Asking

The most important thing to remember about receiving the fullness of the Holy Spirit is that Jesus said that it was as simple as asking our earthly fathers for the things that they naturally want to provide for their children. (Luke 11:11-13) In other words, we don't have to beg or plead; we just expect that God is instantly ready to give us this great promise. Paul called this confidence in asking, "faith." (Galatians 3:2) In essence, we don't work to earn the gift; we simply expect that God wants to give it to us. We don't have to be good enough; we simply have to be His children.

I have encountered many people who have had difficulty understanding this truth. Some have told me of their failures during their Christian lives and concluded with the evaluation that they don't deserve the gift since their lives have been less than perfect. My response is always that they deserve it more than those who haven't had such failures because one of the works of the Holy Spirit is to sanctify us. (II Thessalonians 2:13, I Peter 1:2) Others have told me that they have waited for the perfect time when God was ready to give them the gift. My response to that is to point them to the passage we have already referred to in which Jesus compared our receiving the Holy Spirit to a father giving his son a piece of bread or a fish. I then say that if they are spiritually hungry, God is as ready to give them the Holy Spirit as an earthly father is to feed his physically hungry children. When one young Filipino man told me that he was waiting for God's timing, I responded that God's timing was in AD 33 and that meant that he was almost two thousand years late in receiving. At that, he instantly burst into tears and a beautiful prayer language began to flow out of him!

Take the Whole Loaf

In Matthew 15:21-28, we read the story of a gentile woman who came to Jesus beseeching Him to deliver her daughter who was grievously vexed by demons. After Jesus first replied with a response that seemed to be a rejection, she countered His statement that bread should be given to the children with a persistent argument that even the dogs can eat of the crumbs that fall from the children's table.

From this illustration, we can learn a lesson about not settling for less than is our legitimate right. Even though the gentile woman was accustomed to being treated like a dog by her Jewish neighbors, she had come to realize that even dogs have rights – and she claimed hers.

As Christians, we are the children of God, and we need to realize that God desires to give us His blessings abundantly. Jesus illustrated this lesson a couple times when He compared our Heavenly Father to our earthly fathers and concluded that He was much more willing to grant our requests than our natural fathers are. (Matthew 7:11, Luke 11:13) Unfortunately, most of the time, we fail to really anticipate what He wants to release into our lives – both physically and spiritually. How often is it that we don't even insist upon the crumbs, much less the whole loaf.

Second Corinthians 9:10 says that God supplies on two different levels – seed for sowing and bread for eating. Several days ago, we learned that He gives us the Holy Spirit at salvation like a seed and multiplies His work in our lives through the baptism in the Holy Spirit as an abundant harvest. Today, I encourage you to enjoy both the seed and the harvest. Take the whole loaf to feed yourself and share with others.

Dirty Money

If you travel outside the country, you will soon discover the necessity of having clean, crisp bills. Once, I was down to my last hundred-dollar bill while traveling in an African country. When I went to exchange it, the money changer noticed a tiny tear and refused to accept it. On another occasion, a traveling companion's money was refused even though it was clean and crisp – but it was printed too many years previously. However, the local currency that they give you in exchange is rarely clean or crisp. In most third-world countries, the bills are so tattered and greasy from continued reuse that they are almost unidentifiable as legal tender. However, the amazing thing is that no matter how dirty, crumpled, or torn those bills may be, they are still worth their face value.

In the spiritual realm, the same is true about our lives. No matter how badly our lives are mutilated and shattered, to God we are still worth the eternal price of His own Son's life. Certainly, He desires that our lives be clean and crisp like international-quality hundred-dollar bills, but He doesn't discredit us or deduct from our value because of all the degrading situations we have been dragged through or the devaluing actions we have participated in. That's what salvation is all about – seeking and saving the lost. (Luke 19:10)

Did you realize that US currency can still be redeemed for its full face value no matter how badly it has been damaged by fire or torn from overuse or being run through a washing machine or even decayed from being buried in the ground – as long as the serial number can be proven. Spiritually, our lives never lose their value as long as the seal of the Spirit is intact. (II Corinthians 1:22; Ephesians 1:13, 4:30)

Boldly Before the Throne

Let us therefore come boldly unto the throne
of grace, that we may obtain mercy, and find
grace to help in time of need. (Hebrews 4:16)

The book of Esther presents the saga of a beauty queen turned literal queen – well, at least she became part of the royal harem. However, it seems as though she had the highest ranking among the king's wives in that it was said that the king loved her above all the other women in his harem and that she was given the title of queen as the replacement for Vashti who was labeled as the queen, not just one of the royal consorts. However, the story has one perplexing overtone – the fact that Esther, even as the queen and the king's favorite, did not have immediate access to her own husband's presence. (Esther 4:11) However, at the insistence of her uncle Mordecai, she made the bold decision to take her life in her hands and approach the throne uninvited. (Esther 5:1-2) The interesting aspect here is that she obtained favor as she approached the king.

In contrast, the New Testament principle is that we have already obtained favor with the King of kings. The word "accepted" in Ephesians 1:6 is the same word translated as "highly favored" in Luke 1:28. Since we are already in His favor, we do not need to be reluctant or cautious about approaching God. Unlike the Old Testament queen who had to call a three-day fast before visiting her own husband, we have a standing invitation (Matthew 11:28) and are always welcome into His presence without an appointment (Luke 18:7).

May 21
Digging

Have you ever noticed that the unfaithful steward in the parable of the talents dug a hole to bury his talent (Matthew 25:14-30) while the unjust steward said that he would not dig (Luke 16:1-8)? It may seem like an insignificant coincidence between the two parables, but it is also possible that Jesus purposely made reference to the same activity in the two parables – although from totally different perspectives.

The point that we can see here probably isn't so much about digging as it is about the attitudes the two men had concerning the same action. One man engaged in digging and discovered that it was totally against his master's will. The other man refused to dig but did so in a way that was also against his master in that he had to find a way to cheat his master in order to avoid having to dig.

In our own lives, there are things that some people do in direct rebellion to the will of God while others make certain that they would never be guilty of the same activity but find themselves just as guilty of being out of the Lord's will. Let's take for instance some of the things that we normally consider sins – adultery, for example. Those who do such a thing do so in direct rebellion to the Ten Commandments (Exodus 2:14); yet, many who refuse to do so develop a holier-than-thou attitude (John 8:3-11) which is just as contrary to the will of God as is the action of sexual impurity.

The bottom line is to remember that specific actions are not what matters; the fact that we are stewards and accountable to the Master is what is most important. We must genuinely learn the heart of our Lord Jesus and live in harmony with His heart.

May 22

Dear Ann Landers

Someone once wrote the popular advice columnist Ann Landers:

"A while back, you wrote some wise words about the Protestant work ethic. A recent survey that appeared in the San Francisco Examiner supports my hunch that if the Protestant work ethic is not dead, it is in very poor health. Here are the facts: The survey by Accountemps, an agency that provides temporary help in bookkeeping, accounting and data processing, asked one hundred twenty personnel directors and managers across the country, 'What percent of a typical employee's work day do you estimate is NOT spent working?' The responses ranged from under ten percent to fifty-five percent. The overall average was thirty-two percent. Assuming these results are accurate, the average worker is fooling around almost four months out of each year. If this is true, those idle hours represent a productivity gap that could be a threat to the nation's economy. Is this great country of ours going to hell in a handbasket because people don't want to work anymore?"

I do see a lot of people goofing off when they pretend to be working. Especially with so much work today being done on computers, it is especially easy for employees to be surfing the web while putting up a pretty good façade. Of course, the same principle is played out in every arena of life. I recently sat in the back of a college class and watched one of the students spend a whole class period doing online shopping.

The real tragedy is that we are just as lax when it comes to our spiritual lives. Let's not let our world go to hell in a handbasket!

The Returned Gift

Someone challenged me with the argument that salvation is a work done in us, by God. He went on to say that we have not earned it – nor can we un-earn it. He then went on to suggest that if we think of salvation as a gift, the only way that a gift can be given back is if the gift-giver desires to take it, or is willing to accept it back. His conclusion was that Jesus will not do either. He promised to keep us eternally.

However, there is a major problem with this conclusion. A gift doesn't have to go back to the giver. It can be thrown away by the one who received it or stolen by another individual.

The discussion continued with the argument that eternal life is not conditional or temporal; it is permanent, starting at the moment Jesus saves us and continues on into eternity. Therefore, it would not be eternal life if we could lose our salvation.

The issue here is the matter of who is a believer. Although Paul did say that he was persuaded that nothing could separate him from the love of God (Romans 8:38-39), the scriptures do not make such guarantees to individuals who have abandoned their faith through becoming apostates or even neglecting it through becoming unconcerned about their relationship with God through attachments to the world and the things in the world. Paul actually goes on to say that he is determined to *endure all things for the elect's sakes, that they may also obtain the salvation which is in Christ Jesus with eternal glory. It is a faithful saying: For if we be dead with him, we shall also live with him: If we suffer, we shall also reign with him: if we deny him, he also will deny us.* (II Timothy 2:10-13) He apparently realized that his salvation was not automatic.

The Debate Continues

My contender went on to add, "Well, your conclusion begs the question, 'What is denied to us?' It can't be our salvation, for verse ten speaks of "eternal glory" and verse eleven says *we shall also live with Him.* The context of verse twelve is about our rewards; and this verse (*If we believe not, yet he abideth faithful: he cannot deny himself*) assures us of His faithfulness. We are His body, we are one with Him, and He cannot deny Himself.

I countered the argument with the observation that it was interesting that the verse is supposedly about rewards – an idea that is not at all introduced in the passage. I then added that it must also be noted that the verse is clearly in the subjunctive mood, suggesting a possibility rather than a confirmed reality. In other words, the obtaining of the irrevocable salvation has not yet been accomplished. When it will be accomplished is not specifically defined. I then asked if it might be possible that all this actually occurs at the end of one's life, at which point there is no possibility of altering one's state?

I then went back to the verses from Romans mentioned in yesterday's lesson about the inability of external conditions to separate the believer and questioned why there was no mention of the believer's personal intentional decision to separate himself. I then tossed a monkey wrench into the gears by noting that the verse is about being separated from God's love – not salvation. I followed that observation with a question and a comment, "Isn't it possible to be separated from salvation and still loved by God? After all, that's the condition we were all living in prior to our accepting Jesus as savior."

Memorial Day
No Man Can Pluck Us out of God's Hand
And I give unto them eternal life; and they
shall never perish, neither shall any man
pluck them out of my hand. (John 10:28)

The discussion went on with my opponent's comments, "No one can 'pluck' us out of His hand – and that includes us. We can't 'pluck' ourselves out of His hand. His grasp is tighter and stronger than anything we can do." I contended that anyone with a basic knowledge of the English vocabulary will readily see that "pluck" conveys the meaning of being pulled against one's will. When a farmer plucks apples off a tree or when a woman plucks her eyebrows, it is quite different from when the apples fall off the tree or the eyebrows fall out naturally. Interestingly, the whole question that originated our discussion was based on Galatians 5:4 – the verse referring to the possibility of falling (as opposed to being plucked) from grace.

At that point, my friend felt that we needed to discuss being sealed by the Holy Spirit (Ephesians 1:13, 4:30) – a concept that many feel makes it impossible to negate the work of grace in our lives (Jude 24-25). Before I make a comment about the theological issues with the interpretation of the seal of the Spirit, I have to note some possible implications with the passage in Jude. Just because Jesus is able doesn't mean that He will do everything that He has the capacity to do. He is also able to heal every sick person and save every sinner – but He doesn't. His policy is that we must act in faith toward Him in order to be saved and healed. Isn't it just as logical that we must act in faith toward Him if we want to have this eternal keeping power?

The Final Statement

I found the introduction of the idea of the seal of the Spirit to be very intriguing in that the debater did not want to comment on the idea of grieving the Holy Spirit; he only wanted to emphasize that He has sealed us. My position was that it was a lopsided argument to stress the Holy Spirit's role in sealing us and ignore the possibility of our grieving Him. Additionally, he refused to even discuss the possibility that a seal can be broken – a fact that should be taken as a given. Other than junk mail that goes directly into my trash, I break open the seal on every letter that comes to my mailbox. Furthermore, I break every tamperproof seal on all the packages that I buy in the grocery store and pharmacy in order to use the products inside.

Finally, I left him with a whole list of passages that I felt he should look at through honest and unbiased glasses: Matthew 7:21-23, 13:22,; Mark 4:18-19; Luke 8:14, 9:62, 17:32-33; Acts 1:25, 5:1-10, 8:13-23; I Corinthians 5:5, 5:11-13; I Timothy 1:19-20, 5:8; II Timothy 2:15-18, 4:10; Hebrews 6:4-6, 10:26-27, 10:38-39; II Peter 2:20-22; I John 2:14-17; Jude 5-6, Revelation 3:5, 22:19.

My point isn't to be dogmatic – just to be open-minded enough to look at both sides of the discussion. Additionally, I feel that it is necessary to be cautious with our theology because we could jeopardize our eternal destiny and that of others by promoting false security rather than genuine eternal security. God's gift of salvation is secure and eternal, but we don't want to endanger anyone who may neglect it by thinking that it is not to be treasured and protected. (Hebrews 2:3)

May 27
Don't Miss Out

Two interesting stories in the Old Testament express the principle that our unwillingness or unbelief doesn't hinder God from doing what He wants to do, but our lack of faith and obedience can certainly leave us "out in the cold." When Mordecai approached Esther about helping the Jewish citizens escape Hamman's genocide plan, she was reluctant at first; however, his response to her was that her refusal to help would not stop God from delivering His people even though it would disqualify her and her family from that salvation. (Esther 5:14) When the Syrian blockade of Samaria left the people so devastated that they turned to cannibalism, Elisha promised that God would bring them unimaginable abundance within twenty-four hours. However, the king's chief advisor sarcastically responded that such a thing could not happen even if God were to open the windows of heaven and pour out food. The prophet confidently replied that the advisor's cynicism would not stop God's miraculous supply but that he would only get to see it happen with his eyes and never taste a morsel with his lips. As the story unfolds, God does release lavish resources to the people and the advisor was appointed to collect a "gate fee" from the people as they entered the compound. Of course, no one who is so depraved that he would stoop to eating human flesh is going to politely stand in line and pay an entrance fee when an extravagant feast awaits a few steps away. The end result – the advisor was trampled to death by the masses as they rushed in to get the food. (II Kings 7:1-20)

When God promises a blessing, be the first to rush to the front of the line rather than the one who misses out!

This Ain't Scott

In Pontiac, Michigan, a bar bouncer who claimed he inadvertently had sex with the wrong woman was convicted of first-degree criminal sexual conduct and faces up to life imprisonment for the incident. Bruce Parrish insisted he thought he was having consensual sex with a woman he hadn't met, but who had phoned to invite him to her home. Having never seen the woman, the defense argued, Parrish couldn't have known that the woman with whom he'd had sex in a dark room was someone else. The twenty-seven-year-old victim testified that she drank six or seven beers the night of the encounter and, when she woke up later, she thought the man in bed with her was her boyfriend. When she whispered, "I love you, Scott," Parrish answered, "This ain't Scott, Baby."

Pretty sordid story – right? Well, I shared it simply because it is reminiscent of a couple biblical stories – the story of Jacob and Leah (Genesis 29:21-25) and the account of Lot and his two daughters (Genesis 19:30-36). Both of these biblical stories resulted in consequences far more significant than the life sentence that Bruce Parrish is facing.

But there is a contemporary parallel that the Apostle Paul points out in I Corinthians 10:20 when he says that we can actually join ourselves with the devil and not know what we are doing – a spiritual encounter that is so intimate that it partners us with him in the same way that physical sex makes two people into one flesh. With such consequences looming before us, it is no wonder that the Apostle also commanded us to wake up, keep our eyes wide open, not walk around in darkness, and be sure to watch out where we step! (Ephesian 5:15)

May 29
Ignorance is Bliss

One year during my seminary studies, I taught high school in the morning and attended classes in the afternoon. On one particular day, I arrived at my normal time and walked into my class with my usual jovial attitude. To my amazement, my classmates all responded to me in shock when I addressed them happily. I eventually discovered that the somber pall over the campus was due to the unexpected death of one of the professors that morning. When he didn't show up for class, one of the other professors went to his home and found him dead in his bed. As a widower, he lived alone; so, there was no one in the house to inform anyone about his death. When the news got back to the campus, everyone was so shocked that they went into deep mourning. Due to the fact that I arrived after the announcement, I was unaware of the whole situation and was totally unaffected by it.

My point is that we can be protected from some things simply by being ignorant of them. In fact, I believe that this is one reason that God gives His children the gift of tongues. Paul says that our minds are not involved when we are praying in the spirit (I Corinthians 14:14); on the other hand, our prayers are totally directed by the Holy Spirit who knows the very mind of God. Let's suppose that you had an undetected cancer growing inside your body. If you were to know about it, it may cause you fear, anxiety, and worry. Therefore, God – in His sovereign mercy – allows you to pray about it in the spirit without letting your mind in on the process. The result is that you can be healed and never know that you were even under attack! Your ignorance has kept you in bliss while the Holy Spirit went to battle on your behalf!

What is Your Calling?

I recently had a meeting with two Christian leaders who had been having an ongoing feud for a number of years. I asked them what they felt their calling was. One said, "Pastor"; the other answered, "Teacher." I then opened my Bible to Ephesians 4:1-4.

> *I...beseech you that you walk worthy of the*
> *vocation wherewith ye are called...*
> *Endeavouring to keep the unity of the Spirit*
> *in the bond of peace...even as ye are called*
> *in one hope of your calling.*

I then shocked them both by insisting that they had both given the wrong answer to my question. I followed up with the statement that one may function in the ministry of a pastor and the other in the ministry of a teacher but that the Bible declares that there is only one calling and that we all share that one unique calling – to keep unity in the Body of Christ in the bond of peace. No matter what else we may accomplish, if we don't walk in unity, we have failed to fulfill our calling.

One Christian leader in Brazil worked for a year to organize the churches for the annual March for Jesus. What might have, at first glance, seemed to be a success, he was able to rally four thousand Christians for the parade. A few weeks later, the homosexual community decided to march to draw attention to their agenda. The result of about a month's preparation was an army of ten thousand strong flooding the streets of the city. The churches all had too many personal agendas to fulfill to take the time to unify for one common cause, but the gay community happily pulled together to make a statement. Apparently, they know more about their calling than we do!

May 31
Have You Ever Wondered?

When your pet bird sees you reading the newspaper, does he wonder why you're just sitting there, staring at carpeting?

Why is it that you must wait until night to call it a day?

What if the Hokey Pokey is what it's all about?

How do you know it's an "endless loop"?

Why is football played by hand?

If it rains to make flowers grow, why does it rain on sidewalks?

Man to taxi driver: "Can you take a joke?" Driver: "Yes, where do you want to go?"

What happens if you can't pay the bill at an outdoor café? Do they throw you inside?

After a long introduction, the speaker got up and said, "Now I know how a pancake feels when they pour a lot of syrup on it."

Two farmers each claimed to own a certain cow. The attorneys for each farmer cried out, "Keep pulling," as they milked the cow.

When the mom told the toddler not to tell the dad about the fender bender, he was very obedient: "Dad, whatever you do, don't look in the garage."

What God will say when you meet Him at heaven's gate – "Well done" or just "Well?"

Man prayed for prosperity but only got job offers

Boss yelled at employee at 5:01 PM, "Wake up! You're sleeping on your own time!"

Why we go on spring vacation when we are having the best weather of the year at home?

What's the difference between a person of interest and an interesting person?

What about "Miracles don't just happen" and "Miracles just don't happen."

June 1

Something to Think About

A bank is a place that will lend you money, if you can prove that you don't need it.

Whenever you fill out an application, on the line that says, "If an emergency, notify:" why not write, "A doctor"?

I didn't say it was your fault, I said I was blaming you.

Why does someone believe you when you say there are four billion stars, but check when you say the paint is wet?

Women will never be equal to men until they can walk down the street with a bald head and a beer gut, and still think they are sexy.

Why do Americans choose from just two people to run for president and fifty for Miss America?

Behind every successful man is his woman. Behind the fall of a successful man is usually another woman.

A clear conscience is usually the sign of a bad memory.

You do not need a parachute to skydive. You only need a parachute to skydive twice.

The voices in my head may not be real, but they have some good ideas!

Always borrow money from a pessimist. He won't expect it back.

Hospitality is making your guests feel like they're at home – even when you wish they were.

What's the difference between "beefing up" a story and "hamming it up" as you tell it?

Why do we work so hard to get grass to grow in the lawn and it won't come up; however, it grows in the cracks in the driveway?

June 2
And Now for Some Real Words of Wisdom
A leader who keeps his ear to the ground allows his rear end to become a target.

You cannot paint the Mona Lisa by assigning one dab each to a thousand painters.

Establishing goals is all right if you don't let them deprive you of interesting detours.

Success has nothing to do with what you gain in life or earn for yourself. It has to do with others.

Democracy is like a raft. It won't sink, but you'll always have your feet wet.

You don't stop laughing because you grow old. You grow old because you stop laughing.

Good sense is easier to have than to use.

We must accept finite disappointments but never give up infinite hope.

A child on a farm sees a plane and dreams of places far away. The passenger on the plane sees the farmhouse and dreams of home.

A glimpse is not a vision. But to a man on a mountain road by night, a glimpse of the next three feet of road may matter more than a vision of the horizon.

Disability is a matter of perception. If you can do just one thing well, you're needed somewhere by someone.

Our language has wisely sensed the two sides of being alone. It has created the word "loneliness" to express the pain of being alone. And it has created the word "solitude" to express the glory of being alone.

To think too long about doing a thing often becomes its undoing.

June 3
Points to Ponder
The next time you're in a meeting, look around and identify the yes-butters, the not-nowers, and the why-notters. It's the why-notters who move the world.

It was your idea; therefore, it rules out the possibility that it was the wrong thing.

Learn to forgive your enemies. It'll drive them crazy.

Goal = Success

        God – not tower of Babel

        Ordeal – Garden of Gethsemane

        Attitude – determination, not for self, but for God

        Love – I Corinthians 13 – let love be your aim

The road to success is paved with good inventions.

Phone system for atheists – you dial, and nobody answers.

Lightning – angels taking pictures.

Children get dirtier than adults because they are closer to the ground.

We like someone because; we love someone although.

There's no traffic jam on the extra mile.

Smile: passport to anywhere you want to go.

Conscience: inner voice that says that someone is looking.

Get someone else to blow your trumpet. The sound will carry twice as far. – Will Rogers

Laughter is an instant vacation. – Milton Berle

Never tell a lie – unless lying is one of your strong points.

People who eat forbidden fruit will wind up in a jam.

Your checkbook is your autobiography.

June 4
More Points to Ponder
A friend is one who walks in when the rest of the world walks out.

Triumph is what you get when you add some umph to your try.

Success is not escaping problems, but facing them creatively.

You probably wouldn't worry about what people think about you if you could know how seldom they do.

Don't be afraid of opposition. Remember that a kite rises against the wind.

Our days are like identical suitcases. They are all the same size, but some people can pack a lot more into them.

Success is laying a firm foundation with the bricks that others throw at you.

Where can you always find success, wealth, and happiness? In the dictionary.

If you belly-laugh, you won't belly-ache.

Minds are like parachutes. They are only useful when open.

Even a mosquito doesn't get a slap on the back until he starts to work.

Good luck often has the color of perspiration on it.

Life is a journey. Some take the highway while others just go for the dead ends.

Some people remind me of blisters. They show up after the work is done.

A person without a sense of humor is like a wagon without springs – jolted by every pebble in the road.

Laughter is like changing a baby's diaper. It doesn't permanently solve the problem, but it makes things more acceptable for a while.

June 5

Even More Points to Ponder

Egotist: I specialist

Fat: penalty for exceeding the feed limit.

Net profit: what a fisherman makes

Every path has a puddle.

You grow up the day you learn to laugh – at yourself.

The only things that children wear out faster than shoes are parents and teachers.

There is hope for any man who can look into a mirror and laugh at what he sees.

The trouble with the rat race is that even if you win, you're still a rat.

Youngster's evaluation of church: The music was great, but the commercial was too long.

If we could forget our troubles as quickly as we forget our blessings, the world would be very different.

Home is the chief school of human virtues.

You have a gold mine in your goal mind.

Plan ahead – it was not raining when Noah started building the ark.

Genius: Someone who aims at something that no one else can even see – and hits it.

The opposite of a procrastinator: Someone who spent tomorrow's money yesterday.

The pastor cut himself shaving while thinking about the sermon. The solution: next time, concentrate on shaving and cut the sermon.

If you snooze, you lose. If you snore, you lose even more.

The best thing to give your children after good habits is good memories.

Every one of us has in him a continent of undiscovered character. Blessed is he who acts like the Columbus of his own soul.

June 6

Still More Points to Ponder

Imagination is only intelligence having fun.

Curiosity is a willing, proud, and eager confession of ignorance.

A problem is a chance for you to do your best.

A child is an island of curiosity surrounded by a sea of question marks.

Very often, a change of self is needed more than a change of scene.

The greatest obstacle to discovering the shape of the earth, the continents, and the oceans was not ignorance but the illusion of knowledge.

He's not afraid of work. I can tell by the way he fights it.

The reason I have such a wonderful memory for names is because I took that Sam Carnegie course.

If you judge people, you have no time to love them.

Success is a ladder that cannot be climbed with your hands in your pocket.

Taking joy in living is a woman's best cosmetic.

Optimism is a cheerful frame of mind that enables a teakettle to sing though in hot water up to its nose.

Folks who think they must always speak the truth overlook another good choice – silence.

Don't tell me how hard you work. Tell me how much you get done.

When you reach for the stars, you may not quite get one, but you won't come up with a handful of mud either.

Television is called a medium because nothing on it is rare or well done.

When there is an original sound, it awakens a hundred echoes.

Victory is won not in miles, but in inches.

June 7

And They Just Keep Coming

Catching a fly ball is pleasure, but knowing what to do with it after you catch it is business.

A land developer is someone who wants to build a mountain cabin this year. A conservationist is someone who built his mountain cabin last year.

Life is like riding a bicycle. You don't fall off unless you stop pedaling.

Praise can give criticism a lead around the first turn and still win the race.

If you don't want anyone to know, don't do it.

Good humor may be said to be one of the very best articles of dress one can wear in society.

Love and time – those are the two things in all the world and all of life that cannot be bought, but only spent.

People who go to the second service on Sunday morning: later-in-the-day saints.

The most solid stone in a structure is the lowest one in the foundation.

Ideals are like stars. We never reach them, but like mariners on the sea, we can chart our course by them.

Some people have procrastination in their blood; their ancestors came over on the Juneflower.

It's amazing how quickly a little gossip can divert attention from an intelligent conversation.

The problem with being punctual is that there is no one there to appreciate it.

The problem with ignorance is that it picks up confidence as it goes along.

The problem with experience is that it teaches you a lesson that you really didn't want to know.

June 8
And They Just Don't Quit
The problem with making intelligent suggestions is that you're apt to be appointed to carry them out.

Character is what you are, not what others think you are.

The fewer the facts, the stronger the opinion.

One way to prevent conversation from being boring is to say the wrong thing.

Sometimes, the smallest things in life are the hardest to take. You can sit on a mountain more comfortably than on a tack.

There is victory in good work, no matter how humble.

An idea can turn to dust or magic, depending on the talent that rubs against it.

It is better to debate a question without settling it than to settle it without debating it.

Always acknowledge a fault frankly. This will throw those in authority off their guard and give you an opportunity to commit more.

Talking about fixed income, I wish someone would fix mine.

I have no problem meeting expenses, every time I turn around, there they are.

Plagiarism: the unoringinal sin.

Some people know a lot more than they tell. Unfortunately, the reverse is also true.

An optimist laughs to forget. A pessimist forgets to laugh.

In school, you are taught a lesson and then given a test. In life, you are given a test and then taught a lesson.

Growing old is mandatory, but growing up is optional.

I can live a week on one good compliment. – Mark Twain

June 9
Just One More Day of Ponder Points

If you do not think about the future, you cannot have one. – John Galworthy (Nobel Prize winner)

Where can you always find a happy ending? On a puppy; he is always wagging his tail.

The wedding planner was happy because the ceremony went off without a hitch.

An idea is a fragile thing. Turning it off is much easier that keeping it lit.

When you buy a horse, you buy both ends.

Reality is the leading cause of stress among those who are in touch with reality.

It's discouraging to think about how many people are shocked by honesty and how few by deceit.

What you don't know can hurt you; only you won't know it.

Every child is an artist. The problem is how to remain an artist once he grows up.

People who have an hour to waste usually try to spend it with someone who doesn't.

A hunch is creativity trying to tell you something.

Saints are sinners who kept trying.

I finally know what distinguishes man from the other beasts – financial worries.

Some people strengthen society just by being the kind of people they are.

The greatness of a man can nearly always be measured by his willingness to be kind.

You are not here by choice. You were appointed. God expects you to excel in everything you do.

A man is determined by what he thinks, not what he knows.

Meditation is thinking answers; worry is thinking problems.

June 10
Characteristics of True Leaders
Willing to submit to others in authority (Matthew 8:9)

Willing to work with others for the common good (Acts 15:6)

Able to make decisions and recognize that the "buck stops here" (Ezekiel 3:18, 20)

Dedicated to his followers as well as to the common cause (II Corinthians 11:23-28)

Willing to set an example for others (I Peter 5:3)

Willing to lead by being the first one into the battle (I Samuel 18:16)

Able to rule his own family (I Timothy 3:4)

Willing to lay down his life for others (John 15:13)

Humble (Mark 9:35)

Never demonstrating the "Big I and Little U" attitude (Matthew 20:25-26)

Ready to "roll up his sleeves" and work hard (I Thessalonians 2:9)

Personally involved with his followers (I Timothy 1:2)

Submitting himself to others (Ephesians 5:21)

Praying for those under his leadership (Colossians 1:9)

Setting an example with his own life (I Timothy 4:12)

Willing to mentor (II Timothy 2:2)

Seeking the good of others before his own interests (Philippians 2:4)

Cautious about being overly self-confident (I Corinthians 10:12)

Filled with the Holy Spirit (Acts 6:3)

Filled with the mind of Christ that is willing to become of no reputation and take the form of a servant and sacrifice himself in order to bless those he is called to lead (Philippians 2:5-8)

June 11
The Holy Spirit's Proper Name – Part I

When the gentleman asked the question during the question-and-answer session at one of our pastors' conferences, I was not aware that he was from a "Jesus only" background. Had I understood that point, I would have known that he was trying to drag me into a Unitarian vs. Trinitarian argument by wanting to know what the Holy Spirit's proper name is. Based on the fact that Jesus commanded us to baptize in <u>the name</u> of the Father, the Son, and the Holy Ghost (Matthew 28:19) rather than the three names of three different entities, the argument he was trying to present was that there is only one name for all three. Then, referring to the fact that the disciples responded by baptizing in the name of Jesus (Acts 2:38, 8:16, 19:5), his argument would have continued that the proper name for all three members of the Trinity is "Jesus."

Had I been aware of where he was trying to lead the discussion, I would have been armed with the rebuttal that the audiences that the apostles were addressing were all Jews who had no issue with being baptized in the name of the Father or in the name of the Holy Spirit; however, for them to be baptized in the name of Jesus was a major obstacle. After all, this was the man that they had just murdered a few days before. (Acts 2:21-23) For them to now have to acknowledge Him as their Savior was a total admission to guilt and a reversal of everything they believed.

But, I did not know that the gentleman was trying to challenge my theology; therefore, the question seemed rather "off the wall." However, the answer that I gave – which we will see tomorrow – not only answered his query but also helped the entire group get a new insight into the Holy Spirit.

June 12
The Holy Spirit's Proper Name – Part Ii

I began by referencing Jesus' statement in John 16:13-15 where He said the Holy Spirit would not testify of Himself but would speak only of the Father and the Son. Next, I asked if anyone in the room knew how the Bible came to be written. Of course, everyone responded with the fact that men wrote as they were inspired by the Holy Spirit. (II Peter 1:21) My next comment was that it was amazing that – with approximately forty men writing over a period of fifteen hundred years – not one of them was inspired to give us the Holy Spirit's proper name. They told us the proper name of the Father, (YHWH or Jehovah) and the proper name of the Son (Jesus), but failed to give us the Holy Spirit's proper name. Why? Because the Holy Spirit was inspiring them to write, and He was interested in only writing about the Father and the Son – not Himself.

Next, I turned to the story of Abraham's quest for a bride for Isaac in Genesis chapter twenty-four. There, I pointed out that it was interesting that the entire narrative never gives the name of the trusted servant that the father sent to find a wife for his son. When the servant found Rebekah, he talked only about Abraham and Isaac without speaking anything about himself. He also gave the damsel gifts that were sent from the father and son but never took any credit for his part in getting them to her. I then suggested that this story was a symbolic foreshadowing of the New Testament in which the Father sends His trusted but unnamed counterpart (the Holy Spirit) to find a bride for His Son.

In heaven, we'll probably learn the Holy Spirit's proper name – just as we learned the name of Abraham's servant. (Genesis 15:2) But not right now!

June 13
You're Not So Young
With my birthday coming up in a couple days, someone shared this encouragement with me.

You're not so young when:

Your back goes out but you stay home.

You and your teeth don't sleep together.

You try to straighten out the wrinkles in your socks and discover you're not wearing any.

You hear snap, crackle, pop at the breakfast table, but you're not eating any cereal.

You wake up looking like your driver's license picture.

It takes two tries to get up from the couch.

When your idea of a night out is sitting on the patio.

When happy hour is a nap.

When you're on vacation and your energy runs out before your money does.

When all you want for your birthday is to not be reminded of your age.

Your idea of weight lifting is standing up.

It takes longer to rest than it did to get tired.

Your address book has all names that start with "Dr."

You sit in a rocking chair and can't get it going.

The pharmacist has become your new best friend.

The twinkle in your eye is only a reflection from the sun on your bifocals.

The iron in your blood turns to lead in your pants.

It takes twice as long to look half as good.

You sink your teeth into a steak and they stay there.

You give up all your bad habits and still don't feel good.

Rocking in a rocking chair feels like a roller coaster ride.

You finally "have your head together" but your body is falling apart.

You wonder how you could be over the hill when you don't even remember being on top of it.

Flag Day

Four Freedoms

During World War II, American President Roosevelt and British Prime Minister Churchill held a secret rendezvous on board a vessel in the middle of the Atlantic and created the Atlantic Charter which listed the Four Freedoms: Freedom from want, Freedom from fear, Freedom of speech, and Freedom of religion.

On Flag Day, we honor our flag that represents the liberties that our government ensures to us. However, we must remember that most Americans still live in one form of bondage or another – whether financial, social, physical, or psychological. The problem with civil freedom is that it is constructed by men who are looking from the viewpoint of bondage. The human race has such a history of living in bondage that we have become accustomed to the lack of freedom and see liberty as the exception rather than the rule. God's perspective is that liberty is inherent in the godly character that He originally created in man.

Notice that the Atlantic Charter listed two freedoms as freedom <u>from</u> something and two freedoms as freedom <u>of</u> something. We can actually consider that the freedoms <u>from</u> are demonstrations of the created order looking up to the Creator while the freedom <u>of</u> are demonstrations of the Creator looking down upon His creation. The only way to be free from want and fear is to look up to God and the only way to have freedom of speech and religion is to accept the grace that God extends through godly governments.

Today, let's express full gratitude to the government that grants us liberty – but most of all – let's celebrate the true freedom that only comes from Christ.

Father's Day
Titus, My Son
Last month, we discussed the concept of multiplication in the kingdom of God by discipleship. Today, I'd like to dedicate the Father's Day meditation to the concept of mentorship or discipleship – fathering not only physical sons but also spiritual offspring. Paul provided a great example for us in that he mentored his disciple Titus to the point where he literally called him his son. (Titus 1:4)

The first principle that Paul demonstrated was that he had to know his own identity before he could try to pass it on to Titus. In Titus 1:1, he proclaimed that he knew that he was a servant of God and an apostle of Jesus Christ. He then followed up with the directive that Titus should speak with authority and that he not let anyone despise his youthful inexperience – the kind of result that comes from knowing who you are. (Titus 2:15)

Paul's next foundation for discipleship was knowing what he wanted to accomplish in the life of his disciple. In verse 1:5, Paul spelled out explicitly what he expected to come out of the life of his spiritual son.

In chapter two, Paul came to the heart of fathering – teaching Titus to become a trainer rather than a perpetual student – and to make his disciples trainers of others.

In verse 2:11, the Apostle revealed the key to successful discipleship – that spiritual growth and maturity come by grace, not performance.

Finally, Paul demonstrated the delicate balance between being an encourager and a rebuker. Titus 1:13, 2:6) It is far too easy to fall into the ditch on either side of the road – to only want to speak positively and fail to correct or to correct at the expense of edification.

June 16

True Freedom

*If the Son therefore shall make you free, ye
shall be free indeed.* (John 8:36)

As a follow-up on the Flag Day lesson and the coming Independence Day holiday, I'd like to explore a few more thoughts on freedom.

Let's begin with the idea of true freedom – the kind of freedom that comes only through having the Lord totally in charge of our lives. For an example of this kind of freedom, let's take a look at the life of Joseph. We all know the story of how he was thrown into the pit, sold as a slave, lived for years as a servant in the home of his master, and was eventually falsely accused and thrown into a dungeon without the benefit of a trial. Certainly, his life was not what we would call one of freedom – yet, he was actually the only truly free character in the whole story.

When his brothers, victimized by the famine, showed up in Egypt to look for food, we see that they were still slaves of guilt for what they had done to their brother so many years earlier – even though there was nothing in the present situation that should have prompted them to think of Joseph. *We are verily guilty concerning our brother, in that we saw the anguish of his soul, when he besought us, and we would not hear; therefore is this distress come upon us.* (Genesis 42:21) In chapter thirty-nine (especially verse ten), we see that Potiphar's wife was a slave to lust. Yet, Joseph is never depicted as being subject to any emotional bondages of guilt, resentment, remorse, or depression that could have resulted from all his misfortune. With God as his source, he was free!

Different Forms of Freedom

Freedom – or at least what we perceive as freedom – comes in many forms. As we have already seen, Joseph was free emotionally and spiritually even though he was a slave and a prisoner. All the while, the brothers who sold him into slavery and the woman who put him in jail were imprisoned even though they walked free. Joseph knew true freedom even though he was in chains and behind bars. In the New Testament, we find another prisoner – Paul, who wrote the most liberating letters of all times while locked in a jail cell. In modern history, we read the story of Corrie ten Boom who was incarcerated in a Nazi concentration camp yet grew stronger and bolder while the guards who held her hostage were the true prisoners – slaves to the guilt that drove many of them insane after only a few weeks at their posts.

The story of the thousand Jewish rebels who held out in the fortress of Masada as the Romans conquered the Holy Land gives us another twist on the idea of freedom. As the Roman armies moved in for the final siege, they all committed suicide rather than allowing themselves to be taken as captives to Rome. To them, freedom of spirit – even in death – was more valuable than life itself.

In their decision to release Barabbas rather than Jesus, the Jews made a decision between two kinds of freedom. Barabbas was a symbol of political freedom in that he was integral to the insurrection against Rome. Jesus offered spiritual freedom – a concept that didn't make a lot of sense to those suffering under the tyranny of the empire. What they failed to see was that they also made a choice between temporary freedom and the chance to be eternally free!

June 18

Choosing Freedom

Yesterday's meditation, concluded with the idea that Jesus offered spiritual freedom rather than political freedom. Yet, there is an interesting episode in the gospels that actually comments on this exact idea. In John 6:15, we read that Jesus perceived that the people were ready to take Him by force and press Him into declaring Himself as their king. Escaping the crowd, He resorted to a mountain alone. Although this particular context does not expound on what happened in the solitude of that mountain, we know from other accounts that Jesus used such times of privacy to commune with His Father. It was after these occasions of seclusion with His Father that Jesus stepped back into the scene in a new dimension – sometimes walking on water, sometimes appointing the apostles and enduing them with power over disease and demons, sometimes taking authority over nature…but always demonstrating a renewed and enhanced authority. Amazingly, the people failed to see what was going on. They wanted Him to use His authority to give them political freedom from Rome while totally ignoring the fact that He was continually demonstrating to them that He could offer them a totally different kind of freedom through His authority over all the works of the devil. We can take the discussion even further by remembering that Zebedee's wife asked that her sons be allowed to sit on Jesus' right and left hand in the kingdom (Matthew 20:20-21) and that the disciples were still looking for Jesus to restore independence to Israel even after the resurrection (Acts 1:6).

We must be discerning enough to realize what kind of freedom is really important.

June 19

Freedom with a Pierced Ear

Have you ever noticed how the birds in the zoo continue to sing even though they are in cages and the monkeys play and swing about on the ropes even though they are confined in their enclosure? However, just around the corner, the lions and tigers pace unhappily against the bars of their compounds. Additionally, zoos have to implement breeding programs in order to induce the big cats to reproduce since they tend to shut down reproduction in captivity. The bottom line is that the cats see captivity as a loss of freedom while the monkeys and birds believe that they are still free even while they know that they live in enclosures.

There is an interesting scriptural parallel in Deuteronomy 15:12-17 where we read of the Hebrew slaves who were given the opportunity to go free but decided that they preferred the love and security they had experienced in their masters' homes. Upon making the decision to remain in servitude, they willingly gave up physical freedom in exchange for the benefits that they had come to enjoy in the masters' homes. To symbolize this decision, they were required to have their ears pierced as a physical display of their voluntary state of servanthood. In the New Testament, Paul identified himself as a bondservant of Jesus Christ (Romans 1:1) – essentially, one who had given up the freedom to follow his carnal nature for the security and love that he had found in serving Christ. Even though he probably didn't have a pierced ear, he certainly had his heart pierced and surrendered to Christ.

Like a monkey or a bird, he was free to sing, live joyfully, and reproduce while living under the restraints of obedience to righteousness. (Romans 6:16)

June 20
Misdirected Freedom
In those days there was no king in Israel, but
every man did that which was right in his
own eyes. (Judges 17:6, 21:25)

When there was no legal regulation in Israel, each man became his own judge – a condition that might seem like total freedom. However, it was actually a condition of unrestraint and anarchy. With no one to set guidelines, freedom can actually become a curse rather than a blessing. Because people generally don't recognize the consequences that are inevitably tied to their actions, they usually take freedom as an opportunity for unrestricted actions that will eventually prove harmful to themselves, others, and the environment in general. Proverbs 16:25 speaks to this tendency when Solomon surmised that there is a way that seems right to a man ends but in the ways of death. You see, this Old Testament writer understood something that later became a New Testament principle – no one actually lives free of a master. We all have to choose to be subjects of Christ – or, by default, we become slaves of sin. (Romans 6:23) Either way, there will be consequences – consequences based on the nature of the master we choose to serve: Satan who is a murderer (John 8:44) or Jesus who is a life giver (John 10:10)

If we choose to become slaves to God, we find freedom even in our servitude – freedom from our past, sin, failure, and hate; freedom to our future, righteousness, success, and love; freedom through our present, Christ, faith, and forgiveness.

June 21

Celebrate Freedom

Now that we have a little clearer vision of what freedom is, it's time to celebrate. Every day, we should praise God who created freedom. We should follow that by thanking Him for giving that freedom to us. The next step should be to recognize all the areas of freedom that we have been given and determine to live in them. Of course, we must remember the price that was paid for those freedoms. Just as the rockets' red glare on the Fourth of July are intended for more than just "ooh"s and "ah"s – they are reminders of the mortar fire over the battlefields where so many gave their lives so that we can have a nation that shoots off fireworks – we must also remember the sacrifice that Jesus made so that we can be free. Of course, the true celebration of freedom is to bring others to that freedom by sharing our forgiveness with them so that they are no longer held in the bondage of guilt over their offenses toward us and by leading them to the ultimate freedom through salvation. Next, we celebrate that we are free by using every opportunity to its fullest. We've all heard the expression, "If you've got it, flaunt it." Well, that's the way Jesus expects us to live. Since we are free to love, we should love even our enemies. Since we are free to forgive, we should forgive a minimum of seventy times seven every day. Since we are free to give, we should give to everyone that we find in need. Since we are free to share, we should present the gospel everywhere, all the time, to anyone who will listen. Since we are free to decide which master we wish to serve, we should submit ourselves unto Christ while resisting every influence of the devil.

Let freedom ring! (Leviticus 25:10)

June 22
Addition and Multiplication
There is an interesting mathematical principle presented in the growth of the early church. In Acts 2:47, we are told that as many as were saved were added to the church each day. However, in Acts 6:7, we find that the number of the disciples multiplied greatly.

These two mathematical functions help us to understand a very important principle concerning kingdom growth. Getting people saved does, indeed, increase the kingdom; however, real growth occurs through discipleship. When new believers are nurtured and trained, they also become soul winners – causing multiplication in the kingdom rather than simply addition of new members to the Body of Christ.

If one evangelist were able to win a thousand new souls for the kingdom each year, he would have added sixteen thousand believers by the end of sixteen years of ministry. However, if that evangelist were to win only one person each six months, but were able to disciple that new believer until he also became an evangelist and disciple, he could literally win the world in the same sixteen years. Yes, the start would seem awfully slow, because at the end of six months there would only be two believers – the evangelist and his first convert. At the end of the year, there would be only four – the evangelist, his two converts, and the convert that his first disciple had won. If you were to take the time to do the math and calculate how many people would be affected if this method of multiplication were to continue to reduplicate itself over sixteen years, you would be surprised to find that the result would be that the entire world population could be reached!

The Promise

In the story of the thief on the cross who asked for Jesus to remember him in the heavenly kingdom (Luke 23:42), there is a powerful lesson that we can all learn and use in our daily lives. Notice that Jesus did assure the man that he would be with Him in paradise, but the promise was followed immediately by three hours of darkness. It is the same in our lives – most of the times that we receive promises from God, a period of trial comes before we see the fulfillment.

The first observation that we need to make about this story is that the thief lived through the whole thing. We know that he was still alive at the end of the three hours of darkness because the soldiers had to break his legs in order to hasten his death before the Passover began. On an even grander scale, the disciples had to live through the whole ordeal of the arrest, trial, burial, and three days in the grave while struggling with all the promises that Jesus had given them during their time with Him. The resurrection finally came as a triumphant proclamation of victory. The point is that we'll live through our trying times too!

The key is in Jesus' answer to the thief:

Verily, I say – There is **p**ower behind the promise.

To you – The promise is **p**ersonally addressed to us.

Today – It is a **p**resent guarantee, not "pie in the sky."

You – It is a **p**rivate confirmation, not a general concept.

Shall be – It is a **p**ositive word, not wishing or hoping.

With me – The assurance centers on our **p**osition, or relationship, with Christ.

In paradise – God's promises are the pledge of His eternal care and **p**rovision.

Steps to the Top

Rule #1 – Start at the bottom.

Paul confirmed this principle when he said in Philippians 4:11-12 that he had learned to be content in any condition. While at the bottom, he didn't complain about his situation. He simply allowed God's grace to be his sufficiency. With this approach, he was positioned for promotion toward the top.

Rule #2 – Be a servant.

Jesus taught us that graciously – and even voluntarily – accepting the role of a servant is the key to advancement. (Mark 9:35, 10:43-44) He added that faithfully serving – as opposed to grudgingly fulfilling our obligations – is the doorway to promotion. (Matthew 25:21)

Rule #3 – Bloom where you are planted.

Ecclesiastes 9:10 and Colossians 3:22-23 remind us that, in our roles of servanthood, we must fulfill all our duties as if we are working directly for the Lord rather than our human overseers. This attitude, qualifies us for God's promotion, not just human advancement. (Psalm 75:6-7)

The classic example of how these principles work is found in the life of Joseph. Sold into slavery as a young man, he could have lived and died without anyone – even his master – ever taking notice of his existence. After all, the role of a good slave is to be essentially invisible as he performs his duties. Yet, Joseph applied each of these rules to his service in Potiphar's house and eventually rose to the top position in his organization. After false accusations, Joseph found himself in prison where he again applied all these principles and rose to a position of leadership in the jail – and eventually in the empire.

June 25
Simple Thoughts That Can Change Your Life
Satan may be god of this world, but the earth is an insignificant speck in all the universe.

Lucifer was cast out of heaven so his judgment would begin in the area where we have dominion.

Grace is realizing that you didn't do anything – just like you didn't make the sunrise.

Paul's third prayer over the thorn in his flesh didn't change God; it changed Paul.

Be humble to obtain grace (I Peter 5:5) but approach the throne of grace boldly (Hebrews 4:16).

There are two roads to wisdom – mistakes and mentors.

There is no substitute for excellence – not even success.

If you don't sow seeds, you'll grow weeds.

The fear of the Lord is not being scared of His judgment but having a cautious fear that our actions or attitudes might break His heart.

If you grab hold of a thing, you will lose it and yourself. The separating of the sheep and goats had to do with those who grasped hold of their possessions and those who gave themselves and their goods back to God in service to the least in the kingdom.

Dreams come to pass by action. (Ecclesiastes 5:3)

It's not just gifts and anointing that make a leader – it's also the human side of love that counts.

You're not a leader unless you have someone to lead and understand how to allow each person to use his gift and fulfill his calling.

Look unto Jesus – don't focus on issues.

Ideas are a dime a dozen; people who use them are priceless.

June 26
Reaping What You Sow
Be not deceived; God is not mocked: for whatsoever a man soweth, that shall he also reap. (Galatians 6:7)

I find it interesting that in all the teaching that is so prevalent in the Body of Christ today concerning sowing and reaping, we very rarely hear today's verse incorporated. The whole idea of being deceived in the practice of sowing and reaping and the even more radical idea that sowing and reaping could be a mockery of God are basically foreign to the way we are led to view the principle of seedtime and harvest today. However, they are principles that must be cautiously considered.

Many ministers use the teaching as a way to motivate – and even manipulate – people to give to their ministries. However, the foundational truth is that you cannot sow deception and reap believers. Ministers who have deceptive, ulterior motives in presenting the message will inevitably reap a harvest of followers who give with selfish, ulterior motives – not loyal believers who give joyously and altruistically to the Lord.

Remember that Jacob masqueraded as Esau and eventually discovered that he had had the same identity "switcheroo" pulled on him when he woke up after his wedding night to discover that he was married to Leah rather than Rachel for whom he had served seven years. (Genesis 27:19, 29:25)

When we sow in integrity, we reap Incredibly. Abraham gave up his family when he "sacrificed" Isaac (Genesis 22:9) and reaped all the families of the earth (Genesis 12:1-3).

June 27

I'd Like a Refund

A number of years ago, a guest speaker at our church ministered on self-discipline and changing our mentality in order to change our lives – using himself as the example in that he had lost sixty-five pounds. The funny thing that happened is that, when he came back to the church about a year later, he was as heavy as ever! I honestly wanted to go up to him and ask for a refund on the offering that I had given in the service the previous year.

My thoughts that I want to share today are not so much about getting a monetary refund; rather, they are about the spiritual "refunds" that are "cashed in" when ministers don't back up their messages with their lives. In I Samuel 2:22-25, we find the story of how Eli's sons served as the priests in Israel but their lives were anything but sacred – they committed fornication with the girls who came to worship and they stole the offerings. The scripture clearly states that the result was not simply that Hophni and Phinehas were in sin and rebellion, but that their actions caused the entire nation to transgress – and not just transgressions against one another, but directly against God Himself.

When the person who is in the position of representing God to others lives a life that does not express His true nature, those who see his actions will have no respect for the true nature of God and, therefore, live contrary to the truth. As we have seen in this story, the sinfulness of Eli's sons forced the people into transgression. On the other hand, the Pharisees of Jesus' day lived lives that observed every "jot and tittle" of the law but didn't express the love of God. The result was that they made converts who were actually children of hell. (Matthew 23:15)

June 28

Jehovah Shammah: The God Who is There

When we talk about the nature of God, we often think of His redemptive "Jehovah" names – our Healer, our Provider, our Righteousness. However, there is one Jehovah name that we often overlook because it may not be as spectacular as some of the other names. But we don't have healing or provision or righteousness if God isn't there – Jehovah Shammah. (Ezekiel 48:35)

The classic example of His always being there is found in the story of the three Hebrew men who found themselves in Nebuchadnezzar's fiery furnace. (Daniel 3:24-25) When the king looked in and saw a fourth man protecting, comforting, and fellowshipping with them in the seven-times-hotter-than-normal inferno, he realized immediately that it was the very Son of God. So it must be with us – we must always beware that He has never abandoned us but has gone with us right into the middle of any situation that we find ourselves. (Hebrews 13:5)

A man that hath friends must shew himself friendly: and there is a friend that sticketh closer than a brother. (Proverbs 18:24)

God is our refuge and strength, a very present help in trouble. Therefore will not we fear, though the earth be removed, and though the mountains be carried into the midst of the sea; Though the waters thereof roar and be troubled, though the mountains shake with the swelling thereof. Selah. (Psalm 46:1-3)

June 29

Signs Along the Way

On a veterinary office in Wyoming – Animal farmacy

On an orchard in Michigan – Treemendous fruit

On a car wash in Washington – You auto wash it

On a highway sign in Colorado – Littering is unlAWFUL

On a bakery truck – Drive carefully. The loaf you save may be your own.

In a bar – Ladies are requested not to have children at the bar.

In a restaurant – Customers who find the waitresses rude should see the manager.

Upon arrival at the airport – Please wear your clothes.

In a grocery store – For your convenience, we recommend the courteous, efficient self-check-out system.

At a zoo – Please do not feed the animals. If you have suitable food, please give it to the guards.

At a drycleaners – Drop your trousers here for the best results.

Along a highway – If this sign is under water, the road is impassable.

At an airline check-in counter – We take your bags and send them in all directions.

At a cafeteria – We do not reuse food.

Near a school – School zone, no passing.

On Maui – Hurricane evacuation route, no exit.

Limiting God

Yea, they turned back and tempted God, and
limited the Holy One of Israel. (Psalm 78:41)

The idea that God could possibly be limited may at first seem to be illogical. After all, how could any force possibly thwart the Almighty? In reality, there is nothing that could possibly physically overpower God or outmaneuver Him; however, He has chosen to submit Himself to certain self-imposed rules inherent with His decision to make humans autonomous with freewill. Operating in these restrictions, there are at least five ways that humans can limit God's authority and expression in their lives:

1) Lack of vision – Studies have shown that at least sixty percent of people don't know God's will for their lives. Without a direction and a goal in life, we limit God's ability to help us on the journey.

2) Resistance to change – God is a creator who is always introducing innovation and improvement. Rejection cuts off that creative power in our lives.

3) Fear – We often use the terms "petrified" and "paralyzed" to speak of the debilitating power of fear. When we allow fear to incapacitate us, we are refusing the power of God to take us to new experiences and realities.

4) Unbelief – Truth never changes, but it is our perception of reality that can be altered and distorted. The fact that we decide not to believe any of the promises of God does not make those promises any less real; it just makes them inaccessible to us.

5) Disobedience – Deliberate refusal obviously forces God's intervention out of our lives.

July 1

An Intelligent Man and a False Prophet

And when they had gone through the isle unto Paphos, they found a certain sorcerer, a false prophet, a Jew, whose name was Barjesus: Which was with the deputy of the country, Sergius Paulus, a prudent man; who called for Barnabas and Saul, and desired to hear the word of God. (Acts 13:6-7)

This story makes a very interesting comment on human nature – Sergius Paulus was a prudent (or intelligent) person; yet, he was under the influence of a deceiver. The intellectuals of today's world are guilty of the same kind of deception .

I toured a dinosaur fossil exhibit a couple years ago and listened to the naturalist try to sound intelligent while presenting idea after idea as fact when, in fact, none of them could be substantiated and many were totally against logic and even contradictory to things that she had already said. As I listened to her presentation, Romans 1:22 kept echoing in my head, *Professing themselves to be wise, they became fools.*

Any truly intellectual person would have easily seen the fallacy in her arguments, but the scientific and educational leaders of today are so totally under the influence of Charles Darwin that they can't even see that they have given up reason and logic to espouse his evolutionary theory – a concept that they have adopted as fact and use as grounds for their arguments when they haven't even proven it! In fact, it has become a common practice to reject phenomena evidence that doesn't fit their evolutionary model rather than to honestly examine their theory in light of the evidence.

July 2
Ignored Evidence
Want a really interesting example of how intellectuals are so deceived by Charles Darwin that they can't even see what is right before their eyes? I'd suggest trying to visit the Turnage-Patton Trail in the Paluxy River bed near Glen Rose, Texas. There, you'll see rock-solid proof that dinosaurs and humans lived at the same time, not millions of years apart as the theory of evolution insists.

The length and the beautifully preserved detail of the three trails of dinosaur footprints containing almost two hundred incredibly detailed tracks extending over five hundred feet make this one of the finest displays of dinosaur tracks in the world. In spite of the fact that this find is well accepted in the scientific world, the same paleontologists who laud the dinosaur footprints refuse to acknowledge the fact that fourteen human footprints are also part of the same formation. An additional fifteen human footprints have been uncovered in a nearby excavation, and one other human foot impression has been located in close proximity to the dinosaur tracks. Additionally, other human footprints have been discovered in New Mexico, embedded in geological strata that supposedly predates the time of dinosaurs.

Of course, the evolutionists simply ignore such rock solid evidence because it disproves their imaginary theories. But then, this is exactly the attitude of fallen humanity:

> *Who changed the truth of God into a lie, and worshipped and served the creature more than the Creator, who is blessed for ever. Amen.* (Romans 1:25)

July 3

The Truth on Campus

In an attempt to force out the truth so that the current philosophies could go unchallenged, my alma mater, North Carolina State University, attempted to pass a ruling requiring Christian students to have a permit before talking about Jesus. Fortunately, the Alliance Defending Freedom filed a lawsuit claiming that the Christian students were unconstitutionally prohibited from passing out fliers, leaving their student tables, and talking about Jesus while other student organizations were able to speak freely without a permit. The attorneys argued, "The courts have well established that a public university can't require permits in this manner for this kind of speech – and certainly can't enforce such rules selectively...Unconstitutional censorship is bad enough, but giving university officials complete discretion to decide when and where to engage in silencing students makes the violation even worse...The only permit needed to engage in free speech is the First Amendment."

Actually, the First Amendment guarantees much more freedom of expression of faith on campus than most students and teachers realize. It is totally legal for teachers to pray with colleagues during breaks or at lunchtime. They may lead before- and after-school religious clubs for students. They can answer students' questions about their beliefs honestly, and they may even pray with students outside work hours. It's okay to keep a Bible on their desk and teach about it in class, so long as it fits within the curriculum. Of course, they can always witness for Jesus by acting in a godly manner so that others might be provoked to wonder - and ask - why they have so much kindness and compassion.

Independence Day
The Foundations of Our Nation
We are a Christian people…not because the law demands it, not to gain benefits or to avoid legal disabilities, but from choice and education; and in a land thus universally Christian, what is to be expected, what desired, but that we shall pay due regard to Christianity. – Senate Judiciary Committee Report, January 19, 1853

It is the duty of all nations to acknowledge the providence of Almighty God, to obey His will, to be grateful for His benefits, and humbly to improve His protection and favor. – George Washington

Those who will not be governed by God will be ruled by tyrants. – William Penn

Where can the principles of morality be learned so clearly or so perfectly as from the New Testament? – US Supreme Court, 1844

We are a Christian people and acknowledge with reverence the duty of obedience to the will of God. – US Supreme Court, 1931

The Bible is worth more than all other books ever printed. – Patrick Henry

Of all books, the Bible contributes most to make men good, wise, and happy. – John Quincy Adams

The secret to my success? It is found in the Bible, *In all thy ways acknowledge him, and he shall direct thy paths.* – George Washington Carver

This great nation was founded on the gospel of Jesus Christ. – Patrick Henry

If we abide by the principles taught in the Bible, our country will go on prospering. – Daniel Webster

But for the Bible, we could not know right. – Abraham Lincoln

July 5

Going Deeper in Jesus

The other day, someone mentioned to me her desire to "go deeper in Jesus." The image that immediately flashed into my mind was an illustrated sermon that one of my students had presented in a children's meeting on a recent mission trip. She had a beautifully wrapped gift box with several other equally attractive gift boxes inside. Based on the reference in II Corinthians 9:15 that salvation is a gift, she opened the big box to see what was inside when she accepted the gift of salvation. Of course, the other boxes inside represented all the many other spiritual benefits that the Bible also describes as gifts – righteousness (Romans 5:17), eternal life (Romans 6:23), grace (Ephesians 3:9), and the gifts of the Spirit (I Corinthians 12:4). With this imagery in mind, I envisioned an antique chest that my grandmother had when I was a little child. Always imagining that it was a pirate's treasure chest, my cousins and I always wanted to have the chance to look inside. Suddenly, I could envision that the lady who wanted to "go deeper in Jesus" had finally found the key to that mysterious old chest. I could picture her bending over the open box pulling out one item after another – trying to get to the bottom to find the last treasure that was hidden in it.

With this vision in mind, I turned to my Bible to see what it describes as the things to be discovered when we begin to explore what is in Jesus. To do so, I looked up all the verses that reference *in Christ* and *in Him*. To my surprise, there were over one hundred such references – and I'd like to take the time to explore a few of the most significant ones. In doing so, hopefully we can all go a little deeper in Jesus. Join me on this journey.

July 6
All Fullness is in Christ
The first verse that I'd like to look at is Colossians 1:19 that tells us that it pleased God that all fullness should dwell in Jesus. I couldn't keep myself from interpreting that verse with the image of a scene from a circus clown act when one of the clowns opens a box and a bunch of coiled snakes pop out like a Jack-in-the-Box. Of course the other clowns all stand around laughing at the shock of the one who unwittingly opened the lid. They had taken pleasure in pulling the prank on their friend. Of course, God was not joking when He took pleasure in packing Jesus so full of blessings that they just spring out at us when we begin to explore what it means to live in Him. All of us have experienced this sort of thing when we open a piece of merchandise that was packaged at the factory. Once we take it out of the box, there is no possible way to get all the merchandise and the packing material back into the original box. I've always assumed that this is the manufacture's way of ensuring that we aren't able to return the product for a refund because a requirement for getting our money back is to return the item in the original package!

But back to the topic at hand – it pleased God that He could cause all fullness to dwell in Christ. In other words, He rejoices just like those clowns when He sees the surprise on our faces and the delight in our hearts when we begin to experience the blessings that are ours in Christ – blessings that are more than we know how to contain (Malachi 3:10) and that are more than we could ever imagine or dare to ask for (Ephesians 3:20).

No Void

Additionally, we must realize that Colossians 1:19 tells us that *all fullness dwells in Him*. This means that there is no emptiness in Him. I think that many Christians fail to grasp hold to this reality. A number of popular Christian songs, several faith-based movies, and at least one of the leading daily devotionals on the market today tout the idea that God is often distant, silent, or not responsive. These compositions try to promote a message of patience, endurance, and trust during such times; however, they genuinely "miss the mark" in that they fail to recognize that He is a God who is ever present in our times of need (Psalm 46:1), that He is a friend that sticks closer than a brother (Proverbs 18:24), that He is Jehovah Shammah (Ezekiel 48:35) – the ever-present God who is always with us, even in the fiery furnace (Daniel 3:25). In Jesus, there is fullness – never void or emptiness.

> *John bare witness of him, and cried, saying, This was he of whom I spake, He that cometh after me is preferred before me: for he was before me. And of his fulness have all we received, and grace for grace.* (John 1:15-16)
>
> *Which is his body, the fulness of him that filleth all in all.* (Ephesians 1:23)
>
> *And to know the love of Christ, which passeth knowledge, that ye might be filled with all the fulness of God.* (Ephesians 3:19)
>
> *For in him dwelleth all the fulness of the Godhead bodily.* (Colossians 2:9)

July 8

Salvation

Once we've opened the box and gotten over the recoil at all the treasures inside, the first package that we find inside is labeled "salvation." Second Timothy 2:10 assures us that we'll find salvation in Christ Jesus. Of course, that is the first and foremost selling point that gets most people to turn to the Jesus treasure chest in the first place. We are presented with the alternative that since we are sinners, we have only two options – either to accept Jesus and be saved or reject Him and go straight to hell without passing "Go" and receiving our two hundred dollars. In other words, Jesus is our "get out of hell free" card in life's grand Monopoly game.

I'm sure that we all remember the story of the thief on the cross who asked Jesus to remember him when He came into His kingdom (Luke 23:42), and we've all heard of the deathbed salvations or even the man on death row who prays with the chaplain just before walking that "long mile" to the gas chamber. These individuals have spent their whole lives living selfishly and in sin but turn to Jesus just before drawing their last breath. Of course, we rejoice that these individuals have received eternal life and will not – as the old Pentecostal preachers used to say – "split hell wide open." However, we must lament that they never got to explore all the riches waiting for them in their Jesus treasure chest.

Jesus came that we could have abundant life here on earth – not just eternal life in heaven. John described eternal life not as going to heaven but as knowing God, *This is life eternal, that they might know thee the only true God, and Jesus Christ, whom thou hast sent* (John 17:3) – digging into the treasure chest.

July 9

Redemption

Along with salvation, we also receive redemption (Romans 3:24) – a treasure that illustrates an amazing aspect of God's love. I'd like to tell a little story about redemption. A young boy built a small model boat – a laborious task and labor of love. When he completed the project, he excitedly took his little vessel to the lake to test it out. Delighted, he watched as the wind filled the tiny sails and the boat began to gracefully cut through the waters. Unfortunately, a sudden gust of wind propelled the little boat just beyond his grasp. As he waded into the lake to retrieve the toy boat, the wind continued to push the boat further and further, until it disappeared. Heartbroken, the lad went home thinking that he might never see his little boat again; yet, one day, he was surprised to see it on display in the front window of a local pawn shop. Apparently, someone had found the boat and sold it to the store owner for a few pennies. When he rushed into the shop and told the sales clerk that the boat was his, the clerk's response was that it actually belonged to the store and the only way that the boy could have it would be to pay the asking price. When the lad broke his piggy bank, he discovered that it would take everything he had to pay for the little boat; however, he didn't hesitate to take every one of his coins – to the very last cent – to reclaim his treasured little boat. As he walked out of the pawn shop, he cuddled his prized little boat and exclaimed, "Now, you are twice mine – I made you, and I also bought you." That's the story of redemption – God made us, but bought us back at the terrible price of His own Son when we were lost due to our sins. Our salvation is actually a redemption – God's way of reclaiming us for His benefit – as well as a rescue.

July 10

New Birth

Unless we understand the redemptive aspect of salvation, we run the risk of living our lives just like the deathbed converts – even though we may live for years or even decades after we receive salvation. Until we grasp this concept, we'll not understand how important it is to keep digging in the treasure chest – because it brings delight to Him as well as to us as we discover the jewels inside the box.

As we dig into our Jesus treasure chest, the next discovery we make is that we have new birth as well as salvation. Of course, it is easy to confuse the two because we often use the terms interchangeably; however, let's think back at our own lives and think about our salvation experience. We probably realized an immediate change in many areas.

In giving her testimony, my wife describes the night she was ready to commit suicide and "accidentally" picked up a piece of gospel literature that had been handed to her a few days earlier. After reading the tract and praying the prayer on the last page, she fell asleep with the decision that she could postpone her suicide until the next morning. When she woke up the following dawn, she could hear the birds singing happier songs than she had ever remembered. She could see the sun shining a little brighter than she ever recollected. She had been born again as well as being saved. Had she initiated her plan to take her own life before she prayed that prayer, she would have been saved and even redeemed – but because she gave the Lord a few more hours to work in her, she realized that she had actually become a new creature in Christ and that all the old aspects of her life had passed away as Paul described in II Corinthians 5:17.

Suicide to the Old Man

In all reality, Peggy had committed suicide – she had crucified and mortified the old sinful woman she had been so that she could be reborn as a new righteous woman. (Colossians 3:5) In actuality, she had received two distinct gifts – salvation and the new birth as a new creature in Christ. Unfortunately, some people prefer to stop with just the first gift and never dig any deeper in the treasure chest to discover the wonderful gift that they have as new creatures in Christ.

But that is not the case here; we are excited about going deeper in Jesus – so let's keep digging into the chest. But before we pull out another gift, we realize that the "new birth" package we are holding seems pretty heavy. Maybe there is something inside. Yes, when we open it up, we discover that it is filled with many other gifts just waiting to be discovered. The first one that catches our eye is labeled "righteousness." Second Corinthians 5:21 records that we have been made the righteousness of God in Jesus. What a revelation! No matter how sinful our lives have been, we have been made totally righteous through the righteousness of Jesus who lived His full life without committing one sin. (Hebrews 4:15) As mysterious as it may seem that Jesus (who never sinned) was counted as being guilty of all our sins, it is equally unfathomable to conceive that we (who deserve no credit since all our good deeds are nothing more than polluted rags in God's sight) could be credited with all the righteousness of Jesus. Unthinkable? Yes! Impossible to comprehend? Yes! But true? Even more so, yes!!

July 12

The Bonus Gift

Just as most products come with a warning that they be used properly and with the appropriate safety gear, this package comes with a user's manual notation that it is not to be abused as an excuse for sinning or a license to sin. (Galatians 5:13) In essence, this gift is our license to live free <u>from</u> sin rather than our permit to live freely <u>in</u> sin.

As we marvel at this incredible gift, we realize that it is actually a bonus package with another gift wrapped together with it. This second gift in the same wrapper is labeled "perfection" – a term that almost makes us cringe just to hear it, especially in relationship to our own lives since we all know our own selves well enough to know that our names and the term "perfection" don't legitimately belong in the same sentence. However, God says that in Christ, we have perfection and that it is His intent that we be presented as such. (Colossians 1:28) So what is perfection?

In the letter to the church at Sardis (Revelation 3:1-6), the Lord probed the question of perfection. It is commonly assumed that believers cannot obtain perfection and are, therefore, exempt from striving for it. In fact, that whole philosophy was once flaunted on bumper stickers that proclaimed, "Christians aren't perfect, just forgiven." Such a teaching ignored the testimonies of such biblical characters as Job (Job 1:1), Noah (Genesis 6:9), and Abraham (Genesis 17:1) as well as the words of Jesus Himself (Matthew 5:48, 19:21) and Paul's double admonition in Ephesians 4:11-13. The scriptural context of perfection seems to indicate that perfect people are ones whose actions are perfect because their hearts are perfect.

July 13

Perfect Heart

The scriptures teach that Amaziah, for instance, did what was right but not with a perfect heart (II Chronicles 25:2). He apparently fell into the same category as the believers at Corinth who were doing good deeds – and even operating in spiritual gifts – yet their actions failed to be of benefit because they were not motivated by love. (I Corinthians 13:1-3) On the other hand, David was considered to be a man after God's own heart (Acts 13:22) even though he committed adultery and plotted the murder of the woman's husband. His prayer of repentance in the fifty-first Psalm explained why. His plea before God was that the Lord would not take the Holy Spirit from him and that He would renew a right heart within him. Apparently David understood the necessity of what Paul would later describe as the seal of the Holy Spirit (Ephesians 1:13, 4:30), the quickening work of the Holy Spirit that constantly reminds the sensitive believer of the validity – or lack thereof – of his every thought, motive, and action. In spite of the fact that the focus of the letter is on those who do not have perfect works, the letter acknowledges that some believers do meet the acid test – and gracious promises are extended to them. (Ephesians 5:27, I John 3:3)

There were probably hundreds of young men on the road with the prodigal who could have used new robes and shoes; however, the father only sent his servants for one robe and one pair of shoes because there was only one young man on the road that day who had a heart relationship with him. Like our Heavenly Father in I Chronicles 16:9, the prodigal's father was looking up and down the road, seeking for the son with a right heart toward him.

Acceptance

But the "new birth" box is far from empty; so, let's see what we find next – acceptance. Romans 8:1 says that there is no condemnation when we are in Christ. This means that there is no reason for us to be rejected and every reason for us to be accepted. Well, we all know better than that. After all, we all remember our blunders – some accidental and some deliberately intentional. Certainly, if we have reason to condemn ourselves, God has even more. But this gift says that He doesn't find a reason to condemn us and accepts us anyway. Why? The answer can be found in the companion aspect of this gift – His unmerited favor (also known as grace). It has been said that mercy is not getting what we deserve, whereas grace is getting what we don't deserve. Because of His mercy, God has determined not to cast us away from Himself for our sins; but, because of His grace, He has determined to bring us to Himself without having to earn the privilege. Paul admonished his protégé Timothy to be strong in the reality of this grace that he had in Christ Jesus. (II Timothy 2:1) In essence, understanding this unmerited favor that we have in Jesus should make us strong Christians who can demonstrate that we really are new creatures in Christ through grace, not weak ones who still think and act like the old unregenerate creatures we were before our new birth.

When Paul said in Ephesians 1:6 that we are accepted in the beloved, he used a term that appears only two times in the Bible – here and in Luke 1:28, where the angel Gabriel used this term to tell the Virgin Mary that she was *highly favored*. In other words, our acceptance is not just a toleration; it is a full-blown celebration of our favored relationship in Christ.

July 15

Life

Digging deeper into the "new birth" package, we find another gift labeled "life." According to Romans 8:2, we traded in the law of sin and death for the law of life in Christ Jesus. This means that the very rule that determines our existence is one of life rather than one of death. Let me illustrate this point by sharing a little of the story from my mission work in Nepal. When I first became involved in ministry to Nepal, the country was recognized as the world's only Hindu kingdom, and the promotion of any other religion was strictly prohibited. There were Christians in the country, but they were there solely for humanitarian purposes. In order to have the privilege of staying in the country, they had to agree not to propagate their faith. The nationals who converted to Christianity did so at much peril, facing imprisonment, alienation from family and friends, loss of employment, and physical abuse and persecution. However, during the four years of intercession that led to my first physical ministry in the country, the king granted a new constitution to the people of the nation. One aspect of the new rule was religious freedom – meaning that I could go into the country and minister openly and freely. On one of my early trips, I was questioned about the huge boxes that were part of my luggage. I told the customs officers that they were filled with Christian literature in the Nepali language. I ripped one of the boxes open and started handing samples to all the men in the customs department. Had I been discovered bringing in such literature prior to the granting of the new constitution, I would have been sent to jail or deported, but now I was able to freely give the booklets to the very men who would formerly have been responsible to arrest me.

Liberty

Allow me to continue with my experience in Nepal. Once I got into the country, I could freely stand on any public street and openly distribute my pamphlets. On one occasion when I was being literally mobbed by people wanting to get the free booklets, a police officer came up to see what was going on. When I told him what I was doing and showed him the literature, he responded that I was hindering traffic because of the huge crowd that had gathered. But instead of arresting me or telling me to stop, he asked for one of the boxes of tracts and started helping me pass them out so as to quickly disperse the crowd! This is a powerful example of what it means to move from one law to another. Previously, there was a law that incurred death, but now there was a law promoting life. So it is in Christ – we are translated from a legal system that results in death – dead works, spiritual death, and deadly thoughts and actions – into a new system that allows us to live and do works that bring life to others.

As we hold this glistening jewel of life up to the light, we see that it showers us with a spectrum of vivid colors, one of which illuminates another aspect of this gift – liberty. (Galatians 2:4) Just as the examples from my experience in Nepal have illustrated – moving into the law of life immediately gives us liberty. Prior to the new law, I did not have liberty to bring gospel literature into the nation. In fact, one of my friends spent time in a Nepali prison because the customs officers discovered Bibles in his luggage when entering the country prior. I've often wondered if they might have been the same ones to whom I gave the gospel tracts to the implementation of the new constitution.

Good Lives

This package comes with the safety warning that we should use our liberty in Christ for promoting life rather than allowing it to become a source of bondage through abuse or misrepresentation. (Galatians 5:3)

Associated with the new persons that we have been fashioned into in Christ is the fact that we are given the liberty to live good lives. The Apostle Peter speaks of this reality when he says that we have good "conversation" in Christ in I Peter 3:16 – an old term that today would be translated "lifestyle." The liberty that we have in Christ is not anarchy – the rejection of moral obligation. Rather, it is the freedom to totally embrace moral obligation and to live lives that hallmark graciousness, honesty, and nobility.

Along with this good life that we have in Christ come promises. (Ephesians 3:6) A little later on in the same context, Paul spoke of the things that God was working in us as being more than we could ever imagine or dare to ask for (Ephesians 3:20) – yet, they are all promised to us. Jesus described this in parabolic form when He likened the Heavenly Father to human fathers and illustrated how we humans will do all in our power to ensure that we give our children the best we can afford. Then He surprised His audience by saying that even in doing so graciously, we are still evil. In contrast, God – in whom there is not even a glimmer of evil – gives us even more great and precious promises. (II Peter 1:4) Paul used the terminology of the passing on of an inheritance to an adopted son to make the same point; however, we may often fail to grasp the full meaning of his illustration because we don't know the biblical background of adoption – an idea that we will explore tomorrow.

July 18
Adoption, Inheritance, and Victory
The practice of adoption in biblical times was one of providing an avenue of passing on an inheritance. If a man had no son, he would usually adopt a nephew to become his heir. This practice kept the wealth inside the family rather than letting it be lost to outsiders. Notice that, in the story of Abraham and Lot, it was only after Lot had separated from Abraham (Genesis 13:14) that Abraham became concerned about the fact that he had no heir (verse 15:2). Unlike adoption today, which may be based on sympathy for orphaned children or the loneliness of childless couples, the adoption mentioned here was based solely on the desire to pass on benefits. If we see our position in Christ in this light, we will understand that God is not intending that this benefit be jeopardized. He wants to make an investment in us, and He does not intend to see that investment stolen or destroyed.

But the '"new birth" box is still far from empty. There is another package that catches our attention – victory. Paul boasted in II Corinthians 2:14 that the Lord always causes us to triumph in Christ. That means that if we are in Christ, we can and should experience perpetual victory. In Colossians 2:15 Paul adds, *And having spoiled principalities and powers, he made a shew of them openly, triumphing over them in it.* The literal meaning of "spoiled" is "stripped naked." The verse is actually rendered this way in some modern translations, vividly reiterating the scene being set here. The imagery behind this wording comes from the ancient practice of defrocking the kings and other political and military leaders of conquered nations, but we must wait until tomorrow to fully unpack this truth.

Magnificence

When defeated enemies were brought back from the battle, they were totally humiliated by being marched through the streets naked – no longer with royal robes or regalia of rank. Through the wording he used to speak of our victorious position and the devil's defeated position, Paul painted a vivid picture to awaken his reader to the fact that the opponent against whom we are to stand is an already defeated foe. In Christ, we always stand in this kind of victory.

Another gleaming package in our treasure chest is labeled "magnificence." According to Ephesians 2:10, we are the workmanship of God created in Christ Jesus. Of course, it is exciting enough to realize that we are God's handiwork rather than just the result of a long series of evolutionary accidents that traces our ancestry through monkeys to pond scum. However – as mind boggling as that revelation may be – it is just a scratch on the surface or a drop in the ocean compared to what Paul was really trying to say. The word that he used in this verse actually means that we are more than just God's handicrafts; we are His masterpieces. In other words, each of us is his "Mona Lisa" and His "Michelangelo's David." Yes, there have been millions of paintings of pretty women and statues of handsome men – and all of them are unique and worthy of appreciation because they are the handiwork of talented artisans. However, there is only one Mona Lisa and only one David; they are the masterpieces of genius artists. If Leonardo da Vinci and Michelangelo could produce such magnificent works of art that capture the awe and respect of not only art lovers and critics, but of the common man as well – imagine what it means that you are God's masterpiece.

Enlightenment

For certain, we have not come anywhere near to emptying the "new birth" treasure trove; so, let's get back to digging deeper into the Jesus treasure chest. As we turn our attention back to the bigger box, we come across another parcel labeled "enlightenment" – an aspect that the Apostle John considered so significant that he presented it prominently in the introductory section to his gospel. (John 1:4) In one of his epistles, the beloved disciple came back to this same idea but approached it from the opposite direction by saying that we would be free from deception because there is no darkness at all in Christ. (I John 1:5) Paul explained that we can now have perfect clarity concerning the things of God with his comment that the veil that has kept men from understanding the truth has been taken away in Christ. (II Corinthians 3:14)

What this package ensures is that we can now understand what all the packages that we have pulled out of the "new birth" box really are and how they actually function. In what is probably the most powerful apostolic prayer, Paul interceded for the saints in Ephesus, *That the God of our Lord Jesus Christ, the Father of glory, may give unto you the spirit of wisdom and revelation in the knowledge of him: The eyes of your understanding being enlightened; that ye may know what is the hope of his calling, and what the riches of the glory of his inheritance in the saints, And what is the exceeding greatness of his power to us-ward who believe, according to the working of his mighty power, Which he wrought in Christ, when he raised him from the dead, and set him at his own right hand in the heavenly places.* (Ephesians 1:17-20)

July 21
Cheese and Crackers
A little story from the glory days of Ellis Island and the influx of immigrants into our nation tells about a man who saved every penny he could get his hands on to book passage on a steamer across the Atlantic so that he could start a new life in America. Once he had enough money to pay for his ticket, he took the remaining few coins he had to buy a wheel of cheese and a big tin of crackers. Each morning when the other passengers gathered for a scrumptious breakfast, he retreated to his berth and opened his tin and made himself a meal of cheese and crackers. At noon each day, he enviously eyed his fellow shipmates as they headed again to the dining hall for their lunch. Again, he slipped into his bunk and nourished himself with cheese and crackers. Most tragically of all, his mouth would water as he saw the banquet spread every night for dinner – but, alas, his meal was again cheese and crackers. It was only on the last day of his voyage across the mighty ocean that someone showed him that his ticket read, "All meals included." As heartrending as this story may be, it is even more sobering to realize that it is being played out every day in the lives of millions of Christians around the world who simply haven't dug deeply enough into their Jesus treasure chest to see that their salvation is more than a ticket to a new life in heaven. They don't realize that it is an all-inclusive program while they are on the journey. But in Christ, there is the promise that we can know what we actually already own and that we can understand how to activate those possessions, privileges, and promises.

The Love Package

I can't imagine the surprise that ricochets through our emotions as we reach in to pull out the next package and discover that it is labeled "love." In that love is the basic definition of our relationship with God and even His own personality (I John 4:7-8), it's hard to imagine why this package was buried so far down in the chest. Speaking of the love that we have in Christ, the Apostle Paul says that there is nothing that can separate us from it: not life, not death, not angels, not demons, not things from the present, not things of the future, not things that are high, not things that low – nothing! (Romans 8:39) In light of this passage, it is understandable that we may not really comprehend what God's love is actually about until we have experienced it in times of difficulty. When I first started going to Nepal, it was just coming out of years of persecution of Christians; therefore, I had the privilege of getting to know many individuals who had endured much for Jesus' sake. One such woman was the lady who always found a place on the front row in every service at the church in Kathmandu. Her face was so horribly distorted and disfigured that I decided to ask the pastor about her story. His answer shocked me. When her Hindu husband discovered that she was attending Christian services, he threw battery acid in her face! In spite of the pain and suffering, in spite of the permanent disfiguration, in spite of the humiliation, in spite of everything that could have turned her into a bitter, unforgiving recluse – she was warm and loving, she was joyful and jubilant, she danced and clapped more excitedly than almost anyone else. The love of God erupted from her – the result of digging deeply into the Jesus treasure chest.

July 23

Consolation

The flip side of the love we find in Christ is that we also find consolation in Him. (Philippians 2:1) This is the comfort that comes with resting in His love in spite of the challenges that accompany our decision to follow Him. Let me take you to the African nation of Niger to get a picture of what this means. I want you to meet my good friend in the capital city who hosts me when I come to this country which is ninety-eight percent Muslim. As a fourteen-year-old boy, he heard and received the Good News of Jesus Christ. Well, it was good news to him, but bad news to his strict Muslim parents. No matter how much they tried to convince him to recant, they could not dissuade his new faith. Finally, they did the only thing left to preserve their honor in the community – they disowned their son, declared him dead, and expelled him from their home. Now, barely into his teens, this young man had to find a way to support himself in the crowded city of Niamey. Knowing that no one would give him food or shelter because he had brought shame upon his family by becoming an "infidel," he knew of only one place to turn – the American missionary who had introduced him to Christ. The missionary had little to offer, but he gave the young boy a place to stay and food in exchange for his services in cleaning his house. This is where the consolation comes in – rather than moping about, feeling sorry for himself, my friend modeled himself after Joseph who found himself as a slave and later a prisoner in Egypt. He joyfully cleaned the missionary's house and threw himself into every opportunity he could to learn more and more about his new faith – he wanted to go deeper in Jesus, if you will. And tomorrow, we'll learn the rest of his story.

Blessing

Because my friend in Niger focused on the consolation that he found in Christ, he wanted to know more than what was written in the few books translated into his local dialect; therefore, he learned French (the official language of his region) and then turned to English (the missionary's native tongue). The end result was that by the time he was in his early twenties, he was able to do international business and make a comfortable living – something that would never have happened had he stayed in his father's home or even if he had taken the room with the missionary but done so without letting God give him consolation in Christ.

Reaching into our treasure chest again, we pull out another glistening package – this one is labeled "blessing." The Apostle Paul encouraged us with the fact that we have all spiritual blessings in Christ. (Ephesians 1:3) Let me share a lesson from the Greek language concerning the word "all." It means exactly the same thing in Greek that it does in English – all, every, nothing excluded! I know that it is so easy for us to categorize the blessings of God and believe that certain things belong to certain superheroes of the faith. Yes, we believe that Oral Roberts or Billy Graham can have all sorts of blessings because they are Oral Roberts and Billy Graham; therefore, they are in a totally different category from us and we shouldn't think that such things could ever be ours. Well, have you ever stopped to think of the logic – or, actually, the lack of logic – in that argument? It is not being Oral Roberts or Billy Graham that invokes the blessing; it is the blessing that made Oral Roberts and Billy Graham the men they are in the ministry. The blessings are in Christ – not in the recognized ministers.

July 25

Miraculous Rain

Come with me, if you will, to the island nation of Sri Lanka to see an illustration of the point that blessings belong to all of us – not just Billy Graham or Oral Roberts. A number of years ago, my wife and I arrived in the country to minister in a youth camp that had been arranged for the Christian high school and college students in that Buddhist state. When our host picked us up at the airport, he announced that we were going to have to cancel the retreat. He then went on to explain that the country was encountering a severe drought and that there was no water in the cisterns at the retreat center. Without water for cooking, cleaning, and washing, it would be impossible to house the group at the camp. I explained that we had spent a lot of money in advance to cover the camp expenses and had flown all the way from America for the event. In my mind, it was impossible to cancel the retreat. There had to be a way to make it work. I asked for just twenty-four hours before he made his final decision. That night we asked the Lord for the windows of heaven to be opened in some miraculous way, and God answered our prayer in an even more dramatic way than I had anticipated. We had the most horrendous rainstorm I have ever experienced. It didn't just "rain cats and dogs"; it was more like lions and wolves. I had never seen anything like it; the rain came down by the buckets full – no, barrels full. Not only did the cisterns fill to overflowing, the drought that was crippling the nation's agriculture was immediately alleviated. As a result, we were able to go forward with our plans for the retreat where we saw many young lives changed and destinies set. But the story doesn't end there! I'll share the rest tomorrow.

Simplicity

It wasn't until I revisited the Sri Lanka almost thirty years later and was asked by one of the prominent pastors of the country to preach in his church that I saw proof of the remaining effect of the night that the windows of heaven were opened. That pastor – who is now a significant leader in the country – was called into the ministry as a high school student in that camp that would have been canceled had God not opened the windows of heaven.

My point in telling this story is that it didn't take Oral Roberts or Billy Graham to bring the rain that night – the blessing was in Christ, not in any minister, and I could access it as readily as Oral Roberts or Billy Graham could have. And so can you – if you decide to go deeper in Jesus and keep looking into your Jesus treasure chest.

As we have seen with many of the packages we've opened so far, there is often a flip side to the package. And such is the case here. The back side of the blessing package is labeled "simplicity" – a corrective to overindulgence or misdirection of the blessings that we have in Christ. Paul actually used the word "fear" when he spoke of his concern that the believers could be enticed to abandon the simplicity that is in Christ. (II Corinthians 11:3) But before we go too far in this discussion, it is necessary that we understand that "simplicity" does not mean "depravity." Unfortunately, many Christians think that living in simplicity means that they give up all the niceties of life in order to be godly. There are several problems with that mentality, which we will examine over the next couple days.

Wrong Images of God

The first misconception is that it prompts a wrong image of God – one that portrays Him as barely having enough to go around. Yes, it's wrong and unchristian to take a second helping when there are others who haven't had their first helping, but the truth is that our God is El Shaddai, the God who has more than enough so that everyone can have seconds! We need to develop a both-and rather than an either-or mentality about the blessings of God. Let me take you to a behind-the-scenes meeting among several ministers who were working on a project to raise money for a humanitarian program to feed orphaned children in Africa. When one of the men reached across the table to take a roll from the bread basket, his sleeve pulled up enough to reveal his expensive high-end watch. Another one of the ministers at the table commented, "Just think how many children we could have fed with what it cost to buy that watch." The first gentleman responded, "You have no idea how many children I fed before I bought this watch." You see, there was no error in having the watch because he did not defraud anyone out of a meal in order to get it.

A second error that results from the simplicity-depravity confusion is the subjective evaluation of blessing. Had the first gentleman's watch been of the same price range as the second gentleman's timepiece, the discussion would never have occurred. The point that we need to understand is that we cannot subjectively set the standard for defining blessings; we must go by the objective standard that God has already set. And that is that He wants to pour out (not just sprinkle) blessings on us to the point the we cannot physically contain them. (Malachi 3:10)

Lavish

In Ephesians 1:8, Paul speaks of wisdom and prudence that He made to abound toward us. The New International Version translates this clause as *He has lavished upon us*. One fast-food restaurant puts the meat on a scale to make sure that the customer gets exactly the right number of ounces. If the scale tips a little high, the counter attendant tears off a little so that the customer gets exactly the amount he pays for – and not a bit more. "Lavish," on the other hand, means that there is no scale. God's blessings are spread out for us like an all-you-can-eat buffet. "Lavish" implies an over-the-top excess – like the world-record-breaking three-hundred-thirty-eight-pound hamburger produced at Mallie's Sports Grill and Bar in Southgate, Michigan. It was three feet high, had more than half a million calories, and took twenty-two hours to cook. Why did Mallie's make such a monster of a hamburger? Because they could. Why does God lavish His blessing upon us? Because He can. We serve a God named El Shaddai, the God of More Than Enough. He lavishly gives us abundance, *good measure, pressed down, and shaken together, and running over.* (Luke 6:38)

One other point that we should understand in regard to this concept is that it promotes a mentality that actually makes the devil look more generous than God when we see non-Christians enjoying prosperity that we Christians have deprived ourselves of in the attempt to be simplistic. King Solomon didn't ask for wealth, but God placed more than the top four hundred present-day billionaires combined into his lap! His wealth made him the envy of pagan kings instead of the other way around.

July 29

Satisfaction in Our Relationship with Jesus

Having said all this, now it is time to actually define what the simplicity that we have in Christ really is. It is a heart attitude in which we realize that our real satisfaction is in our relationship with Christ – not in complicated theological explanations about Him or in what He has given to us. One of the greatest influences that I have had in my life was Dr. Lester Sumrall, one of the great Christian authors, broadcasters, missionaries, and pastors of the last century. Due to our deeply personal relationship, I often found myself in private personal prayer time with him. Let me reiterate exactly who this man was. He was the pastor of a three-thousand member church, the author of over one hundred publications, the founder of a Christian educational system that covered all the bases from daycare to doctoral degrees, the president of a broadcasting system that owned a dozen television stations and five shortwave radio stations that literally blanketed the globe with the gospel, director of a world-wide humanitarian program that operated two cargo ships and a cargo plane bringing food, medical supplies, and the gospel to every continent in the world – and the list could go on and on. Now back to the prayer room – I will never forget his earnest prayer, "Lord, I want to know you." Even after more than sixty years in active full-time ministry, he was still wanting to go deeper in Jesus and dig further down into His treasure chest! There was no shortage of blessings – he handled millions of dollars each year – but his simplicity was in his relationship with the God of the blessings, not the blessings of God. That's the simplicity that we must have to balance out the abundance that we have in Christ.

Confidence

Well, what have we here? The next item that I've snared in my treasure chest is marked as "confidence." First John 5:14 assures us that we have confidence in Christ that all our prayers will be answered when we pray according to His will. This confidence is not because of our great ability to fashion eloquent prayers that impress or convince God with our mastery of the art of praying. Neither does it come from our ability to force God's hand through our sincerity or earnestness in moaning, groaning, straining our voices, or starving ourselves through fasting. No, the confidence that we find in our treasure chest is simply because all the promises of God are guaranteed in Christ. Paul emphasized that they are doubly sure when he proclaimed that they are *yea* and *amen* – certainty to the second power! (II Corinthians 1:20)

Have you ever had the experience of having to find a store that was open on Christmas morning to buy the batteries that you failed to get to go along with the "batteries not included" toys that you just presented to your children? At our house, there is a standing joke that I give all my sons – and now my grandsons – a package of batteries every Christmas even if they don't get gifts that require them. Well, when we pull out the next package from our chest, we discover that it is labeled "faith" – exactly the gift that we need to activate the previous gift of confidence in the divine guarantees that are in Christ. Paul spoke of the Colossians believers as being steadfast in the faith that they had in Christ (Colossians 2:5) and of the abundance of faith that Timothy had in Christ (I Timothy 1:14) – the empowering aspects of faith that takes us beyond just wishful thinking, pipe dreams, and hopeful dreams.

July 31
The Walnut Tree – Part I

Some of my favorite stories on the topic of confidence have to do with giving in faith for missions.

While I was dean of the Bible college in Indiana, in the backyard of our home stood a giant walnut tree whose upper limbs brushed the very heavens. It was the home of a multitude of grey squirrels that scampered up and down its trunk and ducked into its hollow knotholes only to reappear on the other side of the tree ten feet further down the tree's trunk. This disappearance and reappearance of the furry little creatures became a little discomforting to us since it meant that the tree must be hollow for some major section of its trunk. Since the tree leaned across the roof of our house, we began to feel that it endangered our home and our lives if it were to be blown over. Several severe storms took their toll of limbs from other trees in our yard; yet the giant walnut remained intact even though it rocked and creaked with the violent winds. I talked to several companies about removing the tree but was constantly offered bids that were far beyond my price range. One friend of mine who did tree removal as a sideline volunteered to take it down for us as a favor. But, after climbing the tree and surveying how much actually reached over the house, he descended and rescinded. We tried to postpone the removal until a later date when we might have the extra cash to pay for the service. But when a violent windstorm raged through our area bringing down one of the trees in our yard, my wife insisted that we act immediately before the next storm razed the walnut that, in turn, would crush our home.

And tomorrow, we'll see what this walnut tree has to do with confidence in God's promises.

The Walnut Tree – Part II

Since the next week was our annual campmeeting and I knew that I would be busy morning, noon, and night, I promised, without fail, to call a tree company immediately after the conference. In one of the sessions, Dr. Sumrall took a special offering for missions, and I responded by making a five-hundred-dollar donation on my credit card. This was a real step of faith because I knew that I would have to pay around eight hundred dollars to get the tree removed the following week. Now I was adding an additional obligation of five hundred dollars more. Where would I get an extra thirteen hundred dollars before the end of the month? I had no idea, but I had confidence that I had to obey the Lord on the missions offering and my wife on the tree removal.

When I went home for lunch after the service in which I had made the missions pledge, I found a stranger standing in my backyard. I went to find out what he wanted and was greeted with a proposal that I sell him the walnut lumber from the tree. He had been in the area for some other wood procurement and had spotted this tree towering on the skyline. It seemed ideal for his veneer business and he was willing to pay five hundred dollars for it. I quickly settled the deal and arranged for free removal – saving me the eight hundred dollars that it would have cost me to have a tree removal company take it down. l also pocketed the five-hundred-dollar check and used it to pay off my missions pledge. I'm still amazed at how the man was driving in my neighborhood and showed up in my backyard on the very day that I planted a missionary seed. Not only that – he offered me the exact amount that I had given in the offering!

August 2
More Confidence Stories
As a college student, I organized my funds by taking my monthly check and dividing my spending money into four envelopes – one for each week. One night at a special missions rally, I felt impressed to empty my wallet for the offering. This left m e a full week behind on my finances, but when I opened my envelope for the next week – much to my surprise – there was twice as much as I had put there! Another experience while I was in college was when I felt directed to empty my wallet in a missionary offering one Friday evening. I knew that that meant I would be penniless until the next weekend, but I also knew that my God would somehow take care of me. When I got back to the dorm that night, there was a note on my door directing me to call one of the college professors that night – no matter how late it was that I got in. Even though I hated to call at a rather late hour, I knew that there was an urgency behind the professor's message; so, I returned his call. He greeted me with the offer to work for him the next day. He had received an opportunity to do some side work and needed an assistant – work that I knew how to help him with. Of course, I agreed and met him early the next morning for a full day's work. At the end of the day, he paid me in cash – more than I had put in the offering the night before. That missionary seed brought me an immediate harvest! Not only that – the business opportunity continued for the professor, and he employed me week after week for a number of months, greatly multiplying the seed I had sown.

August 3
Authority and Anointing
Along with faith come two other powerful evidences of what we have in Christ – authority and anointing. Revelation 1:6 informs us that we are in the position of kings and priests in Christ and that dominion (authority) has been attributed to Him. The only logical conclusion is that this authority is to be executed through His ordained officials – meaning us! The beloved disciple assures us that there is an anointing that we received in Christ and that this anointing abides – or is readily available – in us at all times. (I John 2:27) So, how do authority and anointing function? To illustrate the point, let's look at a few testimonies of encounters with demonic forces that really drew upon the gift of faith and the authority and anointing birthed from it.

It was a dark and stormy night – well, actually it wasn't stormy, and it wasn't any darker than any other ordinary night. But the events of that evening seem to fit so perfectly into one of those "dark and stormy night" stories that I just couldn't resist the intro line. I was visiting the University of North Carolina's Wilmington campus. Since it was only a few miles from Wrightsville Beach, our group had decided to stay with a friend who managed an old beachfront hotel on the Atlantic Coast. The old building had long since seen its better days and was soon to be bulldozed down to make way for the parking lot for a modern condominium. After checking into our rooms, we headed back to town for a Bible study on the campus. About halfway through the study, a young lady sort of floated into the room. With an out-of-this-world daze in her eyes, she looked around and asked, "What is this place?" And over the next couple stormy nights – or mornings – we'll see what happened next.

August 4

The Occult Books

We responded that it was a Bible study and that she was welcome to sit down and join us. Her reply was that she was just walking down the hall when "the spirit" told her to come in, so she took a seat and glared around the room as we completed our session. After the meeting, several of the students talked and prayed with her until it was time to leave the room. At that point, one of the students who was traveling with me suggested that our guest come back to the hotel with us for some further counseling. She decided to accept the invitation, and we headed for the beach. As soon as we parked, I began to feel the uncanny sensation that I was walking into a horror movie. The eeriness continued to mount as we entered the back door. Inside, the kitchen was vibrant with an unearthly presence. On the table we found a large box with a note attached. It was from a young man who had just received Jesus into his heart that day. It explained that, with his new life, he wanted to totally break from the old one that had involved a lot of occultism. The box contained all his occult books that he wished to destroy but was afraid to do by himself. His request was that we burn them for him. Eager to rid the house of the unholy manifestation, we grabbed the box and headed for the fireplace. In that it was winter and that this relic of a hotel was anything but airtight, a roaring fire was already waiting for us in the lobby. All the lobby furniture was huddled around the fireplace as a resort for all the guests as we tried to defend ourselves against the chilly ocean breezes that blew almost as freely through the hotel as they did on the windswept sand dunes outside. Our group, including the new guest, grabbed seats close to the open fireplace as we began to toss the occult books into the flames.

August 5

The Deliverance

Our new friend, in an almost hypnotic voice, began to talk about each of the books as she pulled them out of the box, "This is an expensive book; we can't burn it. This is a nice one; why do you want to destroy it?" We all knew that something was wrong, but no one knew what to do or say. Upon our insistence, every book made it to the inferno, but the evil presence remained. It was at that point that we realized that the demon was not in the books but in the co-ed from the campus – so we began to cast it out. None of us had ever done that before, so we were novices using the trial-and-error method. At one point, we asked the young lady if she wanted Jesus to come into her heart so that she could go to heaven; the response was, "Oh, heaven will be boring – just sitting around playing a harp." At that instant, I realized that I had not been talking to the young lady at all, but that my conversation was with a demon that was speaking through her. I demanded that the spirit be quiet so that the girl could hear and respond. Calling her name, I commanded her to answer me and to receive Jesus into her heart and join me in commanding the demon to leave. She did – and she was free. No longer did she stare with hollow eyes into space. No longer did she speak in a monotone. No longer did she move catatonically. Suddenly she was a vibrant, vivacious young girl. But, she had one major problem – she didn't know where she was or how she had gotten there. Looking at her watch, she exclaimed, "How did it get this late? I've only been gone about ten minutes!" In actuality, she had been in the hotel lobby at least two hours plus all the time she was in the classroom on campus. The spirit that had been controlling her had actually obliterated all reality out of her consciousness.

August 6
Authority and Anointing Against Demons
Since that day at Wrightsville Beach, I have met many others under the devil's control and have seen them set free in the name of Jesus. When I rebuked the spirit in one man who came to my office for prayer, the demon threw him across the room, and he crashed into the wall. When he picked himself up, he began to hop around the room like a frog as his mouth began to spew out the vilest forms of blasphemy and profanity. Yet, at the name of Jesus, he was instantly free and stood to his feet a new man. When he came back for follow-up counseling the next day, he stopped at the receptionist's desk and asked to see me. The receptionist called to inform me that a gentleman <u>claiming</u> to be the one who had been in the prior day was there for an appointment. She added, "But this isn't the same man; I've never seen this man before." He was so radically changed that it showed on his face.

Another young man came to me for counseling and prayer. Under terrible bondage of low self-esteem, he refused to look up. Recognizing this as a demonic torment, I put my hand under his chin and forced him to raise his head and look me straight in the eyes. After ministering deliverance to him, I took him with me to a Christian fellowship meeting. Before long, people who had known the lad for several months began to come up and welcome the "newcomer" to the group. They had never seen him with his head up and did not recognize him as the same person they had known for a number of weeks.

These changed lives were possible because I had found authority and anointing in my Jesus treasure chest. *Behold, I give unto you power to tread on serpents and scorpions, and over all the power of the enemy.* (Luke 10:19)

August 7
Why Am I Here?

Well, let's get back to digging into our Jesus treasure chest. First, let's take a breather and set the stage for our next jewel. All of us want to fulfill our destiny. Each of us has asked the questions, "Why am I here?" and "What is my purpose?" We are all born with a sense of purpose and the feeling that there is a reason for our being on the earth. I am certain that even atheists and evolutionists share these same feelings even though they refuse to acknowledge the fact that there is a Master Designer behind everything and that He gives purpose to the lives of human beings. In fact, He gives purpose to everything, whether human or not, whether animate or inanimate. Just try to find anything in the created order that does not serve a significant function. Even the evolutionists – who claim to believe that everything is nothing more than the result of one very long string of random accidents – will fight to preserve every species of toads no matter how insignificant and every ecosystem no matter how remote. Why? Because they believe that every aspect of nature is vital to the rest of our environment. They would never admit that these very feelings contradict and disprove the very foundational premise of their philosophy. If they are correct in their theory that life as we know it today is the result of a series of unorchestrated events, then most of what we see in the world would be the leftovers from the failed trials. To prove this theory, all we have to do is visit any craftsman's workshop. One of the prominent fixtures will be a trash bin where he tosses all the imperfect specimens, scraps from his projects, and his failed attempts. There is probably more refuse going out the backdoor than sellable product going out the front door.

August 8

From Microcosm to Macrocosm

Now, if we apply yesterday's illustration from the microcosm of a workshop to the macrocosm of the earth, the logical conclusion would be that only a minor portion of what exists in the earth today is significant and valuable – an assumption that would lead us to exploit and pollute with no concern for the consequences. Yes, that is exactly the mindset that once dominated our thinking. But we have since learned that the South American rainforest must be preserved if we hope to sustain life elsewhere on the planet. We have learned that every living creature – from the aardvark to the zebra – serves a vital role somewhere in a chain that supports the entire livelihood of the planet. As the old saying goes, a chain is only as strong as its weakest link. Today, we realize how important every link is and we all go to any length to strengthen every one because we see how vital each one is to the whole. Amazingly, the crusaders who campaign the strongest are those who refuse to admit that such a delicate interdependence could only be the result of the work of a deliberate, intelligent Designer! If their theory that everything is the result of random accidental chance were true, then most of what they are so adamantly protecting is actually nothing more than the sawdust on the floor and the refuse in the waste bin and dumpster rather than the actual crafted masterpiece of the craftsman.

I said all that simply to say this – we have a tendency to treat the owls, whales, and rainforests as if they are significant parts of a grand masterpiece even when we don't acknowledge that there is a Master Creator behind them all.

Lifetime Purpose

Once we acknowledge that there is a Creator at work, the whole process becomes logical and more significant. At this point, we must conclude that if the Creator gave significance to the aardvarks and the tree toads, certainly He had a purpose for each of the humans He created – and there is more to that purpose than just working in a factory or office all week and drinking beer in front of the football game on television.

The Apostle Paul wrote that he had been separated from his mother's womb for the assignment that Jesus gave him on the road to Damascus. Now, that is a pretty radical idea – especially when we realize that it was probably more than three decades between these two events and that Saul had worked harder than any of his contemporaries trying to do exactly the opposite of what Jesus had planned for him. Our first introduction to Paul is as Saul of Tarsus, a persecutor of the early Christians. He grew up as a freeborn Roman citizen in the city of Tarsus, which he called *no mean city*, indicating that it was far above the average city of his time. It was certainly no average place in that it was a major center of commerce, education, and military power. With the excellent education that Paul possessed as his writings demonstrate and his Roman privilege coupled with the strong ethic his Jewish upbringing afforded him, Paul would have been a success in any field he would have chosen to pursue: business, military, academics, etc. Yet, he chose to abandon any of these lucrative pursuits and give himself to the study of theology at the rabbinic school of Gamaliel in Jerusalem, a career that rendered him so little financial security that he had to augment his livelihood by making tents.

Misdirected Purpose

The biblical records indicate that Saul was bothered by anything that deviated from the theological doctrines he had learned in the synagogue and the rabbinical school; that's why he was persecuting the church. (Acts 9:2) He was adamant that the Christian movement – which he considered to be a blasphemous perversion of the Jewish faith – be crushed to death before it had a chance to spread its infectious heresy any further. As a personal disciple of Gamaliel, Saul gained an excellent command of biblical and traditional knowledge and the expertise to expound on these concepts, and it is also likely that he gained influence in the Jewish community through his association with the prominent rabbi and Sanhedrin member. (Acts 5:34)

It was probably this association that afforded him access to the high priest who granted him papers to go to Damascus in his attempt to eliminate the Christian faith before it penetrated this pivotal city. (Acts 9:2) Damascus was a terminal and transit point for all the major trade routes of the time – the frankincense route coming out of the Arabian Peninsula, the gold route coming out of Africa, and the silk route coming out of the Far East – all connecting to the Roman highway system that brought these goods to the capital of the world. Saul knew that if this new religion were able to become entrenched in the city of Damascus it would soon spread like a contagious disease along these corridors of commerce until it had infected the entire known world. Thus, he used his influence, connections, and eloquence to gain permission to implement his strategic plan to excise this religious "cancer" before it entered the bloodstream of the society.

August 11
The Road to Damascus
It was on his campaign to eradicate Christianity in Damascus that Saul encountered Jesus and was converted to the faith that he was so adamantly persecuting and attempting to eradicate. Acts chapter nine describes the dramatic encounter in which Saul was knocked to the ground and blinded by the brilliant light that emanated from the Risen Christ. Those with him were also impacted by the encounter but did not hear the words that Jesus spoke to His captive that day, *Saul, Saul, why persecutest thou me? I am Jesus whom thou persecutest: it is hard for thee to kick against the pricks. Arise, and go into the city, and it shall be told thee what thou must do.* (Acts 9:4-6) With the help of his companions, the blinded crusader found his way to a home on the main street of the city of Damascus. After three days of fasting and soul searching, Saul's conversion was completed when the Lord sent a reluctant evangelist to find him. When the Lord spoke to Ananias, he immediately refused with the logical objection that Saul's only motive for being in Damascus was to arrest Christians – and Ananias could think of a whole lot of better things to do that day than to walk directly into such a trap. The Lord continued to deal with His messenger, telling him that He had already shown Paul a vision of a man by the specific name of Ananias coming to him. With that kind of preannouncement before the Lord even spoke to him about the assignment, Ananias decided that there really wasn't an alternative. Through Ananias' ministry that day, Saul was healed, baptized in water, and filled with the Holy Spirit. Additionally, Ananias was able to speak into Paul's life concerning the Lord's will for his future. (Acts 9:15-16)

August 12

Foreordained Purpose

It seems that Paul's predetermined destiny is not unique but that this lifelong purpose is universal. *According as he hath chosen us in him before the foundation of the world, that we should be holy and without blame before him in love: Having predestinated us unto the adoption of children by Jesus Christ to himself, according to the good pleasure of his will, To the praise of the glory of his grace, wherein he hath made us accepted in the beloved.* (Ephesians 1:4-6)

Yes, Paul was a man who was destined by God to become His apostle and servant. But, he emphatically proclaimed that the same provision has been made for every believer. God has been working a plan for all of our lives – even from before the foundation of the world.

As I was growing up, I always enjoyed reading the World Book Encyclopedia and National Geographic Magazine. I always took a lot of ribbing about wanting to stay inside and read when I could have been outside playing. Now, don't get me wrong – I did enjoy playing outside, riding bikes, building tree houses and forts in the woods behind our house, and chasing the neighborhood girls out of our backyard – but I also loved to read about other places in the world and about the cultures and religions of the people who lived there. It wasn't until I was an adult that I realized that all that reading was God's way of preparing me for a lifetime of cross-cultural missions work around the world. I believe that God preordained a path for my life and designed my temperament and interests so that I would be perfectly fitted for the job – He gave me an interest in the world so that I could go to His disciples around the globe and encourage them in their faith.

Finding Destiny

If He did it for me, I'm totally convinced that He's done it for you as well. Therefore, if you are asking those universal questions about your destiny, I suggest that you simply look at who you are because the Lord fashioned you specifically for your unique destiny. Is there something that you are specifically good at? Where do you think that talent came from? God, of course – and He gave it to you so that you could fulfill a specific calling that could never be accomplished without that ability.

As we have seen, Paul had great giftings that could have propelled him far in life; however, he came to realize that the will of God for him was to serve in the role of an apostle. (I Corinthians 1:1, II Corinthians 1:1, Ephesians 1:1, Colossians 1:1, II Timothy 1:1) He learned the lesson that we all must remember – God's call on your life is a heavenly GPS, giving you a locater of where you are and where you are to go in life.

I think of a couple of the greatest musicians in American history who, as young men, said that they had been called to preach the gospel. Unfortunately, they decided to pursue secular careers with the gift of music that God had given them as part of the ministry that He had intended for them to pursue. Both men made great fortunes and obtained fame that will live on for many, many years after their deaths. I just wonder how powerful their lives would have been had they pursued their callings rather than exploiting their gifts.

As we dig deeper and deeper into our Jesus treasure chest we will see that all the jewels inside only have true meaning if we are using them in alignment with the calling of God upon our lives.

August 14
Gifts and Calling
I need to back up a step and warn you that just because you have an ability in an area doesn't mean that you should assume that any opportunity which involves that gifting is your specific calling. A few years ago, I was offered a position with an international mission ministry – a position that was very tempting to me because of the opportunity to work closely with some of the cutting-edge advances that are happening in the present-day arena of world evangelism. However wonderful the opportunity might have been, it would have required my full time and total commitment. That meant that I would have to surrender much of the mission work I was doing and the classes I was teaching at the Bible college. As I began to pray about the decision at hand, the Lord directed me to the reference to *gifts and calling* in Romans 11:29. Until that particular day, I had always assumed that gifts and calling were essentially the same; however, I suddenly realized that they are actually two different entities. Our gifts are our God-given abilities; whereas our calling is our divine appointment in life. The gifts are given to us as a means to an end – that end is our calling. In the particular situation I was facing, I was being asked to accept a position that would focus on the gift of administration and organization that God has given me. I could have done the job that was offered to me, and I could have done it very well because I have the necessary gift for the position. However, I would have been neglecting the call upon my life – that of a teacher. Since the whole purpose for the gifting of God in our lives is to serve the calling upon our lives, I knew that I had to turn down the position in order to fulfill a higher purpose.

August 15

What Makes You Happy?

The next thing that you should ask yourself is what makes you happy. Now, just in case you are tempted to answer, "Sitting in front of the TV with a beer watching football," I'll warn you in advance that this is not the right answer. Perhaps I should phrase the question with the term "joy" rather than "happiness." Joy is the spiritual quality that most closely parallels our human emotion of happiness. It is the reality that we experience in the presence of God Himself. (Psalm 16:11) Of course, God is in your living room when you are watching football, but you are likely not aware of His presence at the moment. However, there are many other times when we experience happiness that seems to penetrate our full being – all the way into our spiritual man. That is the joy that helps us determine where our destiny lies. When you experience such happiness in a task that you would be willing to pay to do it rather than being paid, you've found a career that brings you joy – follow it! That's what Paul did – he found so much fulfillment in preaching the gospel that he ran a side business of sewing tents so he could pursue his passion. He famously wrote to the Corinthians that he would willingly spend and be spent for the privilege of ministering to them. (II Corinthians 12:15)

There are times when we see a need with the excitement of an entrepreneur, relishing the adventure of being the one who has an answer to other people's problems. When this happens, we are filled with a God-ordained joy that jumps out at us telling us that it's time to start rolling up our sleeves because we've just found God's will for our life and are headed toward our destiny!

Your Complaints

Other things you should consider are the needs that you see around you. Be aware that we can see needs in a number of different ways and that even negatives can be the gateways to positives.

Someone once said that what you complain about is your divine assignment. Remember that we said that Paul was bothered by what he interpreted to be the rise of a heretical movement – and that this was an indication of his calling into the ministry of teaching and preaching divine truth. So, sometimes it is our negative experience to a situation that prompts us to become the solution.

I always love to illustrate this point by giving the example of a church startup in a rented hotel ballroom. Everyone has worked for two or three hours to get everything ready for the service. They've hauled in all the musical equipment, set up the sound system, and arranged all the chairs. Now, they are all ready to enjoy the praise and worship time and the preaching of the Word. But one mother's crying baby is disrupting the whole atmosphere. Everyone is muttering under his or her breath, "Why doesn't that mother do something about that baby? Doesn't she know that it is ruining our whole service?" That is – everyone but one young lady who is questioning, "That poor baby! Why didn't someone think about renting a second room so there could be a place for the babies and little children to be cared for rather than having them held captive in this adult service?" That's the person who is called to start the nursery and children's ministry in the new church!

August 17

God's Will

As we continue our quest into the seemingly bottomless trunk, the next parcel that we retrieve is titled, "God's will" – exactly what we've been hoping to find! Now, that is reassuring because a couple packages ago we were promised confidence when we prayed according to the will of God. The logical conclusion we can draw from that is that we are not guaranteed answers to our prayers if we happen to be praying prayers that are not in accordance with His will. Now we have a promise that tells us that His will is also available in Jesus. Although I Thessalonians 5:18 specifically speaks of thankfulness as an element of God's will in Christ, we can extrapolate that there is much more – and, in fact, the entirety – of God's will that is in Christ. If we know that we are in God's will, then our lives have purpose and we know that we have a destiny. Both are guarantees that we can find as we go deeper in Jesus. (II Timothy 1:9, Ephesians 1:4)

Wherefore be ye not unwise, but understanding what the will of the Lord is.
(Ephesians 5:17)
Having made known unto us the mystery of his will, according to his good pleasure which he hath purposed in himself.
(Ephesians 1:9)

Many Christians spend their entire lives cluelessly walking around in a "fog" wishing that they knew the will of God for their lives, but the scriptures clearly tell us that we can and should know what His will is. How to recognize the will of the Lord is one of the most important things that any Christian can ever learn. We can come to know the will of the Lord in several ways.

August 18

The Word and the Spirit

The first and foremost way to know the will of the Lord is from the written Word. The written Word tells us what is the will of the Lord. For example, it is God's will that none shall perish but that all should come to everlasting life. (II Peter 3:9) If you are seated next to a sinner on the bus, what is the will of the Lord? The will of the Lord is that the person next to you should not perish but for him to come to the knowledge of everlasting life. Therefore, the will of the Lord for you is that you should help that person move into the will of the Lord for his life. You don't have to ask God if it is His will for you to share the gospel with that person sitting next to you. You already have His will written in the Word, *Go ye into all the world, and preach the gospel to every creature.* (Mark 16:15) The Word of God gives us general direction in what the will of the Lord is. The next step is to allow the Holy Spirit to lead you into God's specific will so that you will know how to approach the individual so as to effectively reach him with the gospel message.

This brings us to another way the Lord reveals His will – through His Spirit. There is an inward witness inside each born-again believer to tell him what God wants for his individual life. God will speak to us; so, it is very important for us to get to the place where we can hear the voice of the Lord. So many people come up to me saying, "If God would only show me what to do, I would do it." It is very likely that He is speaking, and they are not recognizing His voice. When we get very close and personal to the Lord, we are able to hear His voice.

August 19
The Voice of the Shepherd
Jesus said that His sheep would hear His voice and follow Him but would not follow a stranger. (John 10:3-5, 27) Notice that He said "sheep," not "lambs." We must mature in our relationship with the Lord in order to clearly recognize His voice. We must stay in close communion with Him so we will distinctly know His voice and obey it. Young lovers can talk for three or four hours about nothing at all. When their mothers ask what they have been doing and why they are coming in past their curfews, they reply, "Oh, we were just talking." It was not facts or knowledge that they were communicating; rather, their communication was developing a relationship. The young man received something of the young lady's personality, and she received something of his personality through the time they spent together. Talking is very important in establishing a relationship – with God as well as with other people. We need to get to the place where we can hear the voice of God and – regardless of the circumstances under which that voice comes – we know that it is the voice of God so that we are able to follow through with what He is saying. A mature Christian should be able to recognize the will of the Lord and not to be confused about it.

In Genesis chapter twenty-seven, we find the story of Isaac and his two sons, Esau and Jacob. We know that Isaac was old and blind, but the Bible doesn't say anything about his having hearing problems. Isaac denied Esau's voice because it didn't match with the circumstances. He blessed the deceptive son because he didn't follow the voice that he heard. We should learn a valuable lesson from this Old Testament story – obey the voice of God regardless of the circumstances!

Three "C"s to the Will of God
Confirmation, Counsel, Circumstances

Another way that we can know the will of God is through supernatural confirmation. God can use supernatural signs and wonders such as prophecy for confirmation of His will; however, He usually does not give us direction that way. Generally, He uses this form of communication as a confirmation of what He has already spoken into our hearts.

We can also know the will of God through the advice and counsel of elders. When there is something that you want to know or have a question about, bring it up before the eldership in your local church. We don't need to go to a leading televangelist for his opinion on it; we need to go to somebody who personally knows us and loves us enough to give us what is really in his heart. Certainly, the evangelist may have a supernatural word that may relate to us, but our pastor or elder – the person who has seen us mature and has spiritual oversight over us – can go before God with a heart of care for us, and he will receive the answer from God.

One final way of knowing God's will is through the circumstances in which we find ourselves. For instance, Paul certainly didn't plan on getting himself bitten by a snake; but when it happened, he realized that God had set up the circumstances so that a revival could occur on the island. (Acts 28:3-10)

Regardless of the method, it is imperative that we learn to know and follow the will of God for our lives and in our day-to-day affairs.

God's Will and His Word

For the sake of solidity in our personal lives, we must also re-evaluate the way we think about the Word of God. The Word of God is a manifestation of the will of God; therefore, we must fill ourselves with it, knowing that it is bringing our lives into alignment with the will and into the favor of the Lord. Jesus said, *If ye abide in me, and my words abide in you, ye shall ask what ye will, and it shall be done unto you.* (John 15:7) In other words, having the Word of God dwelling inside of us will guarantee that we will have answers to our prayer requests. First John 5:14-15 explains how this truth works by essentially substituting the term "will" for "words."

> *And this is the confidence that we have in him, that, if we ask any thing according to his will, he heareth us: And if we know that he hear us, whatsoever we ask, we know that we have the petitions that we desired of him.*

Let's parallel two promises we have concerning our prayers:

1) If we ask according to the will of God, we have confidence that we will have our petitions answered.

2) If we have the words of God abiding in us, we will have our prayers answered.

By combining these two truths, we can see that the cognate principle is that the will of God is the same as the Word of God. Being full of the Word will produce a mind that thinks in agreement with the will of God and a life that is lived out in accordance to the divine will.

August 22

A Lesson for the Prayer Group

I was once part of a group that met early each morning to share requests and then lift up the needs in prayer. Each day they would go around the circle and list all the needs, then one member of the group would be asked to intercede. He would then reiterate all the needs as he mentioned them in prayer to the Lord. Finally, my day came to lead the prayer. I agreed only if they would allow me to do things a little differently. With a nod from the members, I explained that I didn't think that we should spend our time praying the problems but should use the occasion to pray the answers. I challenged each person to give me a biblical promise relating to the need rather than stating the need. Rather than talking about someone's uncle with cancer, I insisted that we talk about the provision Christ had made for the uncle's condition. When I taught them to pray the answer, it changed the entire complexion of the prayer group. They moved from making announcements of bad news to proclamations of the Good News.

> *And Jesus answering saith unto them, Have faith in God...Whosoever shall say unto this mountain, Be thou removed, and be thou cast into the sea; and shall not doubt in his heart, but shall believe that those things which he saith shall come to pass; he shall have whatsoever he saith. Therefore I say unto you, What things soever ye desire, when ye pray, believe that ye receive them, and ye shall have them.* (Mark 11:22-24)

August 23

The Trinity

Surprise! The next box we come to is marked, "the entire Trinity"! (Colossians 2:9) The Father, Son, and Holy Spirit are totally in unity in purpose, nature, and action. The wonderful thing about going deeper into Jesus is that we are drawn into the vortex of the Trinity's unity.

Remember, the Father invited the entire Trinity into His initial plan for man when He said, *Let us make man.* (Genesis 1:26) In like manner, Jesus guaranteed the involvement of the entire Trinity in His final destiny for the human race, the Great Commission to bring the entire earthly family back into relationship with their heavenly family. But the glory of His plan is that He also invited us into that grand experience. In Matthew's account, Jesus promised, *Lo, I am with you alway, even unto the end of the world.* (Matthew 28:20) Luke's account tells us that we must wait for the promise of the Father. (Luke 24:49) In the Acts account, He told the disciples that they would be empowered by the Holy Spirit (Acts 1:8), a promise that is apparently intended in Mark's account even though the exact term is not used (Mark 16:17-18). John's record of the Great Commission lists the involvement of the total Trinity: the Father sent Jesus, Jesus is sending the disciples, and the disciples are to receive the Holy Spirit. When all these passages are considered at one time, we see a remarkable truth emerging – the total Trinity is involved in empowering us to ensure our success in the task Jesus left with us!

> *For there are three that bear record in heaven, the Father, the Word, and the Holy Ghost: and these three are one.* (I John 5:7)

Gifts, Administrations, and Operations

To see how all three persons of the Godhead are involved in our lives, let's take a look at I Corinthians chapter twelve. You may notice that the word "gifts" in verse one is in italics. This means that the word is not actually in the original Greek text. It was added by the translator for what he thought would bring clarity. If we were to translate the verse literally, it would read simply, "I would not have you ignorant concerning spiritual things." Paul does discuss the gifts of the Spirit in this chapter; however, that is not the limit of his interest. He also explains administrations and operations, *There are diversities of gifts, but the same Spirit. And there are differences of administrations, but the same Lord. And there are diversities of operations, but it is the same God which worketh all in all. But the manifestation of the Spirit is given to every man to profit withal.* (I Corinthians 12:4-7)

Paul begins by mentioning that the Holy Spirit will give us gifts – supernatural abilities to do things that we as humans would never otherwise be capable of doing. Next, he tells us that the Lord Jesus gives us various administrations. From Ephesians 4:11, we can understand that Jesus is in charge of placing individual believers into positions so that they can minister with the supernatural gifts that the Holy Spirit has placed inside of them. Finally, the apostle turns to the role of the Father and says that He gives us a diversity of operations. Here, Paul is telling us that it is the Father who puts godly motivations in our lives enabling us to function in the positions in which Jesus has placed us, using the giftings that the Holy Spirit has placed in our lives.

August 25
A Supernatural Message
Paul gives us a listing of the gifts in verses eight through ten, a list of some of the ministry positions (or administrations) in verses twenty-eight through thirty, and a list of the operations in verse thirteen of chapter thirteen: faith, hope, and love. Chapter thirteen emphasizes the futility of the gifts and administrations without the operation of these godly characteristics; whereas, verse seven of chapter twelve guarantees that there will be universal benefit when all three elements supplied by the total Trinity are in alignment.

Just as I was ready to receive the tithes and offerings in church one Sunday morning, a lady in the congregation stood up and spoke out in tongues. Since I was holding the microphone and was in the position to speak out the interpretation so that everyone could hear, I asked the Lord to give me the meaning of her message. After I had spoken what I felt were the words that the Holy Spirit inspired me to give, we went on with the offering and the rest of the service. It wasn't until the next morning in school that I came to understand the significance of the whole event. When one of my students asked me if I knew what had happened, I replied with, "It was a message in tongues and the interpretation. Of course, we all know how that works." His response to me was astounding, "But, you see, I'm from India, and my native language is Hindi. When the lady spoke, she was speaking in perfect Hindi. When you spoke, you gave the exact word-for-word translation of what she said!" If God wanted so badly to get a message across to the people, He could have simply spoken it audibly over the sound system in the auditorium. But that is not His way of doing things. He always works though human instruments.

August 26

God Working with Us – and Us with Him

The promise of divine help was actualized in the lives of the first disciples. In addition to the numerous examples we could cite from the accounts recorded in Acts, at least two scriptures specifically say that God actively did His part:

They went forth, and preached every where, the Lord working with them, and confirming the word with signs following. Amen. (Mark 16:20)

God also bearing them witness, both with signs and wonders, and with divers miracles, and gifts of the Holy Ghost. (Hebrews 2:4)

The reality of divine involvement is so preeminent that some authors have made the clever play on words based on the fact that the prefix *co* means "with" that Jesus left us with a commission – not just a mission. This is exactly what Jesus was intending when He invited us to be yoked together with Him in His yoke. (Matthew 11:29-30)

In truth, we do better to say that we are on God's team rather than suggesting that He is on our team. Paul clarified the order of significance of team members in I Corinthians 3:9 when he wrote, *For we are labourers together with God: ye are God's husbandry, ye are God's building.* In Philippians 2:13, he made it crystal clear that any motivation and any ability to function was not from our side, but totally from God's provision, *For it is God which worketh in you both to will and to do of his good pleasure.* In Romans 15:18, he spoke of what Christ had accomplished through him, and it was in Galatians 2:20 that he spelled out the same truth with unequivocal clarity, *I am crucified with Christ: nevertheless I live; yet not I, but Christ liveth in me.*

He Goes Before Us

God is actually much more interested in the Great Commission than any of us as His team members are. He always takes the initiative to "get the ball in play" and then turns to His team members to bring in the score. The story of Cornelius in Acts chapter ten and the story of Saul of Tarsus in Acts chapter nine are great examples of this truth. Notice how Cornelius had a divine encounter and was given a message to go to Simon the tanner's house to look for a man named Simon Peter – even before Peter was made aware that he was a player in this particular game. We have already seen how the same thing happened to Ananias when God pre-committed him to go on what seemed like a suicide mission to find Saul of Tarsus.

> *And the Lord, he it is that doth go before thee; he will be with thee, he will not fail thee, neither forsake thee: fear not, neither be dismayed.* (Deuteronomy 31:8)
>
> *I will go before thee, and make the crooked places straight: I will break in pieces the gates of brass, and cut in sunder the bars of iron.* (Isaiah 45:2)
>
> *The Lord your God which goeth before you, he shall fight for you, according to all that he did for you in Egypt before your eyes.* (Deuteronomy 1:30)
>
> *For ye shall not go out with haste, nor go by flight: for the Lord will go before you; and the God of Israel will be your reward.* (Isaiah 52:12)

August 28

The Hitchhiker

I often like to illustrate God's strategy by likening it to a football team. The quarterback calls the team into a huddle and directs one player to run down the sideline until he reaches the five-yard line. When the runner makes his turn at the five-yard line, the ball comes to him because the quarterback has coordinated and orchestrated everything to be in perfect sync. All the runner has to do is grab the ball and make a couple steps to score the goal.

The first personal experience of this nature happened when I was a college student back in the 1970s, during the hippie revolution when "sex, drugs, and rock and roll" was the mantra for the day. One day I picked up a young girl who was hitchhiking near the campus. She only needed a lift for a few blocks, but that short ride put her on the most exciting journey of her life – the road to heaven. When she got into my car, she made a comment about the "God loves you" decal on my dashboard. As I began to tell her about the plan of salvation, she shared her story. As an atheist, she had rejected everything anyone had ever shared with her about God or the need for her soul to be saved. However, while experimenting with LSD, she had remained "high" while all the others who were "tripping" with her had come "down." In her drug-induced state, the only explanation she could imagine was that she was dead while all the others were still alive. When she did eventually come "down," she said that something inside of her cried out, "Thank God, I'm alive." At that moment, she knew that she must have a soul and that there must be a God. That divine encounter had prepared her for the conversation I was to share with her that day.

The Man in the Painting

When I walked into the Christian bookstore in Delhi, India, the clerk pointed my attention to a picture of Jesus that hung in the front window and said that he wanted to tell me about what had just happened. A Hindu man had come into the store a few days before asking if he could meet the man in the picture. When the shopkeeper explained that it was a painting of a man who lived many years ago, the customer was perplexed, saying that he had seen the man in his dreams several nights in a row and that he knew he needed to meet him. When he saw the painting, he understood that his quest for this mystery man had finally been fruitful. The store clerk, of course, led this hungry soul to salvation.

The most dramatic story of such a divine "hand-off" comes from the remote mountains of Nepal where one of my friends was doing door-to-door evangelism. One man he met in a very isolated mountain village had been having visions of the various Hindu gods. In fact, he had filled numerous volumes with handwritten narratives of all the stories and revelations he had received about these deities. Then one night, he had a vision in which he was directed that he would be given a revelation about a more powerful deity if he would destroy all the journals he had written about the lesser deities. When he burned the other logbooks, he began to have visions and dreams about another god that he had never learned about before. He wrote the stories and revelations about this new god, but didn't have a name for him – until my friend came to his hut and introduced him to Jesus and showed him that the same stories he was recording had already been written down almost two thousand years before!

August 30

So That's His Name

A little old lady from our church in Indiana traveled into the hinterlands of the Philippines to share the gospel in the unreached villages. In one of these villages, she met a very elderly man who had lived far beyond the normal life expectancy of the people in his area. When Aunty Ruth shared the message of Jesus with the old man, he readily responded with the words, "So that's His name!" He explained that he already knew about this true God through dreams and visions, but had never had an opportunity to know who He was. Only a few days after Aunty introduced him to Jesus, the old man passed away.

Andrew Wommack, the president of the Bible college where I teach, tells the story of introducing himself to a receptionist at a business he was visiting. When she asked what business he was in, Andrew responded that he was a minister. Her next question was, "For whom?" When Andrew replied that he was a minister for Jesus Christ, she immediately interrupted, "Well, then you're the man!" Of course, he questioned her, "What man?" She answered by telling her story. As a Buddhist, she had been going through her religious rituals the night before but felt as if what she was doing was in vain. So she simply prayed, "God, I know that You are real, but I'm not sure who You are. Please show Yourself to me." Instantly, a ball of light invaded her room and a voice spoke to her, "Tomorrow, I'll send a man to tell you who I am." God personally took the divine initiative to reach this woman, but He left the job of scoring the point to one of His ministers. God was working with Andrew Wommack just as He did with the early disciples. (Mark 16:20)

August 31

Dreams and Visions

Today, there are incredible stories like the ones I've just shared, mostly coming from nations behind the Quran Curtain where Muslim men and women are having supernatural dreams and visions that initiate their quest for the One True God. Because I had heard so many stories about these divine visitations, I decided to investigate a little and asked the audience when I was ministering in the country of Niger – which is almost one hundred percent Islamic – if any of them had had such supernatural dreams and visions. To my surprise, almost one fourth of the congregation raised their hands!

God truly is taking the initiative. (John 14:6) He is even more adamant about the Great Commission than we are (II Peter 3:9), but He always passes the ball to His human team members to score the point. Knowing that God is the primary player on the team does take some of the pressure off of us because we realize that we don't have to do it on our own. At the same time, we still need to be vigilant to make our move when the ball is served into our court.

It does no good for a Muslim to have a dream about a man dressed in white unless there is someone who is willing to tell him who that man is. What if no one had built a Christian bookstore in Delhi and hung a picture of Jesus in the window? What if my friend had not gone to the little hut in the remote village of Nepal? What if Aunty Ruth had not climbed over the rugged mountains of the Philippines? What if Andrew Wommack had not stopped to greet the receptionist at that business? What if I had not picked up the hitchhiker? What if you don't follow the Lord's promptings today?

September 1

Paul's Prayers

We are far from emptying our treasure chest, but let's turn our attention to how we access the box itself. Maybe you will remember that my cousins and I never had the key to our grandmother's chest, but there is a scriptural key that can help us unlock this great treasure chest so that we can access all the jewels inside. I suggest that we might start our quest for this key in the prayers of the Apostle Paul. The scriptures actually record four prayers that the apostle prayed for the church. In the first chapter of Ephesians, he prayed that the believers would have the spirit of wisdom and revelation in the knowledge of Christ and that the eyes of their understanding would be enlightened so that they would know the hope of His calling, the riches of the glory of His inheritance, and the exceeding greatness of His power. (Ephesians 1:15-19) In the third chapter of Ephesians, he prayed that they would be able to comprehend and know the love of Christ, which surpasses knowledge. (Ephesians 3:14-21) For the Philippians, he prayed that they would abound more and more in knowledge and judgment. (Philippians 1:9-13) His prayer for the Colossian church was that they would be filled with the knowledge of His will in all wisdom and spiritual understanding and that they would increase in the knowledge of God. (Colossians 1:9-13)

Notice that in these prayers Paul felt that the key to a successful Christian life was knowledge – the same key that Jesus Himself proclaimed, *And ye shall know the truth, and the truth shall make you free.* (John 8:32) If we believe error, we will never have the wonderful riches that are stored in the treasure chest; however, once we learn the truth, we can unlock them.

September 2
Vanity – Part I
Before we actually address the concept of the key of knowledge, let's take a few lines to paint the background so we can see the truth in its proper context. In Ephesians 4:17, Paul directed the believers that they not walk in the vanity of their minds as the gentiles do. Of course, it is easy to immediately define vanity as "emptiness" and go on – totally missing what this verse really has to say. To really catch on to what Paul was trying to communicate, we need to review the book of Ecclesiastes where Solomon defined exactly what vanity entails. In verse 1:14, he concluded that all the works or accomplishments that have been done under the sun are vanity. In verse 2:1, he summarized pleasure and entertainment as vanity. In verse 2:11, he concluded that all forms of employment are nothing more than vanity. Intelligence and education find their way to the vanity list in verse 2:15. Verse 2:17 embraced all of life as vanity. Being in a position of management or authority is also vanity according to verse 2:19. Being in a position to leave behind a legacy or inheritance is also vanity according to 2:21. Verse 2:23 adds diligence and a strong work ethic to the list. Living a moral life falls into the vanity category in verse 2:26. Being human as opposed to simply being a product of evolution still leaves us in the vanity category according to verse 3:19. Verse 4:4 tells us that "keeping up with the Joneses" is also vanity. Struggling to make it "up the corporate ladder" falls in the vanity category in verse 4:7. Actually making it to that lonely place "at the top" is also vanity according to verse 4:8. Verse 4:16 describes even the "Rocky syndrome" of the underdog making unexpected achievements as vanity.

September 3
Vanity – Part II

We are far from finished with Solomon's list of vanities. Verse 5:10 pulls fiscal security into the discussion of vanity. Verse 6:2 amplifies this truth by adding that – even when it is obvious that wealth is a blessing from God – it can be fleeting and, therefore, vanity. Even long life and a prominent family do not ensure that one's life doesn't end as vanity according to verse 6:4. Verse 6:9 adds desire to the vanity list. Verse 7:6 adds a fool's comments. The inequities between good men and evil men fall on the vanity list in verse 7:15. Verse 8:10 tells us that the things that are forgotten as soon as our obituaries are written are nothing but vanity. The fact that just men seem to get the rewards of the unjust and vice versa is obviously vanity according to verse 8:14. Verse 9:9 says that even a happy home can belie the underlying vanity of the relationship. Verse 11:8 adds that even a long life can be only a camouflage for vanity under the surface. Youthfulness makes the list in verse 11:10. And the concluding summation that everything is vanity is found in verse 12:8.

That leaves us with essentially "no stone unturned." Business, industry, finance, education, politics, religion, entertainment, family – every area of human interest and endeavor is included as being vanity. Thus, it becomes obvious that the Apostle Paul wasn't saying that the gentiles don't have anything in their brains; rather, he was trying to tell us that the things they occupy their minds with have no substance. Even if their plans and schemes move nations, transfer fortunes, and change the course of history, they are still vanity in God's sight.

September 4

The Knowledge of God

In that nothing is left off of the vanity list, we must question what it is that must be planted so that our minds as believers will not be focused on such vanity? Paul answered this question by sharing his own testimony, *Though I might also have confidence in the flesh. If any other man thinketh that he hath whereof he might trust in the flesh, I more: Circumcised the eighth day, of the stock of Israel, of the tribe of Benjamin, an Hebrew of the Hebrews; as touching the law, a Pharisee; Concerning zeal, persecuting the church; touching the righteousness which is in the law, blameless. But what things were gain to me, those I counted loss for Christ. Yea doubtless, and I count all things but loss for the excellency of the knowledge of Christ Jesus my Lord: for whom I have suffered the loss of all things, and do count them but dung, that I may win Christ.* (Philippians 3:3-8)

In this passage, Paul gives us a pretty impressive list of accomplishments and pedigrees that would certainly qualify as the "stuff" of success in almost every dimension of life. Yet, he says that all these things are essentially dung – vanity, if you prefer a little more polite description – to him. The one thing that he says is worthy of his consideration is *the excellency of the knowledge of Christ Jesus my Lord.* The truth is that the New Testament abounds with confirmations of the fact that the knowledge of God is the essence of the Christian life. (Romans 1:28, 10:2, 11:33; I Corinthians 15:34; II Corinthians 2:14, 4:6, 10:5; Ephesians 1:17, 3:4, 3:8, 3:19, 4:13; Colossians 1:10, 3:10; II Peter 1:2, 1:3, 1:8, 2:20, 3:18)

September 5

The Christ Hymn

It is the knowledge of our Lord and Savior Jesus Christ that must be planted in us to take the place of the vanity that will otherwise fill the thoughts of our minds and hearts. (Ephesians 3:17 Colossians 1:23, 2:7) But does this mean that we must always go about thinking about God and Jesus like monks cloistered away from the rest of the world in a monastery somewhere? No – a thousand times no! We must find a place of balance where we can continue to live in and have an influence upon all the dimensions of society – yet not be sucked into the vacuum of their emptiness. (John 17:15) The key is to realize that Christ is the true essence of every aspect of life – business, industry, finance, education, politics, religion, entertainment, family, and every other element of life. (I Corinthians 8:6, Ephesians 1:10, Colossians 3:11)   The exquisite "Christ hymn" of Colossians 1:14-20 expresses this truth with such grandeur:

> *In whom we have redemption through his blood, even the forgiveness of sins: Who is the image of the invisible God, the firstborn of every creature: For by him were all things created, that are in heaven, and that are in earth, visible and invisible, whether they be thrones, or dominions, or principalities, or powers: all things were created by him, and for him: And he is before all things, and by him all things consist. And he is the head of the body, the church: who is the beginning, the firstborn from the dead; that in all things he might have the preeminence. For it pleased the Father that in him should all fulness dwell; And, having made peace through the blood of his cross, by him to reconcile all things unto himself; by him, I say, whether they be things in earth, or things in heaven."*

September 6
Really Knowing
Knowing Christ involves much more than mental assent to the truths that we know about Him. Knowing goes far beyond simply hoping or wishing that God is on our side; it involves an unquestionable assurance that comes from actually experiencing the reality of His life in us and our life in Him. Notice in each of the following scriptures from three different New Testament authors that each writer tells us that his key is that he <u>knows</u> something:

> *My brethren, count it all joy when ye fall into divers temptations; <u>Knowing</u> this, that the trying of your faith worketh patience. But let patience have her perfect work, that ye may be perfect and entire, wanting nothing.* (James 1:2-4)
>
> *For ye had compassion of me in my bonds, and took joyfully the spoiling of your goods, <u>knowing</u> in yourselves that ye have in heaven a better and an enduring substance.* (Hebrews 10:34)
>
> *Not only so, but we glory in tribulations also: <u>knowing</u> that tribulation worketh patience; And patience, experience; and experience, hope: And hope maketh not ashamed; because the love of God is shed abroad in our hearts by the Holy Ghost which is given unto us.* (Romans 5:3-5)

September 7

Thoughts That Exalt Themselves
Against the Knowledge of God

Let's look at another passage that demonstrates the all-important role of our knowledge of Christ, *For though we walk in the flesh, we do not war after the flesh: (For the weapons of our warfare are not carnal, but mighty through God to the pulling down of strong holds;) Casting down imaginations, and every high thing that exalteth itself against the knowledge of God, and bringing into captivity every thought to the obedience of Christ.* (II Corinthians 10:3-5)

For many years, I interpreted this passage to mean that God had given us spiritual weapons to pull down the strongholds established in our lives by thoughts that exalted themselves against the knowledge that God existed – ideas like atheism that says there is no God or Hinduism that says that Vishnu, Krishna, Ganesh, or any one of the other millions of their deities is God, or Buddhism that claims Gautama to be divine, or even New Age that tells us that we all are gods. However, the "Ford Better Idea Light Bulb" came on one day when I realized that the serpent in the Garden of Eden did not challenge God's existence; he simply coerced Eve to accept an inferior view of Him. Before the conversation with the devil in snakeskin, Eve knew God as totally benevolent; after allowing the insinuations of the enemy to infiltrate her thinking, she began to suspect that God had a hidden agenda. She allowed a thought that exalted itself against the true knowledge of God to take a toehold in her mind. Before the conversation was over, it had established a stronghold in her heart, and she was ready to betray Him.

September 8

Magnifying God

The same is true with each of us – if we allow thoughts that are contrary to the biblical revelation that God is our healer, our provider, our righteousness, our victory banner, and our all-in-all to take root in our minds, we will soon believe that distortion and lose our faith and our relationship with Him. Psalm 78:41 says that the people of Israel limited the Holy One of Israel by failing to remember how He had delivered them from Egypt. They allowed thoughts that minimized their God to dominate their minds. If we want to think about God properly, we must always be careful to magnify (Psalm 69:30) rather than to minimize Him and His love for His children. Allow me to define "magnify." When we put a specimen under a microscope or examine it with a magnifying glass, we don't actually change its size; all we do is alter our ability to see it. Magnifying has nothing to do with the reality; it only has to do with correcting our inability to see what already exists. Therefore, when we magnify the Lord, all we are doing is adjusting our view of God.

The Holy Spirit helped me adjust my focus one day when He prompted me to realize that I still harbored thoughts that exalted themselves against God. He questioned me as to what I knew about God. I responded by reciting the redemptive names of God. The Holy Spirit then replied that any time I thought that my healing was in the medicine cabinet I was actually entertaining a thought that was exalting itself against what I knew about Jehovah Rapha and that every time I thought that my provision was in asking my boss for a raise I was again entertaining thoughts that exalted themselves against the true knowledge of Jehovah Jireh – and so on.

September 9

God's Redemptive Names

Our weapons are strong enough to destroy the arguments against the knowledge of God. There are many areas of truth that we should know about God; however, we often don't comprehend and live in them. We know that God exists, but we fail to attain the true knowledge of who God is and what He does.

God is Jehovah Tsidkenu – the God of our righteousness. The day that Jesus came into our lives, His righteousness came into us. However, the devil will come to each and every one of us with accusations to combat any awareness we have of this righteousness. Just like David's stone found that tiny eyehole in Goliath's armor, the devil will aim for this vulnerable spot. If that lie penetrates into our minds, he begins to build a stronghold against the knowledge of God's righteousness within us.

God is also Jehovah Rapha – the God who heals all of our diseases. The devil wants to plant lies inside us saying that our ailment is either too big for God to heal or too insignificant for Him to notice. The truth is that God is just as willing to heal the little aches and pains as He is to heal major diseases. He is just as able to heal the most dreaded plague as He is to cure a minor ailment.

We can go through all the redemptive names and qualities of God to learn what we should be thinking about God. Any time we allow thoughts contrary to these truths into our hearts, we have permitted the enemy to use his deceit to begin to erect strongholds in our minds.

Be not conformed to this world: but be ye transformed by the renewing of your mind, that ye may prove what is that good, and acceptable, and perfect, will of God. (Romans 12:2)

September 10

Epignosis

The Apostle Peter opened his second epistle with a dramatic contrast – offering us two radically different options: the knowledge of God or lust.

Grace and peace be multiplied unto you through the knowledge of God, and of Jesus our Lord, According as his divine power hath given unto us all things that pertain unto life and godliness, through the knowledge of him that hath called us to glory and virtue: Whereby are given unto us exceeding great and precious promises: that by these ye might be partakers of the divine nature, having escaped the corruption that is in the world through lust. (II Peter 1:2-4)

If we choose to pursue the knowledge of God, we are promised an end result of becoming partakers of the divine nature. In other words, the very DNA of God will be evident in our lives. If we choose to pursue lust, it will end in corruption (putrefied ruination). Interestingly, the apostle adds the special Greek prefix epi to both "knowledge" and "lust" making both words intensive so that they should be read "all-encompassing knowledge" and "all-encompassing lust." Think about how your epidermis, or skin, covers your whole body. In the same way that no part of your body is left without a covering of skin (epidermis), no part of our lives should be left without a covering of the knowledge of God (*epignosis*). Just as we are vulnerable to infection If the epidermis is punctured or cut, our spiritual lives are endangered if we are not blanketed with the knowledge of God. The apostle leaves us with no middle ground – either we whole-heartedly seek God, or we will be overwhelmingly swallowed up with lust, greed, and an ever-spiraling desire for more and more material possessions.

September 11
How We Think vs. What We Think

An insightful glimpse into this scenario of never-ending escalation of self-centeredness came when a reporter asked a billionaire how much would be enough. With a little twinkle in his eye, the financier responded, "Just a little more." In similar fashion, we as Christians must become possessed with an insatiable desire for the knowledge of God rather than a self-centered desire for the things of this world. In the immediately following verses, Peter admonishes the believers to diligently pursue maturity by adding layer upon layer to our spiritual lives, ending with a warning that to fail to do so would result in becoming barren and unfruitful in the knowledge of Christ. Paul presented the identical options in Galatians 6:7-8 when he said that we will reap everlasting life if we sow to the spirit, but corruption if we sow to the flesh.

This all-encompassing knowledge of God is more about how we think about God, not what we think about Him. The issue is not just a matter of knowing that He is all-powerful, but of understanding that He is using this unlimited power to bring blessing and benefit into our lives. We know that God is omniscient – all-knowing. However, we can apply that knowledge about His omniscience in different ways. We can assume that – since He is all-knowing – He knows about all our failures. In this case, we will live our lives in condemnation and defeat. On the other hand, we can apply our knowledge about God's omniscience with an awareness that He knows the intents of our hearts and understands that they are much more noble than the outward failures He has seen. With this in mind, we live victoriously and free of self-condemnation. The key is in how we think about what we know.

September 12

Cars, Girls, and Money

Proverbs 23:7 proclaims, *As he thinketh in his heart, so is he.* Notice that Solomon uses the word "as" indicating that it is how we think – not what we think – that determines who we will be. If what we think about were the determining factor, all American boys would become convertible sports cars by the time they were sixteen; by the time they were twenty-one they would all have turned into girls; and they would all become a million dollars by age thirty. In raising my sons, I was keenly aware that my role as their father was to guide them in <u>how</u> to think. Thinking <u>about</u> cars would never make them actually become automobiles, but the <u>way</u> they thought about cars would determine the kind of drivers they would become. I knew that I needed to focus on helping them think of cars as something other than toys, status symbols, and weapons – otherwise, it would be dangerous to be on the road at the same time with them. Thinking <u>about</u> girls would never make them actually become women, but the <u>way</u> they thought about girls would determine the kind of husbands they would become. I knew that I needed to focus on helping them think of girls as something other than sex objects or ego enhancers – otherwise, they would become abusive husbands with no hope of happy, stable marriages. Thinking <u>about</u> money would never make them actually become dollar bills, but the <u>way</u> they thought about money would determine the kind of spenders and investors they would become. I knew that I needed to focus on helping them think of money as a tool to accomplish their goals and as seed for sowing into the future – otherwise, they would be facing a future characterized by unhealthy greed and debilitating debt.

September 13
New Perspectives

The way we think about God will radically determine the way we live our lives. When I was working in a campus ministry in the 1970s, I traveled – almost like a circuit-riding preacher – from campus to campus, leading Bible study groups. In one of the groups I visited every couple of weeks, there was a young man who was confined to a wheelchair. When I challenged him to believe God for his healing, he said that he felt that God had put him in the wheelchair to keep him humble. I responded, "Keeping us humble is the work of the Holy Spirit, not a wheelchair." That idea was too radical for him to take, so I admonished him to think and pray about it until my next visit. By the time I returned, he had taken the time to reconsider his view of God and now believed that God was a healer, not one who made His subjects sick. When I prayed for him, strength instantly came into his legs, and he was able to abandon the wheelchair altogether! He had been more crippled in his mind than in his legs!

I ended a class on the gifts of the Holy Spirit by asking the students if they felt that God was calling them to operate in any of the giftings. When one young man responded that he felt that he was to operate in healing, I asked if anyone was sick so that he could begin to minister in his calling. One lady had suffered a back injury a number of years before, but was expecting to be healed at a certain evangelist's meeting. I told her that the same God who works in the evangelist's crusades is just as powerful in our little classroom. When she agreed to have her fellow student lay hands on her, she was instantly healed. Her problem was that she was having faith in God's man rather than in God Himself.

September 14

Hiding in the Trunk

Several days ago, we made mention of Paul's testimony in Philippians chapter three where he declared that his whole aim in life was to know Christ and that he considered everything else in life pointless in comparison to the excellency of the knowledge of Christ Jesus. But today, I'd like to revisit that same passage and pick up on one other goal that Paul had – to be found in Him. (Philippians 3:9)

When I read this statement, 1 envision what would have probably happened had my cousins and I ever had the chance to get into our grandmother's trunk – we would have literally gotten into it! After all, we have all watched little children unpack their Christmas gifts, scatter the toys all over the living room floor, and then crawl into the boxes to play "fort." This is exactly what Paul was expressing – a desire to not only take possession of the gifts in the Jesus treasure chest and to know the Giver of those gifts, but to literally crawl into Him as his fortress and habitation.

In Colossians 3:3, Paul took this concept even one step further when he made reference to our lives being hidden with Christ in God. Not only are we hidden in Christ, we – along with Christ – are also hidden in God. This means that as we go deeper in Jesus, we actually go even deeper into God the Father as well. Of course, none of this happens without walking in the Spirit. The bottom line is that the entire Trinity is beckoning us into an ever-deepening and more intimate relationship.

> *When...the Spirit of truth is come, he will guide you into all truth...he shall receive of mine, and shall shew it unto you. All things that the Father hath are mine...he shall take of mine, and shall shew it unto you.* (John 16:13-15)

September 15
From the Roman Jail Cell
Let's make one more visit to Philippians chapter three and notice one additional statement from Paul's testimony. In verses twelve and thirteen, he says that he has not yet attained or even apprehended his goal of knowing Christ and being found in Him. Not only was the apostle aware that he hadn't achieved his goal in life, he realized that he did not even fully understand what it involved! The question that immediately pops into my mind when I read this statement is, "When did Paul make this observation?" Although there is uncertainty as to the actual timeframe in which this epistle was penned, most biblical scholars tend to believe that it was probably written during Paul's Roman imprisonment. In other words, it was during the last few years – or possibly, months – of his life. Paul had lived his full life and completed his total ministry and was still digging deeper into his treasure chest.

The same is true for us. No matter how much we know and experience, there are still more unfathomable depths awaiting us as we go deeper into Jesus. Remember the story about Dr. Lester Sumrall's prayers? Even after more than sixty years, his daily prayer was, "Lord, I want to know You."

It is said that a thousand-mile journey starts with one step. Even though we've spent two and a half months journeying together, we're hardly beyond the first few steps in this lifelong quest to go deeper in Jesus. Keep digging deeper into the Jesus treasure chest!

September 16
Soul Prosperity
If thou draw out thy soul to the hungry, and
satisfy the afflicted soul; then shall thy light
rise in obscurity, and thy darkness be as the
noon day. (Isaiah 58:10)

This passage comes from Isaiah's discourse on fasting which he calls *afflicting the soul.* (verse 3)   The prophet declares that the people had abused the practice of fasting and then goes to great lengths to explain what should really be involved in a true fast.   He says a godly fast involves a change of heart that gets our concentration off of ourselves and focuses our attention on the needs of others.   Furthermore, it frees the resources that we would normally consume upon ourselves so that we now have the wherewithal to actually affect a change in the situation of the needy.   Having thus afflicted our soul through denying its self-centeredness and greedy nature, we are now able to change its orientation by drawing it out and directing its attention on those who are less fortunate than we are.   Prosperity is a matter of the soul.

The idea is continued in the parable that Jesus told about a man whose fields produced so abundantly that he had no place to store all his revenue.   Although some people might look despairingly at this gentleman because of his wealth, we need to remember that he is actually an example of the biblical promise that God wants to bless us to the point where we can't contain all He gives us. (Malachi 3:10)   However, when the man told his soul to take its rest, the Lord called him a fool. (Luke 12:19-20)

The point is that prosperity does not have to do with what you have, but whether you are selfish with it.

September 17

Everything's Gonna Be OK

How many times have we heard someone say to a person who has just gone through a great trauma or is in the middle of a devastating situation, "Everything's gonna be OK," or "It's all gonna work out"? Of course, we have to also be honest enough to ask how often we've been the one out of whose mouth these words rolled so easily. Certainly, it is great to have a positive attitude that makes us feel that there is always a "silver lining behind every black cloud": however, I'd like for us to take a step back and look at these words of encouragement from a broader perspective.

Many Christians base their idea that everything's gonna be OK on the biblical promise that all things work together for good for those who love God and are called according to His purpose. (Romans 8:28) In fact, I've heard people quote that verse in all kinds of tragic conditions – prolonged illnesses that ran up insurmountable hospital and medical bills complicated by the loss of income due to not being able to work, loss of an automobile due to an accident with an uninsured driver or loss of a home that was not adequately covered by insurance, and the list could go on and on. When faced with such a horrible situation, it is definitely necessary to keep a positive attitude and believe that what the devil meant for evil God will turn around for our good (Genesis 50:20); however, if we really understood the power of this verse, we would never have to use it to encourage ourselves that everything's gonna be okay because this verse is actually intended to help us live victoriously over the attacks that are intended to get us in the destructive condition in the first place.

Tomorrow's lesson will help us see why.

September 18

In Context

The one thing that I always notice about people who reference Romans 8:28 as proof that everything's gonna be okay is that they fail to include the first word in the verse – "and." Since the sentence begins with a conjunction, we must include the previous thought in order to accurately understand the verse. The previous thought begins in verse twenty-six which says that the Holy Spirit will help us when we don't know how to effectively pray about things. The thought continues in verse twenty-seven where the Apostle tells us that such prayers are always in the will of God because they are formulated by the One who knows the mind of God. What is the source of the weakness and ineffectiveness of our human prayers? It is the lack of unquestionably knowing the mind of God on the issue. The truth is that we often limit the hand of God because of our instant prayers for one thing when God is just waiting for us to quit begging Him to do that thing so that He can do something far bigger and better for us. After all, He is the God who does things that are more extravagant than we could ever imagine or dare to ask for. (Ephesians 3:20) On the flip side of the coin, what is the key to effective prayer? Knowing that the petitions we are making are in direct correlation with what God already has in mind to do for us. (I John 5:14-15) At this point, it is important to remember that the thoughts that He is thinking toward us are always good and never harmful and that they are to bring us prosperity and success. (Jeremiah 29:11) In other words, He doesn't intend for us to get into situations where we need for everything to be okay and look for a way for things to work together for our good. Everything should always be okay and good for us.

September 19

The Spirit Helps Our Infirmities

Let me share just one example of how Romans 8:26-28 should be properly applied. When Dr. Lester Sumrall was traveling in Tibet during a tumultuous time in the nation when outlaws, bandits, and rebel forces ruled the land, he was faced with a decision as to which route to take to get to a certain city. After prayer, he felt impressed to go on one specific road. When he arrived at his destination that evening, he discovered that everyone else who had taken the other road had been slaughtered before they reached the village. Had he not heard the voice of the Holy Spirit directing him to go left rather than right (Isaiah 30:21), he would have also lost his life that day. Everything did work together for his good because he totally avoided the area where the ambushes had been set.

Trying to imagine how someone might try to apply Romans 8:28 without its full context, I can only conclude that they would have Dr. Sumrall take the road that everyone else did and be attacked by the marauders, robbed, severely beaten, left for dead, and somehow miraculously survive. After tortuously dragging himself through the hostile terrain to reach the village where the gracious folks would spend the next several weeks nursing him back to health so that he could limp away penniless, someone would look at him and say, "See how everything is okay and it all worked together for your good because you survived when no one else did." Yes, that would have been a testimony, but how much more of a testimony was the fact that God didn't allow any weapon that the enemy intended against him to prosper (Isaiah 54:17) or for any harm to come to him in the first place (Psalm 91:10-11).

September 20
Have You Ever Stopped to Think That...?
The jawbone of an ass is still a dangerous weapon.

You don't get to the top by being full of hot air.

It's nice to be important, but more important to be nice.

Activity should not be confused with accomplishment.

Zero times anything is still zero.

Idleness is disobedience.

Being the rider is better than being the horse.

Being fruitful is better than being fretful.

You should pick battles that are big enough to matter and small enough to win.

If happiness truly consisted in physical ease and freedom from care, then the happiest individual would be neither a man nor a woman; it would be an American cow.

Because the centurion understood submission, he understood that Jesus could stand in one place and triumph over the devil in another place. He did not need to enter into hand-to-hand combat.

If you get rid of it, you don't have to organize it.

To get what you haven't had before, you have to do what you haven't done before.

We ask for daily bread, but why not ask for donuts?

God allowed a hundred years for the building of the ark so that the snails, tortoises, and sloths could get there.

You should make an action that puts you at a point of no return.

You should always weigh the pros and cons and be wary of those people who are pros at being cons.

When you say to the mountain, *Be cast into the sea,* you should be listening for the splash?

If you know "what" and "how," you will always have a job; if you know "why," you will be the boss.

September 21
Think it's Hot?

Do you think that it has been hot this summer? Well, The Anderson (SC) Independent reported that it was 889 degrees one recent September day!

Of course – according to the general media – it would probably be good for us to prepare for weather reports like that. The idea of global warming has become so widely accepted that it has essentially become recognized as a given fact rather than the scientific theory that it actually is.   The US government spends twenty-two billion dollars every year (more than forty thousand dollars per minute) on global warming, and private businesses spend several times that amount, racking up a one-and-three-quarters-billion-dollar budget.   Yet, the world temperature has risen by only a third of a degree in thirty-five years with most of the warming being between 1979 and 1998 followed by gradual cooling since then. It was predicted that the polar ice cap at the North Pole would be gone by 2014, but it has actually grown by about two thirds.

The point of today's meditation is that we realized that the 889-degree temperature was obviously a typo. However, we readily accept as factual other climate reports without considering all the possible prejudice and error that might have occurred in the research, analysis, and reporting of the data.

Ephesians 4:14 tells us not to be like children who are tossed about by all sorts of ideas that are perpetrated through the *sleight of men and cunning craftiness* by those who wish to deceive us. This passage refers to erroneous theology, but we really must apply this same diligence to ferret out fake news in every area of life. If we allow deception a toehold in any area, it will establish strongholds in all areas.

September 22
Working with Nothing

When asked to return to my home church as a guest speaker one Sunday, I prepared a message on Rahab, the harlot who became a hero the day that she saved the lives of two Israeli spies in the city of Jericho. I thought the message went well until I read the next Sunday's bulletin, "I think we were all spellbound by the timely message by Delron Shirley. It made us realize more and more that God can take nothing and make something out of it." Of course, I knew that the pastor was referring to Rahab as the nothing, but the statement did have a sobering effect when I realized that he could have just as easily been referring to me!

Paul made it clear in I Corinthians 4:7 that any ministry we may have is simply a gift from God and that there is no room for boasting about our ability since it isn't our ability at all. Jesus explained the point in a more general context when He said that He is the vine and we are the branches that sprout from that vine; therefore, we have nothing that doesn't originate in Him and that we are totally and utterly helpless without Him. (John 15:5)

Any cleverness or insightfulness in interpreting the scriptures and communicating the truths therein is simply the Holy Spirit (who authored the scriptures) whispering to us the message He hid there in the first place. Thus, the greatest merit we can accept is our ability to hear His voice. At least fifteen times, the New Testament admonishes all who have an ear should hear. (Matthew 11:15, 13:9, 13:43; Mark 4:9, 4:23; Luke 14:35; Revelation 2:7, 2:11, 2:17, 2:29, 3:6, 3:13, 3:22, 13:9) Therefore, it is obviously expected that we should hear the Holy Spirit's insights. In such a case, simply repeating them should not gain any credit for us.

September 23
Simple Machines
We live in an age of extraordinary technology, but did you realize that in the mechanical world, as opposed to the electronic world, there have been no new inventions since ancient times? There are six simple machines that were invented millennia ago that are the foundation of everything that we have today: the lever, the wheel and axle, the pulley, the screw, the wedge, and the inclined plane. In all honesty, the screw is actually a rolled up inclined plane; therefore, it could be argued that mankind has actually invented only five basic mechanical devices. Every other machine that has been created over the ages is simply a combination of these foundational instruments.

Okay, so this is all interesting, but what significance does it have to me? Well, let's apply it to spiritual truth. Second John verse nine in the Living Bible says, *For if you wander beyond the teaching of Christ, you will leave God behind; while if you are loyal to Christ's teachings, you will have God too. Then you will have both the Father and the Son."* Spiritually, there is nothing new to be revealed since the teaching of Christ – just recombinations of old truths. We must be continually cautious when we hear people advocating new revelations. Unless they are clearly founded on the basic gospel truths that are already established in the Bible, they are dangerous and deadly.

September 24
Increased Knowledge
But thou, O Daniel, shut up the words, and
seal the book, even to the time of the end.
(Daniel 12:4)

Having said that the gospel is like the simple machines that we have had since ancient times, we must take the time to deal with scriptures that seem to indicate that there are secrets not yet revealed.

Before we do that, let's go back to the physical world. There have been significant breakthroughs that have revolutionized society. For example, the invention of the combustion engine and the discovery of electricity which fathered two revolutions – the industrial and technological, respectively. Another great illustration would be air travel. It took the human race millennia to get off the ground – but once they did, there was no stopping them. The Wright brothers made the first flight of eight hundred and fifty-two feet in 1903, but it took only sixty-six more years to send a man to the moon! However, we must remember that these developments only unleashed the ability to better utilize the six basic tools we already had available.

So it is in the spiritual realm. There have been great turning points in the theological world – Martin Luther's revelation of salvation by faith rather than works and the Pentecostal awaking are great examples. However, none of these revelations were new; they were in the scriptures all along. It was when they came to light that revolutionary things happened. In like manner, the secrets that are sealed up until the last days will only be the unleashing of ancient truths. When the seven-sealed book in Revelation chapter five is opened, the truths are ones that date all the way back to the Old Testament.

September 25

Success and Failure

In a study of the most successful people in America, over five hundred of them said that their success came just one step beyond their greatest defeat. Another study revealed that the average American entrepreneur fails between three and four times before he finally achieves success.

These discoveries can help us reorient our attitude toward success and failure. For starters, we see the grace of God in that Proverbs 24:16 tells us, *A just man falleth seven times, and riseth up again: but the wicked shall fall into mischief.* God actually allows us twice as many "goes" at success than we actually need. Failing does not make you a failure; refusing to try again does.

We can come to a place where our latest failure can be our last failure – in two ways. We can get up again and finally find the success that God intends for our lives – thus ending the cycle of failing. Or we can refuse to get up, accepting defeat. In this case, we never have to face another possibility of failing – but we never have another chance at success! Thus, we prove the point that quitting is a permanent solution to a temporary problem.

Joshua 1:8 promises good success to those who know and live by God's laws – which means that there must also be such a thing as bad success for those who gain their place in life outside God's standards. Of course, such a statement needs no proof in that we all have witnessed those people who have achieved their status by cheating, lying, and stealing. Such people are failures regardless of their seeming success in that they failed at the test of integrity and refused to get up and try again.

September 26

Think Big about the God Inside of You

Ye are of God, little children, and have overcome them: because greater is he that is in you, than he that is in the world. (I John 4:4)

We are constantly faced with challenges that are bigger than we can handle. That is actually a great blessing! If we didn't face such challenges, we would never have the reward or experience the thrill of releasing the power of God that is inside us and realizing the victorious growth of our faith that it brings.

Think back to the story about the ten spies who cowered before the giants in the Promised Land, *There we saw the giants, the sons of Anak, which come of the giants: and we were in our own sight as grasshoppers, and so we were in their sight.* (Numbers 13:33) Notice that it was their own evaluation of themselves that determined their defeat. Now, let's fast-forward forty years to the testimony of Rahab to see how the people of Canaan actually felt about the Israelites.

I know that the LORD hath given you the land, and that your terror is fallen upon us, and that all the inhabitants of the land faint because of you. For we have heard how the LORD dried up the water of the Red sea for you, when ye came out of Egypt; and what ye did unto the two kings of the Amorites, that were on the other side Jordan, Sihon and Og, whom ye utterly destroyed. And as soon as we had heard these things, our hearts did melt, neither did there remain any more courage in any man, because of you: for the LORD your God, he is God in heaven above, and in earth beneath. (Joshua 2:9-11)

The spies imagined their own defeat and never even gave God a chance to prove Himself strong.

September 27
The Greatest Barrier Against the Devil

It may seem like a random coincidence, but maybe it is worth some serious consideration. In the book of Ephesians, the section in chapter five that deals with the family leads directly into the discussion of spiritual warfare in chapter six. As I have just said, this may be totally random; however, it would be totally out of character for Paul since he was a very orderly author who demonstrated purpose in everything that he wrote.

Actually, it seems that we can make a connection from the very first pages of the Bible to the very last ones and find a theme that confirms the conclusion that there is a definite link between these two seemingly random topics. In Genesis 15:18, God made a covenant with Abraham that he and his family would inherit the land that is bounded by the Euphrates River. In Daniel 9:27, there is a reference to a covenant that will be established by the Antichrist with Israel – the family of Abraham – thus voiding the covenant that was established with their father Abraham. The result is described in the book of Revelation when four demons are loosed from the Euphrates (Revelation 9:14-15) and three frog spirits are released from the same river (Revelation 16:12-14). In other words, as long as the family of Abraham held onto the God-given promises of their father, the devil was held at bay. As soon as Abraham's family abandoned the faith of their father, the enemy was no longer restrained.

But it is not just theology; this principle works in real life. A study done among Lutheran families showed that homes in which the Bible is read on a daily basis are seventeen hundred percent less likely to divorce.

September 28
The Real Reason for Divorce
Having touched on the topic of divorce, perhaps it would be good for us to explore the subject a bit. My first consideration on the topic would be to explore why we are experiencing such a high incidence rate in the church and in the world. Jesus actually gave us the clear answer in His discussion with the Pharisees in Matthew 19:8 and Mark 10:5 – hardness of heart. In this discussion, He explained that divorce was not part of God's original plan. A man was to cleave to his wife with an inseparable bond as if they were stuck with Gorilla Glue. However, the callousness of men's hearts against the laws of God, the emotions of their wives, and the conviction of the Holy Spirit demanded that God develop a Plan B. Thus, divorce was instituted as an expression of God's grace, allowing Him an alternative to manifesting His judgment. In other words, they got an exception to God's general rule and specific commandments.

> *Therefore shall a man leave his father and his mother, and shall cleave unto his wife: and they shall be one flesh. (Genesis 2:23-24)*
> *Thou shalt not commit adultery. (Exodus 20:14)*
> *Thou shalt not covet thy neighbour's ...wife. (Exodus 20:17)*
> *What therefore God hath joined together, let not man put asunder. (Matthew 19:4-6)*

The thing that we should see here is that – all the while holding onto the hardness that is in our hearts forcing us out of His perfect will in Plan A and into the necessity of accepting His grace through Plan B – though subtle, this is still a trick of the devil.

September 29
Divorce Options

When we find ourselves in the situations that could lead toward a divorce, we often start to panic like a hiker lost in the woods who responds by running faster and getting himself even more lost rather than calming down and looking for landmarks that could help him find his way back home. In our frenzy, we fail to realize that divorce simply leads from one bad problem to another. Perhaps the major landmark that we will overlook is found in the story of the woman with five husbands and a live-in boyfriend and the story of the woman caught in adultery. (John 4:3-30, 8:2-11) In these stories, we see the element of hardness of heart expressed in the Jews who snubbed their noses at the Samaritan woman and in the Pharisees who wanted to stone the adulterous woman and were later convicted in their own consciences when Jesus confronted them with the challenge that the sinless one should cast the first stone. We also see the redemption story in that God forgave both of these women and gave them a second chance at life – and apparently without having to leave their mates! We see an even more dramatic story in the Old Testament book of Hosea where the prophet's wife left him for a life of prostitution, but he not only took her back but actually pursued and brought her back at his initiative. He did, however, insist that she face her failures and accept his graciousness in redeeming her.

The bottom line is that we must deal with both partner's failures, realizing that God has a total solution. (Isaiah 1:18, Ezekiel 26:36, II Corinthians 5:17, I John 1:8-9)

September 30
Options for the Divorced Person

Someone once said that marriage is like a harp; when the music stops, the strings are still there. Even after a divorce, there are still strings attached – legal strings, financial strings, emotional strings, relational strings... And the Bible addresses these issues head-on. Paul is pointblank in his counsel that divorce should be avoided if possible but that there are obligations that must be taken seriously if the dissolution of a marriage becomes unavoidable.

> *But and if she depart, let her remain unmarried, or be reconciled to her husband: and let not the husband put away his wife.* (I Corinthians 7:11)

Here, he offers three options: divorce and remain unmarried, get back together, or simply stop the whole thing short of the divorce.

> *For I would that all men were even as I myself. But every man hath his proper gift of God, one after this manner, and another after that.* (I Corinthians 7:7)

Here, he makes a footnote to the option of remaining unmarried – yes, it is the better choice, but not the only one. Elsewhere, he explained that his state of singleness was his choice because he wanted the freedom to fulfill the call to travel the nations as a missionary – a call that not everyone has.

> *If the unbelieving depart, let him depart. A brother or a sister is not under bondage in such cases: but God hath called us to peace.* (I Corinthians 7:15)

The bottom line is that God wants us to live in peace, not bondage. If the divorce was unavoidable, we are free to move forward with our lives.

October 1

Sacrifice

All my life – and my guess is that this is also true with you – I've heard people, especially preachers, talk about sacrificing for the Lord. They often say things like, "You haven't really given until it hurts." But let's take a look at the scriptures to see if God has a different perspective on the topic:

> And I will very _gladly_ spend and be spent for you; though the more abundantly I love you, the less I be loved. (II Corinthians 12:15)
>
> How that in a great trial of affliction the _abundance of their joy_ and their deep poverty abounded unto the riches of their liberality...first gave their own selves to the Lord, and unto us by the will of God. (II Corinthians 8:2-5)

The Old Testament background of sacrifice was that it was actually a time of celebration in that the people gave to God out of the abundance that they had been blessed with; therefore, it was not a painful thing. On the contrary, it was actually an occasion to rejoice in the overflow of their blessing. Additionally, the bulk of the Old Testament sacrifice – with the exception of the whole burnt offering – was given back to the worshipers for them to enjoy as a celebratory meal with their families.

Yes, the passage we are looking at today speaks of how the believers gave out of their poverty – but it was only their monetary poverty, not their spiritual poverty. In fact, they abounded spiritually, which is the source of financial blessing.

Let's not be reluctant to give sacrificially. Rather, count it an occasion to celebrate the blessings of God.

October 2
Embracing the Suffering

A few years ago, there was a particular daily devotional that hit the top of the charts in the Christian publishing field. I think that I received four gift copies that Christmas. One was leather-bound with my name engraved on the cover, and another was a gift from one of the most prominent Christian leaders on the international scene. So, I decided to read through it; however, I was actually rather disturbed that there was a repeated message presented. One quote from the book encapsulated its general philosophy, "To appreciate the joy, you have to embrace the suffering."

No matter how good this message may sound, it isn't biblical. The message of the scripture is that we are undeserving orphans who have been adopted by a gracious God (Ephesians 1:5) whose intent is to bless us with an abundant inheritance (Ephesians 1:18) that comes with no strings attached (Proverbs 10:22).

We must face the fact that bad things do happen along the way in our Christian lives. Trying to deny that would be delusional. But the truth is that bad things also happen to non-Christians as well. In fact, there are more bad things, and with much more intensity, that happen to unbelievers than to believers. Just look at the hospitals, drug rehab centers, the homeless shelters, and the jails – and calculate the percentage of believers versus unbelievers you find there. Christians certainly are not exempt. The Bible straightforwardly admits, *Many are the afflictions of the righteous," but it continues with a promise, "but the Lord delivereth him out of them all.* (Psalm 34:19)

My point is that suffering is intrinsic to the human situation; it is not a steppingstone to God's grace and blessings.

October 3

Experience

I recently heard a Christian recording artist make the statement, "God makes me live out what I write and sing about." He then went on to explain how that he had written songs about living and walking by faith and suddenly found himself in situations where he had to actually apply the principles that he had put into his songs. You can't imagine how that statement made me cringe on the inside. My spirit cried out, "You should have lived it out before you tried to minister about it."

To be honest, I think that it is probably the majority of Christian preachers, writers, and singers who are guilty of this same error – not just this lone songwriter. So many of us try to live off of theoretical ideas that we glean from other ministers or maybe even from the Bible itself without actually knowing how – or even if – those principles work. And, in His divine wisdom, God has a way of testing us to see if we can live by our own teachings.

The Bible uses two different metaphors to speak of spiritual truth. One is milk (I Corinthians 3:2, Hebrews 5:12-13, I Peter 2:2), and the other is meat (I Corinthians 3:2, Hebrews 5:12-14). The difference between milk and meat is in the digestion. A mother eats meat, digests it, produces milk from the nutrients she received from the meat, and feeds her baby with that milk. So it is with ministers. We must ingest spiritual truths, let them work inside our lives, experience how those truths really work in actual circumstances, produce a digested and digestible version of those, and then feed others with those truths. Anything short of living the Bible out in our own lives is just taking a sip of milk and passing on the carton.

October 4
Different Flesh

Andrew Wommack made an insightful statement about the carnal nature of Christians, "We all have different manifestations of the flesh. Some people get drunk and commit adultery. I watch too much TV when I get into the flesh." A simple statement like this can help bring a totally new perspective on our Christian lives. We probably all remember having to read The Scarlet Letter in junior high school. The story line is about a woman who was forced to wear a big "A" as her punishment for committing adultery. The punchline of the book is the revelation that her partner had been the preacher who had doomed her to this display of public shame. Was her succumbing to sexual temptation any more evil than his hypocrisy? On a similar note, I've often wondered about the emphasis that many Christian preachers place on how women are to dress. In some circles, women are required to dress so out-of-fashion, wear their hair in such unflattering styles, go without make up, and refuse jewelry to the point where they become so ugly that no man would ever be interested in them. My concern is that, if the preachers were properly training the men how to deal with their carnality, there wouldn't be a concern about how the women were dressed. Notice that Galatians 5:19-21 lists hostility, strife, jealousy, and anger right alongside adultery and fornication as works of the flesh.

Romans 8:13 and Colossians 3:5 tell us that the way to deal with our carnal influences is not to try to suppress them by wearing long dresses and no make-up but by literally putting those fleshly impulses to death – a process that can only be accomplished through walking in the Spirit.

October 5

Legion – Part I

The story of Legion may seem lightyears away from anything that relates to our lives. After all, how many of us have ever encountered a wild man running naked in the graveyard? However, if we stop long enough to look at the story within the story, we'll probably realize that this story is about life as we experience it every day. Beyond the sins of this particularly tormented man's saga is the story of almost every person we meet – likely even including ourselves.

The demoniac of Gadara lived in the tombs. This isolation is characteristic of the devil's work. When the enemy gets a foothold in an individual's life, he separates him from others – husbands from wives, parents from children, neighbors from neighbors, one tribe from another, one nation from the next, and the scenarios can go on and on. The end result is mistrust, suspicion, divorce, estrangement, hostility, violence, and war.

The demoniac was said to spend his time crying – an indication of deep emotional trauma, distress, and anxiety. Such deep inner turmoil is often too hurtful to bring out into the light and share with others; since victims can't open up and talk about it, they are doomed to tears of agony and wails of heartbreak.

When we stop to look at these individual torments that afflicted the poor man rather than his overall catastrophic condition, it is easy to see that the story is not some extravagant tale that is beyond our daily experience. On the contrary, it is a story that gives the extreme scenario so that we can have hope in every situation that we face. If there was a cure for this beyond-measure incident, there is hope for the ones we face.

Legion – Part II

The next observation that the gospel writer made about Legion's condition was his self-destructive act of cutting himself with stones. Self-destruction is a classic indication of the devil's work in a person's life. Sometimes, it is suicide; sometimes, it manifests in mutilating oneself; but, generally, it is far more subtle in negative thoughts and words about oneself. Low self-worth and a poor self-image victimize their subjects into seeing themselves as less intelligent than others, less attractive than their peers, less fortunate than those around them, and less accepted than the rest of society. Such feelings drive their victims into destructive lifestyles such as isolation, lack of motivation, not making attempts at advancement due to fear of failure, becoming critical and judgmental of others who are successful, the quest for escape through self-medication that leads to drug or alcohol addiction, joining with bad companions such as a gang, or living in a harmful co-dependent relationship in order to find acceptance.

In John 10:10, Jesus said that the enemy comes to steal, kill, and destroy. Each time that we encounter death – whether physical death or death of dreams, ambitions, or relationships – we have encountered the enemy. Any time we encounter loss – physical, relationally, or emotionally – we have encountered the enemy. Every time we encounter destruction – whether from an outside force or from our own self-destructive actions or attitudes – we have encountered the enemy. The good news is that Jesus went on to say that He had come to give life and to give it abundantly. We have the promise that we, like Legion, can also encounter Jesus and find full restoration.

October 7

Legion – Part III

The story of Legion doesn't end with the three negative observations about the man when he was under the influence of the devil. It also includes three observations about his condition once he met Jesus – he was sitting, he was clothed, and he was in his right mind.

The fact that he was sitting indicates that he was no longer wild and untamed. The man who previously could not be held in place by chains and fetters was now willingly sitting at the feet of Jesus listening to His teachings and taking part in the fellowship of His disciples – totally cured from the anti-socialism that once drove him into the graveyard where his only companions were haunting, disembodied voices. He was clothed – indicating that he had now come to a place of self-respect and acceptance of himself within community. No longer was he crying out in emotional distress; he had found a place where he belonged and the agony of his inner man was now replaced with respect for his outer person. The tranquility of the inner man was manifest in his outer persona. In his right mind, he no longer was tormented with the negative self-destructive thoughts, vain imaginations, and lies that once tormented him to the point of lunacy.

Yes, it is easy to read through this description of Legion's deliverance and restoration without actually seeing that it contains a promise for all our distresses and for the agonies of those we meet every day. No longer must we – and those we meet – live in isolation, trauma, distress, and anxiety, or in physical or psychological self-destruction. There is an answer – and it is as easy for us today to find as it was for the man in Gadara two thousand years ago.

October 8

Legion – Part IV

The story of Legion is still far from being finished. When the local people realized that Jesus had just knocked the bottom out of their local economy by allowing the demonic spirits to go into the herd of swine that immediately drowned themselves, the residents of the community ran Him out of town. As the Lord was leaving town, Legion ran after Him, asking to become part of His entourage. Jesus responded with another proposal – that Legion stay at home and share with his own friends and family the story of all that had happened to him. Mark records that he did just that and the news of his deliverance soon spread through all of Decapolis. A few weeks later when Jesus returned to the same region, the people welcomed Him with open arms. In fact, the meeting that followed was likely the second largest crowd in the entire ministry of Jesus – a congregation of four thousand men plus women and children, with the largest gathering being five thousand men plus women and children. What caused this incredible reversal – from being chased out of town to receiving such a warm reception? Legion's testimony. The point here is that the deliverance that sets us free from our bondages should never stop with us; we need to pass it on so that everyone we meet can enjoy the same freedom that we are experiencing.

In our world filled with isolation, distress, and self-degradation, there is only one hope – that we acknowledge the drawing of the Father and verbally surrender to it. When we do, we will find communion, healing, and acceptance. But not only will we find restoration for ourselves, we'll discover a life that can bring that same glorious transformation to others.

October 9

Legion – Part V

Before we leave the story of Legion, there is one other observation that I think is worthy of our attention – there were two distinct dimensions in Legion's transformation. Before Jesus ever spoke to Legion or did anything to affect his life, Legion ran to Him, fell at His feet, and worshiped Him. The first dimension in Legion's deliverance was an internal recognition of the authority of Jesus. A demoniac who was so controlled by the devil that he ran naked, lived in a cemetery, and brutally abused himself somehow recognized Jesus and confessed that He had authority over him. This obviously supernatural recognition is what John was speaking of when he said that no man can come to Jesus unless the Father draws him. (John 6:65, 14:6) It is that internal tug that goes beyond – and sometimes, against – our normal human logic, making us realize that there is a void in our lives and that there is nothing short of God Himself that can fill it. The next dimension of Legion's deliverance came when Jesus spoke to the demonic forces that controlled him. It was in this verbalization that Legion's transformation occurred. This is the message that the Apostle Paul so succinctly expressed in Romans 10:8-10 when he said that we believe unto righteousness in our hearts but it is with our mouths that we confess unto salvation. Legion's heart reaction was to worship, but it took Jesus' verbalization for the salvation to be completed.

> *That if thou shalt confess with thy mouth the Lord Jesus, and shalt believe in thine heart that God hath raised him from the dead, thou shalt be saved.* (Romans 10:9)

Columbus Day
Columbus' Bible
In his book, <u>The Bible in America</u>, Steve Green wrote about the first Bible that found its way to the shores of the New World:

But in the captain's cabin of the flagship was a handwritten copy of *The Latin Vulgate,* a well-worn Bible that had guided not only the captain's spiritual life, but his epic voyage as well. Years later he stated his reasons for such a risky endeavor, "It was the Lord who put into my mind (I could feel his hand upon me) the fact that it would be possible to sail from here to the Indies. All who heard of my project rejected it with laughter, ridiculing me…There is no question that the inspiration was from the Holy Spirit, because He comforted me with rays of marvelous inspiration from the Holy Scriptures…I said that I would state my reasons: I hold alone to the sacred and Holy Scriptures, and to the interpretations of prophecy given by certain devout persons."

The year was 1492 and the captain was Christopher Columbus (1451-1506), a man driven by faith as much as he was driven by fact. History would prove that he was mistaken on many fronts. The world was nearly twice as large as he had calculated. And it wasn't a passage to India that he had found. He had discovered a land mass of huge proportions. Though he didn't know it at the time, the inspiration he had taken from the Bible had resulted in the Bible being taken to the unknown continent for the first time. The Bible had come to the Americas – and the Americas and the world would never be the same.

October 11
The "Allness" of Prayer
Praying always with all prayer and supplication in the Spirit, and watching thereunto with all perseverance and supplication for all saints. (Ephesians 6:18)

In this one sentence, Paul proclaims the universality of prayer. He says that we must pray:

1) All the time
2) With all manner of prayer
3) For all the saints

In other words, there is no time and no situation in which there is not some form of prayer that is appropriate. There are prayers of rejoicing when things are going right. (I Corinthians 7:30) There are prayers of supplication when things are not going so well. (Hebrews 5:7) There are prayers of intercession for others in need. (I Timothy 2:1) There are prayers of thanksgiving when we need to step back and get a proper perspective on what we are wishing for in relation to what we already have. (Philippians 4:6) There are prayers of fellowship when we just want to spend time with the Lord. (Matthew 14:23) There are prayers of watching when we need to be cautiously aware of the traps that could ensnare us. (Matthew 26:41) There are forgiving prayers in which we let go of offenses that could cripple us. (Mark 11:25) There are prayers of endurance when we feel that our physical strength will fail us. (Luke 18:1) There are prayers of defiance that prove that we are more than conquerors even when the circumstances seem to dictate otherwise (Acts 16:25) There are healing prayers that bring health and deliverance (Acts 28:8).

Pray without ceasing. (I Thessalonians 5:17)

October 12

The Exquisite Fragrance of Victory

God leads us from place to place in one perpetual victory parade...everywhere we go, people breathe in the exquisite fragrance.
(II Corinthians 2:14-15, Message)

We often think of this passage in the context of the victory march that we as Christians are to participate in as we live our lives in triumph over the devil – which is exactly the message of the scripture. However, today, I'd like us to consider one other aspect of the message that we might easily overlook – the exquisite fragrance that all the people breathe as we participate in that triumphant march.

Paul says that there are two different aromas given off during this parade – one of death to those who are part of Satan's camp and one of life to those who are with Christ. Obviously, the stench of death has to do with the fact that the forces of the enemy have been defeated and are therefore humiliated as we parade about in our triumphant glory. However, it might seem that there is a bit more to the fragrance that the believers are to experience. It seems that it is more than just the celebration of victory. If we read the passage in the context of the whole chapter, we see that Paul begins the section by talking about his desire to come to the Corinthian believers in unity. He goes on to include a statement about the need to beware of Satan's devices, a segway into the discussion of the victory march. It seems likely that Paul is actually trying to communicate to us that the exquisite fragrance that all believers are to enjoy comes not just through defeating the external attacks of the enemy but also those he executes internally within the church.

October 13

Twenty-first Century Noah

The Lord came unto Noah, who was now living in America and said, "The earth has become so wicked that I need to send a flood. You have six months."

Six months later, the Lord questioned Noah when He saw that he had not even started on the construction of an ark.

"Forgive me, Lord," begged Noah, "I can't get the necessary building permit. I've been arguing with the boat inspector about the need for a sprinkler system. My neighbors claim that I've violated the neighborhood by-laws by building the ark that exceeds the height limitations. The local council and the electric company are demanding a ton of money for the future costs of moving power lines. I can't get the wood because there's a ban on cutting local trees in order to save the Greater Spotted Barn Owl. The environmentalists won't listen when I try to tell them that I am trying to save the owls. The American Society for the Prevention of Cruelty to Animals insists that it is cruel and inhumane to put so many animals in a confined space. The Environmental Protection Agency wants to conduct an environmental impact study on the proposed flood. The Human Rights Commission says that I'm not employing enough minorities, and the Immigration Department is checking the visa status of the people who want to work. The unions insist that I hire union workers with ark-building experience. The Internal Revenue Service seized all my assets, claiming I'm trying to leave the country illegally with endangered species."

At that point, God decided that there was no need to destroy the world since the government had already done it!

October 14
The Revelatory Power of Speaking in Tongues
Part I

For he that speaketh in an unknown tongue
speaketh not unto men, but unto God: for no
man understandeth him; howbeit in the spirit
he speaketh mysteries. (I Corinthians 14:2)

Over the years, I have been challenged on many different occasions by people who feel that speaking in tongues is nothing more than some sort of emotional high that those who practice it use in order to escape reality. They say that the words themselves mean nothing and that the only value that the practice may bring is simply the euphoria that the speaker may experience for the few minutes that he or she is disconnected from the real world. On the contrary, speaking in tongues is not an escape <u>from</u> reality; rather, it is a connection <u>to</u> reality.

The first thing that I'd like for us to notice is how Paul describes what happens when a person speaks in tongues – *in the spirit, he speaks mysteries.* With this explanation, it might be easy to understand why some people would discredit the practice, saying that speaking mysteries, or unintelligible ideas, is pointless. But before we jump to any rash conclusions, it is important for us to remember that there is a radical difference between "unintelligible" and "unintelligent."

Just because something is inexpressible does not mean that it is senseless. In fact, the Bible gives us two powerful examples of things that are considered unspeakable, yet to be treasured – the joy of knowing Christ (1 Peter 1:8) and the grace of God we experience in salvation through Christ (II Corinthians 9:14-15).

The Revelatory Power of Speaking in Tongues
Part II

The second area that we should focus on in this verse is the fact that what is being spoken is defined as mysteries. Some might immediately respond that there is no point in focusing on things that are unsolvable – or, at least, unsolved. But exactly the opposite is actually true. To understand this point, let's take a look at some of the things that the Bible describes as mysteries:

> The kingdom of heaven or God (Matthew 13:11, Mark 4:11, Luke 8:10)
>
> Christ and God (I Corinthians 4:1; Colossians 2:2, 4:3)
>
> God's will (Ephesians 1:9)
>
> Christ and the church (Ephesians 5:32)
>
> The gospel (Ephesians 6:19)
>
> The faith in a pure conscience (I Timothy 3:9)
>
> Godliness (*God was manifest in the flesh, justified in the Spirit, seen of angels, preached unto the Gentiles, believed on in the world, received up into glory*) (I Timothy 3:16)
>
> Christ in you, the hope of glory (Colossians 1:27)

Certainly no one would dare to say that any of these subjects is unworthy of consideration and meditation! In that case, it does seem advantageous to speak of them in our prayers – even in prayers that are unintelligible to the natural mind.

October 16
The Revelatory Power of Speaking in Tongues
Part III

The third area of focus that I would like to consider in this verse is that the tongues speaker is described as speaking to God rather than man. Now, let's apply a bit of basic logic to the matter at hand. Let's say that you were having trouble with your car. Would you go ask the local grocer how to get it working properly? Obviously not – you'd go to the automobile mechanic. Why? Because he is the one who knows the answer to the mystery of why your car is not working properly. Need I really take the space on this page to draw out the analogy that it is the all-wise God to whom we need to address these mystery issues. Since it is obvious that we must have an understanding of God, Jesus, the gospel, God's will, His kingdom, and what exactly it means that Christ is in us, it is only logical that we need to address these issues to the proper authority and in the proper way. Romans 8:26-28 explains exactly how this happens.

Likewise the Spirit also helpeth our infirmities: for we know not what we should pray for as we ought: but the Spirit itself maketh intercession for us with groanings which cannot be uttered. And he that searcheth the hearts knoweth what is the mind of the Spirit, because he maketh intercession for the saints according to the will of God. And we know that all things work together for good to them that love God, to them who are the called according to his purpose.

October 17
The Revelatory Power of Speaking in Tongues
Part IV

From Romans 8:26-28, we learn that the Holy Spirit knows that we don't even know how to address the Lord properly concerning these mysteries; therefore, He assists us by praying with words that we would never be able to imagine, framing questions that we would not be able to construct. And He does this in tongues. Because He knows exactly what is in our hearts (our unintelligible – but not unintelligent – questions and concerns) and also knows the exact will of God (as opposed to our limited comprehension of it), He presents our requests in the exact manner that renders the wonderful result of having everything work out just perfectly on our behalf!

But as wonderful as that may be, it seems that there may be even more in this verse – the involvement of the very Son of God, Jesus Christ. Notice that the verse says that the one making intercession is the one who knows the mind of the Spirit – apparently someone other than the Holy Spirit Himself. Of course, we have to be cautious before we jump to conclusions because Greek at the time the Bible was penned didn't use capital letters. Therefore, the word "Spirit" could originally have been written with a small letter, indicating the human spirit rather than the Holy Spirit. In this case, the word "mind" would have to be understood not so much as the brain but the thinking process. If this is the case, then Paul is saying that the Holy Spirit knows what's going on in our spirits as we pray those unintelligible words, and He translates our requests to God in intelligible words. However, if we retain the capitalization, we get a totally new meaning, which we will explore tomorrow.

October 18
The Revelatory Power of Speaking in Tongues
Part V

By retaining the capitalization of "Spirit," the verse is definitely speaking of someone other than the Holy Spirit since it is illogical to say that the Holy Spirit knows His own mind. In that we know that Jesus lives eternally to make intercession for us (Hebrews 7:25), the only reasonable option is that the verse is referring to Jesus. In this case, we have a multiplied benefit when we pray in tongues – not only does the Holy Spirit intercede on our behalf, but His concern catalytically generates more intercession from Jesus Himself – and we know that the Heavenly Father never denies the requests presented by His Son! (John 15:16, 16:23-27)

One other thing that we need to focus on is that Paul acknowledges that the mysteries that are spoken are from the spirit of the speaker – a concept that might be confusing to some readers because they automatically assume that the tongues come from the Holy Spirit. From the very first occurrence of this phenomenon, the scriptures made it plain that the believers in the Upper Room on the Day of Pentecost did the speaking as the Holy Spirit gave them the words to say. (Acts 2:4) Thus, speaking in tongues is a joint operation of the inner heart of the believer and the Holy Spirit. As the spirit of the believer cries out for an answer from God, the Holy Spirit takes that request and molds it into the perfect prayer which is then verbalized in tongues by the outward physical being of the believer. As the mystery is unraveled, everything in the believer's life is supernaturally coordinated to work out just right.

October 19
The Revelatory Power of Speaking in Tongues
Part VI

Now that we have mentioned the physical and the spiritual dimensions of the believer, we need to also incorporate the soulical nature as well. And Paul does just that in I Corinthians 14:14, *For if I pray in an unknown tongue, my spirit prayeth, but my understanding is unfruitful.* The believer's soul is still "out of the loop" at this point. That's why the prayers are considered mysteries – the mind doesn't figure out all the details. But the fact that the mind may still be at a loss doesn't make praying in tongues void or useless. If we would only think for a minute, we'd all realize that major aspects of our lives are controlled by things that don't register as logical in our minds. Let's take love for instance. Can any one of us give a logical, scientific, or mathematical formula or explanation for what happens when a mother sees her baby for the first time or the ongoing love between the parent and the child or what happens when that young man and young woman meet for the first time or how that infatuation turns to affection and matures into a life-long commitment? Of course not, but every one of us has committed his life to that thing called love, whatever it is. In the same way, we can pray mysteries in the spirit and still not have a logical intelligible resolution, but at the same time we will just know everything is all right. It all makes sense in our hearts even if our brains are still at a loss. Paul described this sort of relationship in Ephesians 3:19, *And to know the love of Christ, which passeth knowledge, that ye might be filled with all the fulness of God* – truths which he has referred to as mysteries in verses four and nine of this same chapter.

October 20
The Revelatory Power of Speaking in Tongues
Part VII

How is it possible to know something that goes beyond knowledge as Paul suggested in Ephesians 3:19? Obviously, he is expressing the event in which our spirits have experienced the content of the mystery while our brains are still trying to comprehend all the clues. This same message is echoed in I Corinthians 2:9-10, *But as it is written, Eye hath not seen, nor ear heard, neither have entered into the heart of man, the things which God hath prepared for them that love him. But God hath revealed them unto us by his Spirit: for the Spirit searcheth all things, yea, the deep things of God*, in which he explains that there are truths and realities that are revealed in the spirit that are still not comprehended by the physical personality.

Coupled with the gift of speaking in tongues is the gift of prophecy in which the mysteries that the spirit part of the believer has experienced become comprehensible to the intellect, *He that prophesies understands all mysteries*. (I Corinthians 13:2) Since the Lord wants our total being to be blessed, He actually advocates that we desire this revelatory gift of prophecy above the other gifts which may only benefit one portion of our personality. For example, healing that blesses the physical man or speaking in tongues that can bless the spiritual dimension while leaving the soulical unfulfilled (I Corinthians 14:1); however, when prophecy comes forth, there is a total blessing that benefits us in every aspect. This is why the apostle stressed that the gathering of believers should focus on prophesy and revelation (I Corinthians 14:6, 14:26).

October 21
The Revelatory Power of Speaking in Tongues
Part VIII

I want to beg your indulgence at this point because I want to speculate on some concepts that are not specifically spelled out in the scriptures, but I believe that we can connect the dots without any real violation to reason or the sanctity of the text. We know that once he was converted on the Road to Damascus and then baptized and filled with the Holy Spirit under the ministry of Ananias (Acts 9:17) Paul spent the following three years in Arabia without any contact with other Christians who could have taught him the essence of the faith (Galatians 1:16-17). When he came back from those years in the desert, Paul brought with him an understanding of the gospel that changed the world. How did he come by it since his previous knowledge was totally based on the rabbinic interpretations of the Old Testament, ideas that he literally defined as dung? (Philippians 3:8) Perhaps – and this is the point where I stretch the line pretty far between the dots – this revelation came to him through speaking in tongues and the accompanying gift of prophecy. Although there is no reference to when he began the practice of praying in tongues, we do know that the apostle was an avid tongues speaker. (I Corinthians 14:18) It is likely that he could have begun this practice as soon as he was filled with the Holy Spirit since this seems to be a biblical pattern – the believers in the Upper Room on the Day of Pentecost (Acts 2:4), Cornelius and his household (Acts 10:45-46), and the disciples in Ephesus (Acts 19:6) and possibly the believers in Samaria in that something occurred that was phenomenal enough to make Simon the Magician want the ability to reduplicate it (Acts 8:17-19).

October 22
The Revelatory Power of Speaking in Tongues
Part IX

We assume that Paul was referring to himself when he wrote of a person who was *caught up into paradise and heard unspeakable words, which it is not lawful for a man to utter.* (II Corinthians 12:4) Notice how closely his description of unspeakable words that could not be uttered parallels with descriptions we have already seen him use when referring to speaking in tongues. Now, let's take another line and connect to the next dot that we find just a couple sentences later in verse seven – the fact that, because of the abundance of his revelations, Satan sent a messenger to try to keep the apostle from being exalted or recognized as an authority. If all these dots do indeed connect, we can conclude that Paul spent much of the time that he was isolated in Arabia speaking in tongues so that he could get the revelation of the mysteries of God in his spirit, and then he pressed into prophecy so that the unspeakable truths in his heart would become comprehensible to his mind in such a clear way that he could present a clear legacy of gospel truth for generations to come – the revelation of the mystery that was kept secret since the world began (Romans 16:25), the wisdom of God in a mystery, even the hidden wisdom that God ordained before the world unto our glory (I Corinthians 2:7), and the mystery that had been hid from ages (Colossians 1:26).

If – and even though we can't prove it beyond doubt, it does seem plausible if not likely – Paul's world-changing revelations came to him through praying in tongues, we should eagerly pursue this gift as an avenue to help us have solidity in our Christian faith and security in our daily walk.

October 23

Powerful Quotes on Prayer

Prayer is not given to us as a burden to be borne, or an irksome duty to fulfil, but to be a joy and power to which there is no limit. – A.E. Richardson

When we pray God hears more than we say, answers more than we ask, and gives more than we can imagine in his own time and His own way.

Fretting magnifies the problem, but prayer magnifies God. – John Piper

Prayer is not preparation for the work. It is the work. Prayer is not preparation for battle. It is the battle. – Oswald Chambers

Prayer is the most aggressive pro-active, offensive, invasive action one can take in any situation. Prayer reaches into the spiritual realm and accesses all the power of heaven for the circumstances of earth. – Jennifer Kennedy Dean

More work is done by prayer than by work itself. Hours with God make minutes with men effective. – Martin Luther

You can do more than pray after you have prayed, but you cannot do more than pray until you have prayed. – S.D. Gordon

Pray the largest prayers. You cannot think a prayer so large that God in answering it, will not wish you had made it larger. Pray not for crutches but for wings! – Phillips Brooks

He who has learned to pray has learned the greatest secret of a holy and happy life. – William Law

Quiet waiting before God would save from many a mistake and from many a sorrow. – Hudson Taylor

October 24

More Powerful Quotes on Prayer

To pray is to wage war. To pray is to fight spiritual battles you don't even realize in magnitude. Prayer brings angels down to help, and takes demons down to defeat. Don't underestimate what your praying can do. Never forget "Christ in you is greater than all the demons in the world." (I John 4:4) Because prayer is your most powerful weapon, always obey the impulse to pray. Much prayer – much power. No prayer – no power. – Norman Noramal

The secret prayer chamber is a bloody battleground. Here violent and decisive battles are fought out. Here the fate of souls for time and eternity is determined, in quietude and solitude. – Ole Hallesby

Prayer is his delight because prayer shows the reaches of our poverty and the riches of his grace. Prayer is the wonderful transaction where the wealth of God's glory is magnified and the wants of our soul are satisfied. – John Piper

The Lord delights in the prayers of the upright. – King Solomon

Prayer is the greatest opportunity and privilege offered to a person in Christ. The Father wants the same communion with you that He had with Jesus. – Myles Monroe

Since Jesus ever lives to intercede, any time you pray – day or night – Jesus is already interceding. Every time you go to prayer, you can be Jesus' prayer partner. – Wesley Duewe

Then shall ye call upon me, and ye shall go and pray unto me, and I will hearken unto you. – God

October 25
The No-show Employee
Joaquin Garcia, Spanish government employee who was supervising the construction of a waste water treatment plant, took a six-year break from work and still got paid before his bosses finally discovered the ruse. Garcia started skipping work in 2004 and was not caught until 2010 when he became eligible for a special plaque honoring his twenty years of service. When supervisors tried to contact him about the award, they discovered that no one had seen him for years. The head of the water company said in court that Garcia's office was near his, but for years he never saw the man. The water company reportedly thought government officials were Garcia's bosses, and vice versa.

Garcia says that officials got it all wrong. He claims that he had been bullied in an earlier job, so he switched assignments, headed to the treatment plant, and discovered there was nothing for him to do. He apparently decided to keep his bosses in the dark because he feared he would not be able to find another job at his age.

A Spanish court approved his fine which amounted to more than thirty thousand dollars. Still, that's less than the forty-two-thousand-dollar salary he earned each year without working. He has since retired and is receiving pension benefits.

Preposterous? Yes!! But many of us are guilty of exactly the same scheme. We never report to work as witnesses, church workers, tithers, givers, intercessors, or ambassadors for the kingdom of God – yet, we expect to keep receiving a full salary and reaping all the benefits in the employee package!

October 26

The Will of God

*And be not conformed to this world: but be
ye transformed by the renewing of your mind,
that ye may prove what is that good, and
acceptable, and perfect, will of God.*
(Romans 12:2)

We've all heard it said – and likely been the one who
said it – "I may not be in the perfect will of God, but at least,
I'm in His acceptable will" or "I would like to be in the center
of God's will." Those ideas certainly seem to be defensible
from the verse that we are looking at today. However, we
would have to read only this verse to legitimately believe that
there is anything less than one exact and explicit will of God.
All the other references to the will of God are clear-cut in
describing the will of God as a singular reality – not a multiple-
choice option. In which we can pick either:

     A) the good will
     B) the acceptable will
     C) the perfect will

Actually, if it were a multiple-choice question, the
answer would be:

     D) all the above

There is only one will of God – and it is good and
acceptable and perfect! Remember that Jesus taught us to pray
that the will of God would be carried out on earth exactly the
same way that it is done in heaven. (Matthew 6:10, Luke 11:2)
Is it even imaginable that the angels would ever try to
substitute their strategies for His directives, that they would try
to cut corners, or that they would ever misinterpret or
misconstrue what He meant. Certainly not! God is
anticipating that we find and follow His explicit will just as
accurately and precisely as His angels do in heaven.

October 27
Quips that are not Wisecracks or Jokes

God sometimes responds to our requests with, "I can't answer your prayers because we're not in the same business. I'm not interested in paying your utility bills when you're not interested in spreading the gospel around the world."

He sometimes says that he can't bless our offerings because we need to learn to give simply out of obedience rather than to coerce Him into doing something for us or giving us something.

God made everything out of nothing. When He looks at our lives, He realizes that He has plenty of raw building material – nothing.

If minsters really understood faith, they would burn all the congregation's faith promise cards because the promises were made to God, not the church.

Because we want to appear before God with gold, silver, and precious stones instead of wood, hay, and stubble, we should continually ask ourselves:

What in the world am I trying to do?

How in the world do I propose to do it?

Why in the world do I even bother?

God told the Jews to give fine linen, not rags, for building the tabernacle. We should not give something that cost us nothing.

When the pastor tells the choir director that he didn't want choir members who were "trying to sing" because church isn't karaoke, he needs to remember that the pulpit isn't amateur night at the comedy club either.

And let's not overlook the church dinner – there is a reason we have covered dishes at these carry-ins.

October 28
Speaking to the Mountain
I was with my doctor the other day to review the results of some tests I had taken. When he couldn't get his computer to pull up the results, he kept muttering, "Come on, work. Come on, work." I couldn't help but think about how a highly educated man could stand there in front of one of his patients – who had advanced education degrees – talking to a machine as if he expected the machine to hear him and respond. Of course, it really seems that it is intrinsic in humans to speak to inanimate objects. Just think about the number of times you have yelled, "Come on, start!" to your car when the ignition refused to turn over. And then, once you got the car to start and headed down the highway, how often have you whispered to the gas tank to not run out when the little fuel supply warning light came on, asking for a miracle like the one when the widow's oil and meal didn't run out during the whole of the famine in Israel. Even more preposterous, you kept calling for there to be a gas station at the next exit!

Well, we do it all the time, but for some strange reason we think it radically fanatical when a Bible-thumping preacher tells us that we have to speak to our mountains – telling diseases to get out of our bodies, financial resources to come into our hands miraculously, and obstacles to move out of our way. (Mark 11:23)

The truth is that God built us with an innate awareness that there is power in our words to change the physical world we live in. Let's not let the devil rob us of the reality of that power.

Death and life are in the power of the tongue: and they that love it shall eat the fruit thereof. (Proverbs 18:21)

October 29
Words of Wisdom
It's not what you look at that matters, it's what you see.– Henry David Thoreau

Honesty is the first chapter in the book of wisdom. – Thomas Jefferson

Start with what is right rather than what is acceptable. – Franz Kafka)

A man must be big enough to admit his mistakes, smart enough to profit from them, and strong enough to correct them. – John C. Maxwell

If you don't know where you are going, any road will get you there. – Lewis Carroll

Science is organized knowledge. Wisdom is organized life. – Immanuel Kant

Success has a price; prosperity is priceless.

If a man loves the labor of his trade apart from any question of success or fame, the gods have called him. – Robert Louis Stevenson

A giving church attracts successful people. They march to a different drummer from mediocre people. They are successful because they have a different outlook.

Followship is as important as leadership.

Think beyond your time.

Stop fasting and praying; start feasting and playing.

Build foundations with the bricks that people throw at you.

Your predictability is the devil's greatest tool.

Circumstances weaken weak faith but strengthen strong faith.

It takes force to deal with others; but it takes strength to deal with oneself.

If there is no enemy within, the enemy without cannot succeed.

October 30
The Perfect Storm

I recently had to mediate in a situation that arose between two students in the Bible college. After listening to both sides of the situation, I concluded that what we were dealing with was not a current problem; rather, it was a present-day manifestation of issues that the two have had since their childhoods. Both had been abused for much of their lives – one since childhood and the other during the whole of her married life. Abused people deal with their hurts in two ways: they become abusers themselves or they develop a victim mentality. One of the students had followed path number one, and the other had taken course number two. It was a "perfect storm formula" – throwing into close quarters two people from abusive backgrounds who have responded in these two different ways.

As I sat with these two individuals, I asked the Holy Spirit for an appropriate illustration to help them see what was going on – and I got the most unusual response. The Holy Spirit reminded me of a scene from a movie when someone gets a bit under the influence and says or does something out of character. In such cases, they often excuse themselves with, "It's the wine talking." With that explanation, I was able to get each party to see that the other had no real animosity; instead, it was the abuse talking. With that I helped them see that they did not have a problem with each other but that both of them had problems with their abusive pasts. I was then able to tell them that there is a third way to deal with their issues – to stop coping with their hurt and let Jesus heal it! Just as He did for the disciples on the sinking ship, Jesus walked into the perfect storm brewing in their souls and commanded the wind and the waves, *Peace! Be still!*

Halloween
Want to Hear a Scary Story?

Recent calculations place the number of Christians martyred since the time of Jesus at seventy million. Approximately a million Christians were systematically exterminated in Nazi Germany and fifteen million Orthodox Christians and others were murdered in Russia between 1917 and 1950. In China, at least two hundred thousand Christians and foreigners were killed in the Boxer Rebellion of 1898 to 1900, and another seven hundred thousand were killed in communist China between 1950 and 1980. The number of Catholics killed in Mexico from the late 1800s to 1930 is estimated at more than a hundred thousand, while three hundred thousand Christians are believed to have been killed under Idi Amin in Uganda between 1971 and 1979.

Some of the top martyrdom situations in Christian history ranked by size include:

1921–80 – Soviet prison camps: 20,000,000
1214 – Genghis Khan: 5,000,000
1358 – Tamerlane: 4,000,000
1929–37 – Stalin: 2,700,000
1560 – Conquistadors kill Amerindians: 2,000,000
1925 – Soviets against Roman Catholics: 1,200,000
1258 – Hulaku Khan captures Baghdad: 1,100,000

Today there are thirty-five countries where Islamic extremism has risen to levels akin to ethnic cleansing where over seven million Christians have been killed for faith-related reasons and more than two thousand churches have been destroyed.

November 1
Beware of Demons
A number of years ago, I was visiting a church to hear one of my students preach. When the pastor realized who I was, he invited me to assist with the prayer ministry at the end of the service. Two young girls came up to me and asked for prayer to be baptized in the Holy Spirit. As I was praying for them, I could hear a commotion beginning to stir at the other end of the altar. As the disturbance grew louder, I recognized that it was a demonic manifestation and realized that no one seemed to be able to get it under control. Under my breath, I was praying that the girls would hurry up and start speaking in tongues so I could get free to go take charge of the situation.

Once the girls began to speak in tongues, I motioned for one of the elders to come and continue to minster to them so I could assist with the demoniac. Of course, the girls had heard the ruckus, and looked up to ask what was going on. The elder responded that it was a demon and that they should keep praying in tongues so that it wouldn't jump on them. Thank goodness, I had not stepped away when he said that; it gave me the opportunity to reassure the girls that the demon would not randomly jump on them.

Demons have no authority to invade people's lives without an invitation. King Solomon expressed it this way, *As the bird by wandering, as the swallow by flying, so the curse causeless shall not come.* (Proverbs 26:2) In other words, it is no more likely for the devil to invade your life than it is for a wild bird to fly up and land on your shoulder.

The problem with most Christians is that they give the devil more credit than he deserves and don't give themselves nearly as much credit as they deserve.

Election Day
Get Out and Vote
Here are some interesting statistics about elections:

One third of all Christians are not registered to vote. Of those who are registered, only a little over half (fifty-four percent) actually show up at the polls.

Based on the number of people who actually cast a ballot on election day, it is possible that as small a fraction as eighteen percent of the population actually determines which candidate will be the next President, and as little as thirteen percent of the population can make the decisions that affect one hundred percent of the people.

Only thirty-nine percent of voters bother to make a selection for positions such as governors or senators, and only six percent vote in elections on the city level.

Can we find men on the ballots today who hold the same values as our Founding Fathers?

It is the duty of all nations to acknowledge the providence of Almighty God, to obey His will, be grateful for His benefits, and humbly to implore His protection and favor. – George Washington

We have no government armed with power capable of contending with human passions unbridled by morality and religion. Our Constitution was made only for a moral and religious people. It is wholly inadequate to the government of any other. – John Adams

Before any man can be considered as a member of civil society, he must be considered as a subject to the Governor of the Universe. – James Madison

November 3

What's in the Heart?

I have observed that there are three things that reveal what's in the heart of a man.

1) Legalism – I think that we all have had the experience of not even thinking about doing some particular act – such as walking on the grass – until we saw a sign telling us not to do so. Laws and regulations reveal what's in our hearts – unfortunately, it is generally rebellion. Of course, there are those who are free from rebellion – to such souls, legalism is only a guideline to help them live the orderly lives they desire.

2) Grace – When offered the unmerited, non-judgmental, non-condemning grace of God, people react two different ways. Some say, "Great! Now I know that God is not going to hold my faults, failures, and frailties against me; so, I can live with abandon." Others respond with, "Now that I know that God has unconditional love for me, I want to express my unconditional love for Him as well. I can do this by adopting His nature totally and living above all the faults, failures, and frailties of my former life." The different responses define the heart nature – one that is looking for an excuse and one that is looking for a remedy.

3) Alzheimer's – When I visited my mother-in-law in the memory care unit, I was saddened to see what dementia and Alzheimer's had done to their poor victims. Some who would have never cursed in their former lives did nothing but babble profanity continuously. It had been hidden in their hearts only to be revealed by these diseases. However, when I visited a minister friend in a similar facility, he repeatedly muttered, "Hallelujah! Glory to God!" What was in his heart was what showed up on his lips.

Smooth or Hairy?

I was in college during the 1970s – a very interesting time with the hippy counterculture, the sexual revolution, the influx of Eastern thought...you name it. One of the contemporary thought processes was existentialism – a philosophy that opposed rationalism and empiricism and stresses the individual's unique position as a self-determining agent responsible for the authenticity of his or her choices. Of course, all college students were required to take these unorthodox ideas seriously in order to pass our freshman introduction to philosophy class. So, I ended up attending an existentialistic play as one of my assignments. That was forty years ago, but I will never forget one scene in the play in which one of the actors quoted the Bible, *My brother Esau is a hairy man, but I am a smooth man.* The quote from Genesis 27:11 had absolutely no bearing on anything and had no significance to the context in which it was quoted. The only significance that I have ever been able to place on the use of that passage was an attempt to make the Bible look meaningless and trite and to make those who would want to find meaning in it look like fools or imbeciles.

The truth is that many Christians do wind up looking like fools and imbeciles when they talk about the Bible by taking passages totally out of context, twisting passages to defend their pet conspiracy theories, misquoting the text so as to force it to say what they already believe rather than what it actually says, and truncating the message of the passage by only quoting part of the verse.

Let's stop trying to be such "smooth men" with our "hairy" interpretations of the Word of God.

November 5
Survivors

In a study of people who would be considered survivors in many different aspects of life – cancer survivors; survivors of natural catastrophes such as hurricanes, tornadoes, and earthquakes; survivors of financial calamities; survivors of disastrous accidents such as plane crashes; and survivors of human atrocities such as war, imprisonment, and abuse – these heroic individuals described themselves and identified the defining characteristic or quality in their lives that destined them to survive.

Twenty-eight percent described themselves as "connectors." The ability to draw from the strength of others and the synergistic strength of individuals who determine to work together is a well-documented biblical principle. (Ephesians 4:16, Hebrews 10:25)

Twenty-four percent defined themselves as "realists." James referred to the necessity to be a doer of the Word rather than just a hearer only and then added that this would prevent us from deceiving ourselves. (James 1:22) Although I doubt that too many of the survivors interviewed thought of this biblical passage, it does set the standard for qualifying as a realist.

Twenty–one percent thought of themselves as "thinkers." God gave us a brain to develop and use. He commanded us to meditate on the Word of God so that our ways would be prosperous and that we would have good success and that our minds would not be filled with vain thoughts. (Joshua 1:8, Ephesians 4:17)

Fifteen percent called themselves "fighters." We simply can't survive without resisting. (James 4:7)

Twelve percent said that they were "believers." But isn't this the active ingredient in all the above titles?

November 6

Acceptable Sacrifices

Ye also, as lively stones, are built up a
spiritual house, an holy priesthood, to offer
up spiritual sacrifices, acceptable to God by
Jesus Christ. (I Peter 2:5)

According to this passage, our sacrifices are only acceptable through Jesus Christ. What a revelation! Actually, I would think that we all knew that rather intrinsically, but it is likely that we never really stopped to think it through or analyze it biblically.

Anything that we would want to offer to Him would be either something that we earned, purchased, built, or grew – but none of these things are possible without His help. First Corinthians 3:11 tells us that we cannot build anything worthwhile unless it is laid on the foundation of Jesus Christ. John 15:4-5 assures us that we cannot produce any fruit in our lives unless we are connected to the vine which is Jesus Christ. On a more rudimentary note, there is nothing that we could ever offer to God that was not originally made by Jesus. (John 1:3, Colossians 1:16) Any of our human accomplishments that we would think to offer to Him are simply pointless. (Philippians 3:8)

So, how do we ever arrive at a sacrifice worthy of offering to the Lord? The picture is painted for us in the book of Revelation. There are multiple references to the fact that believers are to be given crowns as rewards for their faithfulness and service. (I Corinthians 9:25; II Timothy 2:5, 4:8; Hebrews 2:7; James 1:12; I Peter 5:4; Revelation 2:10, 3:11, 4:10) In Revelation 4:9-11, we find out what we are to do with those rewards – cast them at the Lord's feet and proclaim that He alone is worthy. Because Jesus gave us the crowns, they are acceptable sacrifices to offer to God.

November 7
Say it Out Loud
That the communication of thy faith may become effectual by the acknowledging of every good thing which is in you in Christ Jesus. (Philemon 6)

Notice that Paul encouraged Philemon to acknowledge – or share – all the good things that Jesus had done in and for him. He stressed that in doing so Philemon's faith would become effectual. In other words, Paul was saying that his testimony would become effective through sharing it.

How many times have you been to a funeral and witnessed someone leaning over the coffin whispering to the corpse, "I wished I had told you this when you were alive"? Well, such a conversation with the deceased is totally pointless. However, had that conversation been held months or years before, the connection between those two lives could have been much stronger.

The same is true with the communication of our faith. Every time we share with others, we have the chance to relive the blessing ourselves and become strengthened by it. Additionally, as we share the story with others, they are encouraged and challenged to expect more in their own lives. Such sharing also produces a synergism in which not only are the two individuals blessed and strengthened, but there is also an invisible bond built between them as they feel that they have jointly experienced the blessing of God.

There is power in verbalizing our feelings and articulating our experiences. Make a determination to share at least one episode of your testimony with at least one person each day.

November 8

Looking After Things That Are Coming

Men's hearts failing them for fear, and for looking after those things which are coming on the earth: for the powers of heaven shall be shaken. (Luke 21:26)

"The sky is falling! The sky is falling!" So said Henny Penny, better known as Chicken Little, in the folk tale about the supposed end of the world. Well, Chicken Little's world did end when she recruited a fox to assist her in her attempt to get the warning to the king. She became the fox's supper that evening.

Notice the intriguing parallel between the folk story and the biblical passage. When Chicken Little went into hysteria over the end of the world, she got outfoxed by a fox. When men become concerned about circulating conspiracy theories, the coming apocalypse, or doomsday, they get taken down by heart failure. There's a lesson to be learned here.

How does the Bible instruct us to react to the fact that the end is drawing near?

Peace I leave with you, my peace I give unto you: not as the world giveth, give I unto you. Let not your heart be troubled, neither let it be afraid. (John 14:27)

And when these things begin to come to pass, then look up, and lift up your heads; for your redemption draweth nigh. (Luke 21:28)

I must work the works of him that sent me, while it is day: the night cometh, when no man can work. (John 9:4)

Not forsaking the assembling of ourselves together, as the manner of some is; but exhorting one another: and so much the more, as ye see the day approaching. (Hebrews 10:25)

November 9

Don't Eat the Apples

For Adam was first formed, then Eve. And Adam was not deceived, but the woman being deceived was in the transgression. (I Timothy 2:13-14)

The other day, I saw a cartoon of Adam and Eve. Eve, holding an apple with a bite missing, was saying to Adam, "He was talking to you – not me – when He said, "Don't eat the apples." I'm sure that the cartoonist was trying to create humor by crafting an absurd it-never-happened conversation between two (what I suppose he imagined to be) mythical characters. And I am even more certain that he had no idea how theologically accurate his depiction was.

The verse that we are studying today makes the point that Adam, not Eve, was in transgression because she was deceived whereas he was not. It further explains that the reason behind the whole scenario was that Adam was formed first. To understand this verse, we have to go back to the chronology given in Genesis chapter two. Adam was created in verse seven; the prohibition against the fruit of the tree of the knowledge of good and evil was established in verse seventeen; Eve was created in verse twenty-two. Since there is no mention that God ever repeated His commandment about the tree after Eve's appearance, we can assume that she got the word second-hand from Adam. Thus it was possible for her to be deceived into taking a bite. However, Adam was in blatant rebellion when he joined her in the treat. The entrance of sin into the world is attributed to Adam, not Eve.

Wherefore, as by one man sin entered into the world, and death by sin; and so death passed upon all men, for that all have sinned. (Romans 5:12)

November 10

Just Receive It

Over the years there has been a lot of teaching about forcibly taking what is rightfully ours – much of it based on Matthew 11:12, *And from the days of John the Baptist until now the kingdom of heaven suffereth violence, and the violent take it by force.* However, the scriptures repeatedly tell us that the kingdom is ours to be received rather than taken by force, earned, or begged for. Time and again we are told to simply receive such blessings as salvation, healing, Holy Spirit, the promises of God, and our spiritual and physical inheritance:

He shall <u>receive</u> the blessing from the Lord, and righteousness from the God of his salvation. (Psalm 24:5)

And all things, whatsoever ye shall ask in prayer, believing, ye shall <u>receive</u>. (Matthew 21:22)

Therefore I say unto you, What things soever ye desire, when ye pray, believe that ye <u>receive</u> them, and ye shall have them. (Mark 11:24)

A man can <u>receive</u> nothing, except it be given him from heaven. (John 3:27)

Ask, and ye shall <u>receive</u>, that your joy may be full. (John 16:24)

<u>Receive</u> ye the Holy Ghost. (John 20:22)

For if by one man's offence death reigned by one; much more they which <u>receive</u> abundance of grace and of the gift of righteousness shall reign in life by one, Jesus Christ. (Romans 5:17)

And for this cause he is the mediator of the new testament, that by means of death, for the redemption of the transgressions that were under the first testament, they which are called might <u>receive</u> the promise of eternal inheritance. (Hebrews 9:15)

A Pebble for Every Devil

In the story of David and Goliath, we often tend to stop at the point where David knocked down the giant; however, that was actually only the beginning of the battle. Had David left his nemesis lying on the ground and begun his victory lap around the battlefield, Goliath would have soon come back to his senses, climbed back to his feet, staggered to his tent, taken a couple Excedrin tablets, and headed off to do David in. But David did more than just knock his opponent out; he stole Goliath's sword and cut off the villain's head with his own weapon. But the story doesn't even end there – the sight of the decapitated antagonist inspired the up-to-this-point cowardly Israelite army to take up their weapons to pursue and defeat the entire Philistine host.

There is a lesson to be learned from this story – don't settle for a victorious battle; go for a totally victorious war! Too often, we are happy with simply solving the issues at hand rather than dealing with the actual root cause of the problem. Let's take finances for example. Knocking down Goliath could be paralleled with the struggle to pay the utility bill for the month. We celebrate when we finally get a miracle necessary to deal with it. However, the utility bill, along with the mortgage, the car payment, the kids' tuition, and the credit card bill will all be due again next month. But if we go after the spirit of poverty that has kept us in the place of always having too much month left at the end of our money, we are cutting off the giant's head so that he can't plague us again. And the beauty of this kind of victory is that it inspires others to release their own faith to pursue and slay their own giants!

The Two Sauls

We all know that the Apostle Paul was originally known of as Saul of Tarsus, but it is likely that we have never stopped to consider that Saul's parents chose his name from the royal history of their nation. Saul was named after Israel's first king – King Saul. Surprisingly enough, it turns out that there was a striking parallel between the latter Saul and his namesake.

After Samuel anointed David to be the replacement for the rebellious first monarch, Saul began to sense that the young soldier and lyre player was a threat to his kingdom and the dynastic rule he hoped to build. Because the women attributed David with slaying ten thousand of the enemy while they credited him with only a thousand, jealousy soon turned to animosity, plots, and all-out violence. He made killing David his top priority; yet, all the while, David determined to respect and honor the king because of the anointing that was upon him as king even though he was not using that anointing legitimately. In the life of Saul of Tarsus, we see some exact parallels. This Saul was a leader among the Jewish religious ranks; in fact, he was the understudy and protégé of Gamaliel – one of their most prominent leaders. Yet, a new personality appeared on the scene who was attracting followers away from the status quo that the religious institutions were enjoying. Jealousy quickly morphed into all-out war and Saul spearheaded the campaign to eradicate the new faith.

Both Sauls thought that they were serving God when in essence they were fighting against Him. But even more striking was the parallel that God refused to fight against either Saul because there was a latent anointing in each of them.

Apprehension

Not as though I had already attained, either were already perfect: but I follow after, if that I may apprehend that for which also I am apprehended of Christ Jesus. (Philippians 3:12)

Paul used a very interesting term to describe his relationship to Christ and His gospel – apprehension. People speak of being born again, of getting saved, of giving their hearts to the Lord, of asking Jesus into their lives or hearts, of receiving the Lord, and any number of other terms – but no one says that he or she has been apprehended, arrested, captured, seized, or taken into custody by the Lord.

Of course, we can give the excuse that he was a rebel going ninety miles an hour in the wrong direction and Jesus had to arrest him in order to stop him long enough to get his attention. But the truth is that we were all rebels, focused on doing our own thing. Maybe your encounter wasn't as dramatic as Paul's Damascus Road experience, but it was actually of the same nature as his – an arrest. And if we could only begin to reframe our thinking about what actually happened to us in that encounter, I'm sure that we would begin to live our lives more seriously. In that we are under arrest, we are no longer free to live the same lawless lives we once enjoyed. Now, we have been taken into custody, we are totally under the authority of the arresting officer. Paul goes on to say that he desires to apprehend the gospel – to arrest it and bring it totally into his authority. It is only when we submit our lives to the authority of Christ that we can then get a full grasp of His Word.

November 14

Joseph – Part I

Joseph is one of my favorite biblical heroes. The way that he dealt with all the hardships that came his way and came out victoriously is an incredible message of inspiration to all of us. However, have you ever stopped to consider that Joseph didn't have to go through everything that happened to him? If he had controlled his tongue and attitude when he got the special coat from his father and had the dreams about how his brothers were to bow down to him, his brothers' jealousy and resentment that led to his being sold into slavery would not have been kindled. After all, he could have taken those revelations and hidden them in his heart the way that the Virgin Mary did when she was informed that she was to be the mother of the Son of God. If he had taken someone with him so that he would not have been in the compromising situation of being in the house alone with Potiphar's wife, he would not have gone to jail. After all, he was in charge of all the other servants and could have assigned one to be with him at all times.

Yes, it does seem that his own words confirm that it was his destiny to go through all these things, *But as for you, ye thought evil against me; but God meant it unto good, to bring to pass, as it is this day, to save much people alive.* (Genesis 50:20) We so often read this passage to say that God meant for good to come out of all the things that happened to him because of the brothers' evil intentions. However, in the original explanation that Joseph gave to his brothers, we get a clue as to what the "it" in this passage is intended to mean, *Now therefore be not grieved, nor angry with yourselves, that ye sold me hither: for God did send me before you to preserve life.*

November 15

Joseph – Part II

The fact that Joseph was sent into Egypt was what God meant for good – the preservation of life. God's plan had nothing to do with the way he was to get there – simply that he had to get there. It is likely that he could have come as an ambassador had he not stirred up his brother's anger. After all, his father was a wealthy and powerful man in the region and could have had influence on the ruling authorities in Egypt.

Once that approach was spoiled by the brothers' decision to kill Joseph, God intervened and changed their minds so that they sold him into slavery – not a very honorable way, but a way to get him to Egypt none the less. If the brothers had killed Joseph, he would never have made it to Egypt – or anywhere, for that matter. Had they sold him to another band of slave traders, he could have wound up any place in the Middle East. But God had a good intent, and He was seeing that it came to pass.

Once in Egypt, God orchestrated that Joseph be sold into Potiphar's household because Potiphar was a man of influence in Pharaoh's court – apparently a step toward getting Joseph into a position where he could gain access to the monarch. As God blessed Joseph and prospered him in Potiphar's house, God was simply moving him up the ranks to poise him for the influence he was destined to have. However, Joseph's failure to safeguard himself sent him to jail as an inmate rather than to the palace as a messenger.

God, in His infinite wisdom, was able to undo all the complications and still fulfill His purpose. It certainly could have been much easier on everyone involved had he used a little more discretion and discernment – a lesson we can all learn from.

November 16

Prophesying According to Faith

Having then gifts differing according to the
grace that is given to us, whether prophecy,
let us prophesy according to the proportion
of faith. (Romans 12:6)

On one of my mission trips to the Dominican Republic, I ministered at a growing congregation that was "bursting at the seams" in their present church facility. When the pastor asked me to pray with him that he would be able to build a larger sanctuary to hold all the people, I felt prompted to tell him that he was going to have the larger building and that the money was going to come from an outside source rather than his own people. Additionally, I sensed that the government would actually be his source. I shared the first two points with him, but I was reluctant to say anything about the government funding. It took very little faith to say that an outside party would help – after all, this happens every day with churches and mission agencies from the US or Europe raising the funds for local pastors and churches on the mission field. But to say that the government would help seemed so unlikely that I could not bring myself to make such a specific prediction.

Later, I learned that there was a very good likelihood that the government would indeed build a building for the congregation. A man with influence in the president's office had zeroed in on this particular pastor to be the one to oversee a proposed educational center in the community. If this project were implemented, the government would buy his present building, tear it down, build a large structure on the site, and allow him to use it for his church as well as for the government-funded community center.

November 17
Prophesying Through Human Channels
And the spirits of the prophets are subject to
the prophets. (I Corinthians 14:32)

In yesterday's lesson, I shared how I had truncated a prophetic word because I simply did not have enough faith to say what was in my heart. Had I had the courage to say that the government was going to help him, it would have been an incredible encouragement to him since the word would have come from someone who had no knowledge of what was actually already in the works. The thing that we must understand from this illustration and the biblical passages on prophecy is that even though the supernatural word comes directly from God, it passes through human channels and can be limited or distorted in transmission. Since the spirit that motivates us to prophesy is under the control of the one who is speaking, we can reduce the message through our lack of faith or enhance the message through our own ego-boosted imagination. We can make the message come out in King James English or preface it with "Thus saith the Lord" to make it sound more spiritual and authoritative, or we can make the message less intimidating by simply saying something like, "I just feel..." I once heard a person prophesying over an individual and prefaced each sentence with, "The Lord would say to you," and then inserted the person's name before giving the prophetic message. The only problem was that the prophet was using the gentleman's brother's name instead of the correct name of the individual. Did that negate the validity of the message? No, it simply affirmed that the divine message was coming through a human vessel.

November 18

Blind Faith

We often speak of "blind faith" as a way of expressing our willingness to step out and do things even though we don't comprehend how they are going to work. Although this expression may describe how we feel at the moment, it is actually a poor description of how the Bible describes faith. In fact, a more accurate description should be, "looking faith." Let me share a few passages that illustrate the point.

In Acts 3:3-4, we read the story of the lame man at the Beautiful Gate. When he first encountered Peter and John, he was described as <u>seeing</u> them. Peter's response was to <u>fasten his eyes</u> on the lame man and command him, "<u>Look</u> on us." Notice the progression from simply <u>seeing</u> to intentional <u>looking</u> – an act of faith that indicates the anticipation of finding something.

Acts 7:55 records the story of how Stephen as he was being martyred <u>looked steadfastly</u> into heaven and saw the glory of God and Jesus standing on the right hand of God. Again, he exerted faith with anticipation that God was going to reveal Himself at this crucial moment.

Hebrews 11:10 reflects on the life of Abraham by saying that he <u>looked</u> for a city whose builder and maker is God. Obviously, this was not a physical city since it is described as being the handiwork of God Himself, not a human construction team. In other words, he was expressing his faith in heaven as he explored the earth.

The real definition of faith is given in Hebrews 12:2 as simply *Looking unto Jesus the author and finisher of our faith.* Maybe we are blind to the way He will answer our issues, but we have 20/20 vision of the Answer!

November 19
The Word of Power
Who being the brightness of his glory, and the express image of his person, and upholding all things by the word of his power, when he had by himself purged our sins, sat down on the right hand of the Majesty on high. (Hebrews 1:3)

We find some interesting phraseology in this particular verse when we read about the *word of His power.* We are accustomed to references to the power of the word (Ecclesiastes 8:4; Luke 4:32, 4:36), but this passage reverses the anticipated order – suggesting a difference in the meaning.

We all know that there is power in the Word of God. It was by His word that the universe was created. It was by one spoken word that Lazarus came forth out of the grave after having been dead for four days. It was through Jesus' spoken words that the blind received their sight, the deaf began to hear, the demoniacs were freed from their torments, and the lepers were cleansed. It is also through our spoken words that we control the power of life and death. In essence, the spoken word is the controlling power of the created order – and it would make perfect sense to speak of the power of God's Word in this sentence as the force that upholds all things in the created order.

The significance of the reversed wording in this particular passage is that it helps us grasp the immensity of the Lord's power by saying that it only takes one word of His power or authority to sustain the entire universe. He is not having to continually work at running the universe and making everything viable. It doesn't take His full resources – just one word!

Draught Conditions

Behold, the days come, saith the Lord God,
that I will send a famine in the land, not a
famine of bread, nor a thirst for water, but of
hearing the words of the Lord. (Amos 8:11)

Several years ago, my wife and I were among the thirty-two thousand residents who were evacuated from our community as it was ravaged by a wildfire. Although our home was spared, close to twenty thousand acres of forest and almost three hundred fifty homes were destroyed. The actual source that ignited the fire that took two lives in addition to all the other devastation has never been determined; however, we know that the force behind the fire was a long and severe drought that dried everything to kindling. The following year, our community was inundated by flash floods that swept away cars, destroyed businesses and homes, and filled the streets with ash-filled mud from the burn scar. In what seemed like a twist of fate, the devastation of the fire left the former forest land barren and set up the potential for the flooding. In other words, the floods were the result of the draught.

Amos speaks of a spiritual draught, but in the very next chapter prophesies the most miraculous harvest imaginable, *Behold, the days come, saith the Lord, that the plowman shall overtake the reaper, and the treader of grapes him that soweth seed; and the mountains shall drop sweet wine, and all the hills shall melt.* (Amos 9:13) Since both passages are introduced with the same phrase, *Behold, the days come, saith the Lord*, it is apparent that they are to be seen in conjunction. The present spiritual draught is actually setting the stage for a coming revival.

Fasting

For though we walk in the flesh, we do not war after the flesh: (For the weapons of our warfare are not carnal, but mighty through God to the pulling down of strong holds;) Casting down imaginations, and every high thing that exalteth itself against the knowledge of God, and bringing into captivity every thought to the obedience of Christ. (II Corinthians 10:3-5)

Please forgive me for the awkward timing of this meditation – right at the beginning of the Thanksgiving-Christmas-New Year holiday season when we are all going to over-indulge in holiday meals, special treats, and delicacies that we wouldn't even think of during the rest of the year. But before I launch into today's lesson, let me remind you of one of the words of wisdom that I learned from Dr. Lester Sumrall, "It's not what you eat between Thanksgiving and New Years that makes you overweight; it's what you eat between New Years and Thanksgiving!"

Today, I'd like to explore the spiritual significance of fasting. In Isaiah chapter fifty-eight, fasting is called *afflicting the soul* on three different occasions. (verses 3, 5, and 10) In other words, fasting is not actually a suppressing of the physical appetite but the mental process that makes us think that we must eat. With this in mind, we can understand that the practice of fasting is actually a spiritual weapon that helps us pull down the strongholds and vain imaginations that are part of our souls. Through fasting, we learn to control our thoughts, impulses, and urges – and take them captive, making them obedient!

Thanksgiving

In Luke 17:11-19 we find the story of a band of lepers who came to Jesus to be cleansed of their disease. Of the ten who were healed, only one returned to Jesus to say "Thank You." One little detail that we might overlook in the story is that Jesus said to the one who came back, *Your faith has made you whole.* The significance of that little statement is that he was not only healed, he was made whole. The others were healed, but apparently, they would still bear the scars that the ravaging disease had left on their bodies. That's why they had to go to show themselves to the priest to have their healing verified. This man was made whole – meaning there was no longer any trace of evidence that he had been a victim.

This Thanksgiving season is a great time to make a decision to live lives characterized by thankfulness. Yes, we can be blessed without thankfulness – the story of the nine other lepers validates that point. However, there is a much deeper and more thorough work that happens when we stop to be thankful – the blessings penetrate into our total being, not just our physical personality. Thankfulness gives us fulfillment in the soulical and spiritual dimensions in addition to the physical blessings.

Someone once coined the little rhyme that we must make a <u>choice</u> to <u>rejoice</u> to verbalize the reality that joy is a decision. I'm afraid that my attempt at a similar play on words is not quite as catchy as that one, but let me share that we must be <u>thinking</u> of <u>thanking</u>. Thanksgiving takes conscious effort because it is so easy to be caught up in enjoying the blessing that we don't stop to think about appreciating the One who made the blessing ours.

November 23
Words of the Wise
The words of the wise prod us to live well. They're like nails hammered home, holding life together. They are given by God, the one Shepherd. (Ecclesiastes 12:11, MSG)

Don't need a majority if you are the remnant.

God is as human as you need Him to be; you are as divine as God needs you to be.

The gospel should wreck us.

NO = Next Opportunity

FAIL = First Attempt at Initial Learning

Perfection is not attainable, but if we chase perfection, we can catch excellence. – Vince Lombardi

Spiders were the original web designers – and we thought that we were so clever to come up with a whole new occupation.

When a preacher introduces his sermon with, "I want to talk for the next few minutes," we should think, "If he's going to lie about that, why should I believe anything else he says?"

You are unique – just like everybody else.

Soap was invented centuries ago; it is even mentioned in the Bible. However, it was only in our lifetime that someone figured out that it could be shaped to fit your hand. It's amazing how we can go so long and totally overlook the obvious.

It's not enough to get rid of the bad harvest; we need to pull up the roots.

Budget cuts can actually raise up men of faith.

Dream for the whole journey but plan for little individual steps.

Learn to discern between your dreams and God's vision.

November 24
Preparing Our Hearts
But this people hath a revolting and a rebellious heart; they are revolted and gone. Neither say they in their heart, Let us now fear the Lord our God, that giveth rain, both the former and the latter, in his season: he reserveth unto us the appointed weeks of the harvest. (Jeremiah 5:23-24)

The prophet described the people as rebellious and revolting in their hearts because they did not decide within themselves that they needed to fear or respect the Lord. Because they did not prepare themselves spiritually for the Lord, He was not able to physically bless them with peace and prosperity. A similar evaluation was made of King Rehoboam, *And he did evil, because he prepared not his heart to seek the Lord.* (II Chronicles 12:14) In contrast, we are told that Hezekiah (II Chronicles 30:19) and Ezra (Ezra 7:10) did prepare their hearts to seek the Lord. In their situations, God was able to intervene and manifest His blessings.

On a practical level, we must understand that we are God's kings and priests in this New Testament era just as Rehoboam, Hezekiah, and Ezra were in the Old Testament period and that, just as nothing good happened in the Old Testament when the king's heart was not right with God, we hold the key to what blessing can come and which ones may be withheld in our generation. We must have right hearts for good things to happen in our dispensation. (I Samuel 7:3, II Chronicles 20:33)

November 25
Fishing for Men
I think that we have all seen the photos of a fisherman standing on the dock beside a huge trophy fish that he has just reeled in. The thing that we have to realize about the story behind that photo is that the fisherman hired a boat and guide for the day. The guide picked the bait, strung it on the hook, took the fisherman to the right spot to fish, and showed him how to actually do the fishing. If the fisherman decided to eat his catch, the guide was responsible for getting it cleaned and packed on dry ice and possibly for even arranging for a cook to prepare it for dinner. The only thing that the fisherman did was reel in the catch and stand next to it for the Kodak moment.

It is not so different in the spiritual world as well. Yes, Jesus did tell us that He would make us fishers of men (Matthew 4:19), but He also said that no one comes to the Father except through Him (John 14:6) and that no one can come to Him unless the Father draws him (John 6:44). In essence, Jesus was saying that He would serve as the fishing guide to ensure that we make the catch and get the credit.

An excellent illustration of this principle happened to my wife on a mission trip to England. The team prayed for God to give them clues as to whom to share the gospel with. One of the team members received several specific words: cowboy boots, a green hat, red shoes, and a guitar. Soon they spotted three musicians – one with a guitar, wearing cowboy boots and a green hat, and one with red shoes! After sharing the gospel with them, they gladly let my wife pray, and two of the three received the Lord. The Guide made the fishing trip a success, but my wife got to reel in the prize and take the photo!

November 26

If

I have never taken the time to count them, but I assume that the estimation is accurate that there are over fifteen hundred conditional promises in the Bible. If this is not accurate, and even if there were only <u>one</u> conditional promise in the scripture, we would have to acknowledge that God's blessings are dependent upon our cooperation with His will and commandments. Some people refuse to accept this idea, saying that it is legalism to believe that we have to do something in order to get God's provisions. However, Jesus Himself (the actual embodiment of grace) and the Apostle Paul (the champion of grace theology) both present us with abundant examples of conditional promises that require our action in order to activate God's provision.

> For *if you forgive men when they sin against you, your Heavenly Father will also forgive you. But if you do not forgive men their sins, your Father will not forgive your sins.* (Matthew 6:14-15)
> *If you believe, you will receive whatever you ask for in prayer.* (Matthew 21:22)
> *If you hold to my teaching, you are really my disciples.* (John 8:31)
> *If you obey my commands, you will remain in my love, just as I have obeyed my Father's commands and remain in his love.* (John 15:10)
> *If you confess with your mouth, "Jesus is Lord." and believe in your heart that God raised him from the dead, you will be saved.* (Romans 10:9)
> *By this gospel you are saved, if you hold firmly to the word I preached to you. Otherwise, you have believed in vain.* (I Corinthians 15:2)
> *If anyone does not love the Lord – a curse be on him.* (I Corinthians 16:22)

November 27
How Healthy is the Church in America?

Every year, approximately four thousand new churches are established in America. But before you start your Hallelujah Dance, let me hasten to add that approximately seven thousand churches close each year in our country. Therefore, we have a net loss of about three thousand churches annually.

Additionally, there are about fifteen hundred pastors who leave the ministry each month. That calculates to a loss of eighteen thousand church leaders who resign for one reason or another each year. In fact, four out of five Bible college and seminary graduates leave ministry within the first five years of serving in the ministry. And those who stay are facing real challenges. Half of them say that they would leave if they could but have no other way of making a living, and eighty percent of them say that they feel unqualified to fulfill the rolls they are in.

Four out of five pastors' wives wish that their husbands were in a different profession, and the majority of pastors' wives say that the most destructive event in their family was the day the husband entered the ministry. It is no wonder that approximately half of the marriages of America's clergy end in divorce.

I'm sorry if I have painted a pessimistic picture. That was certainly not my intent. I simply wanted to report some facts to help us be aware of the situation that we face in the church today. I just want to encourage you to make our church leadership a priority in your prayers. So often we think that they should pray for and minster to us, but we fail to think about the fact that they may need our prayers in order to survive. If Jesus (Matthew 26:28-40) and Paul (Romans 15:30) needed prayer, our present-day leaders do as well.

November 28
Called into the Ministry – Part I

As a follow-up to yesterday's lesson, I'd like to consider a very basic issue that is at the root of a lot of failures within the ministry – the clarity of the calling upon one's life. Let's look at the Apostle Paul as an example to see what clues we can find that would validate his calling and position in the Body of Christ.

In Acts 13:2, we see that he and Barnabas were established in the ministry through the confirmation of the church leadership. Men who responded to the prompting of the Holy Spirit seriously evaluated what they sensed that they had heard through fasting and prayer and then publically ordained them into the ministry. Notice that they did not make the decision lightly. They based it upon what they had already seen in the lives and work of the two candidates and they applied a principle that Paul would later define as refusing to lay hands on anyone suddenly. (I Timothy 5:22) Unfortunately, many ordination boards today simply rely upon paper applications in making a decision concerning whom they will ordain.

But Paul's calling didn't start with the elders in Antioch. It dated much further back to the day that the Lord Himself called him into the ministry. (Acts 26:16-18) On the Road to Damascus, Jesus personally told Paul that there was a divine destiny upon his life. In fact, this calling was actually the defining moment for the apostle – so much so that he continued to proclaim that his apostleship came directly from God, not from men. (Galatians 1:1) How many of the ministers who exit the ministry each year can go back in their lives and say that there was a definite moment when they knew that God had individually separated them for His purposes?

November 29
Called into the Ministry – Part II

We can't even look to the Damascus Road experience for the origin of Paul's calling. In Galatians 1:15, he testifies that his separation (or ordination, if you will) goes all the way back to his mother's womb. Agreeing with such men of God as Isaiah (Isaiah 49:1, 5), Jeremiah (Jeremiah 1:5), and David (Psalm 139:13-16), Paul says that his calling was something that God had been working on for his entire life. Even though he was – as Jesus put it – kicking against the pricks (Acts 9:5, 26:14) – his life showed that he had a destiny in the ministry. Otherwise, he would not have so diligently pursued the training at the feet of Gamaliel (Acts 22:3) and involved himself in the established religion of the day to the point where he had access to the high priest himself (Acts 9:1, 22:5). How many of the pastors in the annual exodus from the pulpit can look back at their lives and see that God's hand was upon them – even in their childhood – directing them toward a divine mission? Perhaps that's the reason that many say they can't do anything else – not because they are not qualified for other positions, but because they are so bent toward the ministry they would not fit.

But even his mother's womb is not the genesis of the call upon Paul's life. In Ephesians 1:4-6, he declared that the divine call and purpose on his life dated back to even before the foundation of the world. Somehow, Paul saw what he was doing as part of an eternally orchestrated plan. With that sense of purpose and destiny it would be impossible to ever quit or decide to pick another occupation! Once we get the glimpse that our lives are actually part of a supernaturally choreographed purpose, how can we ever even think of abandoning it?

November 30
Fuel Trucks Also Have to Have Gas

A survey that was done among pastors several years ago revealed some shocking results. It was discovered that the average pastor spends about seven minutes a day in personal devotional time with the Lord – prayer and Bible study. With such a limited time with the Lord, it's no wonder that they are flocking out of the church doors and then leaving their congregations to close the doors behind them.

After all, it doesn't matter how much fuel is in a gasoline tanker's storage tank. If there is none in its operational fuel tank, it is going to wind up on the side of the road. Ministers need to be filled up by spending time in the presence of the Lord.

Elijah had no hesitation in declaring to the king that it would not rain unless he declared it to be so. Why? Because he had been standing before the Lord and, therefore, knew that the Lord would stand behind him. (I Kings 17:1) And when you have a ministry that produces that kind of results, you would not even think of quitting or closing the church.

The high priest entered the Holy of Holies once each year (Hebrews 9:7), but that one day that he was privileged to spend before God sanctified the other three hundred sixty-four days and gave him the authority to execute all the other ministry.

Draw nigh to God, and he will draw nigh to you. (James 4:8)

Come unto me, all ye that labour and are heavy laden, and I will give you rest. Take my yoke upon you, and learn of me; for I am meek and lowly in heart: and ye shall find rest unto your souls. (Matthew 11:28-29)

December 1

Let the Nations Know

Give thanks to the Lord and proclaim his greatness. Let the <u>whole world</u> know what he has done. Sing to him; yes, sing his praises. Tell <u>everyone</u> about his wonderful deeds...Let the <u>whole earth</u> sing to the Lord! Each day proclaim the good news that he saves. Publish his glorious deeds among the <u>nations</u>. Tell <u>everyone</u> about the amazing things he does...O <u>nations of the world</u>, recognize the Lord, recognize that the Lord is glorious and strong...Let <u>all the earth</u> tremble before him. The <u>world</u> stands firm and cannot be shaken. Let the heavens be glad, and the <u>earth</u> rejoice! Tell <u>all the nations</u>, "The Lord reigns!" Praise the Lord, the God of Israel, who lives from everlasting to everlasting! (I Chronicles 16:7-36, NLT)

On the day that David moved the ark from Gibeon to Jerusalem, he composed a magnificent song of praise and thanksgiving unto the Lord to celebrate that the ark was at home in the new capital of Israel. It is fascinating to notice how much emphasis that he placed on the universality of God's reign. The anthem was not just on the covenant relationship He had with Israel – what would be expected in a song about the ark of the covenant. The essence of the gospel is that, no matter how wonderfully God has acted in your life, it was not for your sake alone. He is always blessing us so that we can be a blessing to others and an example of His goodness that draws them to Him.

December 2

Covered Sin

He that covereth his sins shall not prosper:
but whoso confesseth and forsaketh them
shall have mercy. (Proverbs 28:13)

In Genesis chapter thirty-eight, we find an intriguing story about the patriarch Judah and his daughter-in-law Tamar. Tamar's husband had died without leaving an heir. According to the Jewish law of the time, Judah gave his second son to Tamar in order to produce an heir. He, however, refused to do so – knowing that any child that was born to Tamar would supersede any children that he might have on his own in receiving the family inheritance. When the second son died, Judah refused to give his one remaining son to Tamar – fearing Tamar was a "black widow" and that this last son might die as well. When Tamar tricked Judah into having an illicit relationship with her, Judah tried to hide his offense and desired to prosecute his daughter-in-law to the fullest extent of the law – death. In a shocking turn of events, Tamar proved that it was Judah who had impregnated her and fully exposed his evil deeds. In turn, Judah confessed that Tamar was more righteous than he was no matter what wrongdoing she may have been guilty of.

The point of the story is that God has a way of exposing everything that we so cleverly hide. In the words of Jesus Himself, *For nothing is secret, that shall not be made manifest; neither any thing hid, that shall not be known and come abroad.* (Luke 8:17) However, the wonderful promise of God is even though we can't conceal our sins, He can cover them in the blood of Jesus so that they are never exposed.

December 3

Three Confessions

We all know that Peter denied the Lord three times on the night of His trial, but there is a lot more to the story if we only read it carefully. Actually, Peter had already failed the Lord three times even before the arrest. Jesus had asked him to pray with Him while He agonized before His Father in the Garden of Gethsemane; however, Jesus found Peter sleeping rather than praying on each of the three occasions when He returned to the disciples.

After the resurrection, Jesus met the disciples on the shore of the Sea of Galilee and sat with them around the campfire dining on a meal of roasted fish. As they sat together, Jesus confronted Peter three times with the question, "Do you love Me?" – one time for each of the times he had fallen asleep and for each of the times he had verbally denied Him. But that still isn't the end of the story. The book of Acts records that Peter was arrested on three different occasions (Acts 4, 5, and 12) – giving him three opportunities to refuse to deny the Lord, matching the three occasions on which he failed the same test. It can also be noted that it took him three repetitions of the vision of the sheet filled with unclean animals to come to the place to obey the command to slay and eat.

It seems that God wanted to let Peter see that what had been birthed inside him was sufficient to face the challenge that he had failed at previously. Had Jesus asked Peter only once about his love or had he only appeared before the magistrates one time, Peter might have walked away with some lingering doubts inside himself. But after three hearings, there was no question that he had been totally restored.

December 4

Superhuman God

Seeing that we have a great High Priest who has entered the inmost Heaven, Jesus the Son of God, let us hold firmly to our faith. For we have no superhuman High Priest to whom our weaknesses are unintelligible–he himself has shared fully in all our experience of temptation, except that he never sinned. (Hebrews 4:14-15, J.B. Phillips New Testament)

Although the word "superhuman" is not found in the original Greek text of this passage, its meaning is certainly implied in the context. However, its addition here certainly gives this passage some extra impact, helping it to say explicitly what we all know theoretically but may often fail to apply practically.

We all acknowledge that the incarnation was God coming to earth as a human, taking upon Himself all the frailties and limitations of human flesh; however, we still have a problem actually grasping the concept that He literally emptied Himself of all His divine power and personality. (Philippians 2:6-8) We somehow still sense that He healed the sick, raised the dead, walked on water, and discerned what was in people's hearts because He was God masquerading as a human rather than God actually having become a human. But this verse helps us comprehend that there was nothing extra-human operating inside Jesus as He lived among us here on earth. He operated with exactly the same qualities that you and I have available to us if we simply tap into the power of a renewed mind and decide to be led by the Holy Spirit.

December 5
Are You on the Naughty or Nice List?

There is a vanity which is done upon the earth; that there be just men, unto whom it happeneth according to the work of the wicked; again, there be wicked men, to whom it happeneth according to the work of the righteous: I said that this also is vanity...The righteous, and the wise, and their works, are in the hand of God...All things come alike to all: there is one event to the righteous, and to the wicked; to the good and to the clean, and to the unclean; to him that sacrificeth, and to him that sacrificeth not: as is the good, so is the sinner; and he that sweareth, as he that feareth an oath. (Ecclesiastes 8:14, 9:1-2)

As we enter into the Christmas season, we are sure to hear people asking little children if they have been good all year so that Santa Claus can bring them all the toys on their wish lists. Of course, we all have an innate feeling that good things come to good people – sort of a karma theology – and we are always puzzled when bad things happen to good people and good things happen to bad people. But these verses – from the inspired Word of God – tell us that both good and bad things happen to both good and bad people.

But there is another side to the coin. We actually have the ability to determine that good things will happen in our lives – not by being good people, but by being people who develop a relationship with the Holy Spirit. (Romans 8:26-28, Galatians 5:16-25)

December 6

The Man on the Stretcher

There is a very interesting story in the fifth chapter of Luke. Jesus was teaching inside a house and the crowd was so huge that it overflowed the building and blocked all the entryways into the home. Some men were so determined to get their friend to Jesus in hopes that he might be healed that they refused for the congested situation to hinder them. Climbing to the roof – possibly a trick that they learned from Santa Claus (I'm sorry, I just couldn't pass up the seasonal humor) – they ripped open a hole. They hauled their companion up to the housetop and lowered his stretcher down through the opening.

Of course, this is a familiar story, but perhaps there is one little detail that most of us have overlooked as we have read and recited the tale over and over again. Verse seventeen says that the power of God was present to heal as Jesus was ministering that day. However, as we read the story, there is no mention of anyone else being healed. Certainly, it is possible that there were others, and Luke just didn't think to report them. Although an argument from silence is a very tenuous position, I somehow feel that no one else was healed that day. Furthermore, I believe that the Holy Spirit inspired Luke to make this comment so that we could learn a lesson – just because God has made a provision doesn't mean that we will automatically receive those blessings.

An old saying goes, "You can lead a horse to water, but you can't make him drink." That is exactly the way it is with God's blessing. He wants us well, prosperous, and victorious – and He has made all the provisions for us to have those benefits; however, it is up to us to reach out and receive them.

December 7
Dying for One's Enemies
O my son Absalom, my son, my son Absalom!
would God I had died for thee, O Absalom,
my son, my son! (II Samuel 18:33)

Although Absalom had mounted a rebellion against David, had chased him out of his palace, and violated his concubines, and had led many of David's closest counselors into treason against him, David still loved his son and lamented that he would have died for Absalom. What a moving depiction of the love that supersedes all wrong and injury.

In reality, every one of us is the recipient of exactly that kind of love. Through our sins, we have made ourselves just as much enemies of God as Absalom was to David and we have committed just as blatant tyrannies against God as did Absalom against his father. Yet Jesus laid down His life on our behalf.

Greater love hath no man than this, that a man lay down his life for his friends. (John 15:13)

As the Father knoweth me, even so know I the Father: and I lay down my life for the sheep. And other sheep I have, which are not of this fold: them also I must bring, and they shall hear my voice; and there shall be one fold, and one shepherd. Therefore doth my Father love me, because I lay down my life, that I might take it again. No man taketh it from me, but I lay it down of myself. I have power to lay it down, and I have power to take it again. This commandment have I received of my Father. (John 10:15-18)

For if, when we were enemies, we were reconciled to God by the death of his Son, much more, being reconciled, we shall be saved by his life. (Romans 5:10)

December 8

Europe and Asia

Now when they had gone throughout Phrygia and the region of Galatia, and were forbidden of the Holy Ghost to preach the word in Asia. (Acts 16:6)

Paul was expressly forbidden by the Holy Spirit to minister in Asia but after seeing a vision of a man from Macedonia calling for his help, he set sail immediately for Europe (Acts 19:9-10). As he traveled through the various regions of Greece, the apostle worked many miracles, led multitudes to Christ, and birthed a number of churches – a testimony to his obedience to the call of God upon his ministry. However, just because God refused for him to minister in Asia at one specific point did not mean that there was never again the possibility for him to reach that continent. In Acts chapter nineteen, we read the story of his ministry in Ephesus (in Asia) where he stayed for two years and had an effective outreach to both Jews and gentiles. In fact, his ministry there was so powerful that it was said that all of Asia heard the gospel within those two short years.

The moral of the story has to do with God's timing rather than His arbitrary decision to permit or prohibit our activities. He knew when the season was right for Paul to go to Greece and when it was optimal for him to be in Turkey. Had Paul insisted on staying in Asia, he would have missed the harvest in Europe and would have likely found that the doors of ministry that were wide open upon his later visit to Asia might not have been open at the previous time.

I can verify from my own experience that things I wished to do were delayed but worked out so much better when I did them in God's perfect timing.

December 9
My Christmas Wish List

Ask of me, and I shall give thee the heathen
for thine inheritance, and the uttermost parts
of the earth for thy possession. (Psalm 2:8)

As we are drawing near to the Christmas holiday, I'm sure that all of us have compiled lists – or, at least, made mental notes – of things that we are hoping to receive from friends and relatives. Well, here's a great suggestion of what to ask the Lord for. As a matter of fact, it is a surefire list because He has already told us what to ask for – the nations.

But more than just asking for the nations for our Christmas gift, He said that we should ask for the nations as our inheritance. I came to that realization a number of years ago when I decided that more than anything else in life I wanted to see the nations of the world discipled for Christ. I was willing to give up any kind of financial security that I might be able to accrue in order to travel the world teaching and sharing the Word of God. But the impact of this verse really hit me when the Lord showed me that my thinking was too small since I had focused all my energy on one nation – the country of Nepal. He challenged me to seek for open doors in not just one or two nations but all the world. It was at that point, that my wife and I named our ministry, "Teach All Nations" – a rather presumptuous moniker for our little mom-and-pop ministry. But God has honored it and taken us around the world more times than we can count!

Of course, not all of us are called to actually go to nation after nation, but all of us can have an inheritance of the harvest in these nations through our prayers and financial support for those who do go.

December 10

Asking for Support

Having just mentioned the Christian privilege of financially supporting missionaries and considering the fact that we are nearing the end of the year when many believers like to make special charitable gifts, let's talk about those people who depend upon our free-will offerings for the livelihood of their ministries.

Two great ministers from the late 1800s characterize two radically different approaches to support raising. George Mueller cared for more than ten thousand orphans without ever asking a single soul for even a pence. He believed totally in letting God speak to people about his need. D.L. Moody, on the other hand, said that God is not only the author of supernatural communication but also the author of natural communication. It has been reported that he said, "If there is a millionaire that has not given to my ministry, just give me his address and I will pay him a visit."

Let me share a story about another minister and his approach to raising support. The gentleman would visit people's homes and present his need to them when they opened the front door. If they didn't give him an offering, he would insist upon praying for them – right on their porch in front of all the neighbors and the passing traffic. Of course, they would be embarrassed into giving him something so he would go away – and they would be ready to quickly give him something the next time he approached them.

The lesson we can learn from these three men is that we should give when the Holy Spirit prompts us to – even if the minister has not asked directly. However, we should never allow ourselves to be manipulated into giving.

December 11

Sons of God

But as many as received him, to them gave he power to become the sons of God, even to them that believe on his name. (John 1:12)

Certainly, we all appreciate the fact that we can be born again and become sons of God, but it is likely that we have not really gleaned all that Jesus was offering here. Essentially, He was saying that He wanted to give us the power to become the sons of God rather than the sons of the devil. Paul helped to explain that there is no middle ground between being the seed of the devil and the seed of God when he wrote, *Wherein in time past ye walked according to the course of this world, according to the prince of the power of the air, the spirit that now worketh in the children of disobedience.* (Ephesians 2:2) He says that prior to our becoming the children of God, we were under the power of the devil himself – not just good people who hadn't gotten around to being born again. Jesus was pointblank when He made the statement, *Ye are of your father the devil, and the lusts of your father ye will do.* (John 8:44) Of course, we can try to sanitize the verse by saying that He was referring only to the specific Jews that He was confronting at the time. However, if we read the passage in its full context, we'll see that Jesus was actually talking to Jews who believed on Him. (verse 31) Therefore, they were actually in the transition from the Jewish faith into following Jesus; however, until they were actually born again, they were still children of the devil. As the Apostle Paul would describe it later, they needed to be delivered from the power of darkness and translated into the kingdom of God's dear Son. (Colossians 1:13)

December 12
Inheriting the Kingdom of God
For this ye know, that no whoremonger, nor
unclean person, nor covetous man, who is an
idolater, hath any inheritance in the kingdom
of Christ and of God. (Ephesians 5:5)

In yesterday's meditation, we referenced Ephesians 2:2 in which Paul said that the believers in Ephesus had at <u>one time</u> lived lives that were controlled by the devil and given over to carnal behavior. But today, let's address the issue of believers who are <u>presently</u> still living such lives. Paul said that those who manifest the works of the flesh will not inherit the kingdom of God. (Galatians 5:19-21) John the Revelator makes it even more dramatic when he says that those whose lives are characterized by such activities will have their place in the lake of fire and brimstone, which he defines as the second death. (Revelation 21:8)

These are pretty serious consequences for allowing ourselves to continue in fleshly habits motivated by demonic forces. No wonder Paul admonished the believers in Ephesus that fornication, all forms of uncleanness, and covetousness should not be named among them even one time (Ephesians 5:3) – a radical statement that challenges our contemporary concept that it is a lifestyle, not an occasional slip-up, that determines our eternal destiny.

Even before we face the second death and the lake of fire, our lives of the lusts of the flesh cause us to forfeit our inheritance in the here-and-now kingdom of God that Paul described as righteousness, peace, and joy in the Holy Ghost (Romans 14:17) through guilt and shame.

December 13
The Gospel According to Kids
The following are supposedly excerpts from actual Sunday school papers by youngsters:

Moses died before he ever reached Canada. Then Joshua led the Hebrews in the battle of Geritol.

The greatest miracle in the Bible is when Joshua told his son to stand still and he obeyed him.

David was a Hebrew king skilled at playing the liar. He fought with the Finklesteins, a race of people who lived in Biblical times.

Solomon, one of David's sons, had 300 wives and 700 porcupines.

When Mary heard that she was the mother of Jesus, she sang the Magna Carta.

When the three wise guys from the east side arrived, they found Jesus in the manager.

Jesus was born because Mary had an immaculate contraption.

St. John the blacksmith dumped water on his head.

Jesus enunciated the Golden Rule, which says to do one to others before they do one to you. He also explained, "A man doth not lie by sweat alone."

It was a miracle when Jesus rose from the dead and managed to get the tombstone off the entrance.

The people who followed the lord were called the twelve decibels.

The epistles were the wives of the apostles.

One of the opossums was St. Matthew who was also a taxi man.

St. Paul cavorted to Christianity. He preached holy acrimony, which is another name for marriage.

Christians have only one spouse. This is called monotony.

December 14
The Grand Canyon
Many years ago, I had the once-in-a-lifetime privilege of rafting the Colorado River through the Grand Canyon. There were about a dozen people in our party who had only one thing in common – a desire to participate in this epic adventure. We were all strangers to one another prior to the trip and had simply joined forces by booking the same dates with the river guide. It was a several-day adventure in which we ran the rapids during the day and camped out under the stars at night – giving us a real opportunity to become well acquainted. One evening as we were sitting around the campfire after cooking our supper on the open flames, one of the team looked out at the gigantic rock formations towering nearly a mile above us on the riverbank and began to muse about the millions of years that it had taken the river to cut its path through the solid rock. As soon as he finished his "scientific" discourse, another member of the group began to poetically describe all the impressions that she as an artist had been experiencing as she marveled at the beauty of the monoliths. Finally, I decided to take a turn and began to reference the Bible, speaking of the intricacy of God's handiwork in nature.

The amazing thing is that what we see in each thing that we look at is determined not so much by what is actually there to see but by what is in our hearts determining how we behold everything. And this principle holds true not only with the natural wonders around us, but also with the people we encounter, the things that others do and say, the situations we face in life, and the opportunities set before us. May we have hearts that always focus on the beautiful and positive aspects.

December 15
Hardened Hearts

In yesterday's meditation, we explored the fact that we all see things according to what is in our hearts. One man saw the Grand Canyon scientifically because he had an academic heart. One lady saw it poetically because her heart was that of an artist. I saw it as the handiwork of God because of the spiritual inclination of my heart. Today, I'd like to take that thought just a step further and explore what it is that keeps us from seeing things from God's perspective. The Bible calls this a hardened heart.

In John 12:40, Jesus quotes the prophet Isaiah, *He hath blinded their eyes, and hardened their heart; that they should not see with their eyes, nor understand with their heart, and be converted, and I should heal them.* The fact that Isaiah attributed the blindness to God Himself is beyond the scope and anything that we can discuss in this one page; so, let's leave that issue alone for the time being. The point is that hardened hearts are accompanied with blindness.

We can see an amazing instance of this in the scriptures when the disciples actually took part in distributing the miraculously multiplied fish and loaves but failed to realize the miracle that had just happened because they had hardened hearts. (Mark 6:52, 8:17) Perhaps it was because the disciples were so focused on getting the food to all the multitude of people present that they simply didn't take time to realize where all that fish and bread was coming from. After all, passing out five thousand plus food baskets is a lot of work for just twelve men. The point is that unless we make a point to seek for a heart sensitive to God, we can wind up with hardened hearts right in the middle of His presence. (Psalm 51:10, 101:2)

December 16

Unbelief and Misunderstanding

Let us labour therefore to enter into that rest,
lest any man fall after the same example of
unbelief. (Hebrews 4:11)

Let's lay aside all our pre-conceived ideas for just a few minutes. It would be good to lay them aside for the rest of our lives, but for now I'm only going to ask for just the time that it takes to read this page.

Most of us would immediately think that the thing that keeps us from receiving the promises of God would be disobedience, but this passage says that it is unbelief. Of course, as soon as we stop to think of it, the idea makes sense – if we don't believe that God wants us blessed, we'll never prosper. We have been commanded to believe and to live by faith; therefore, unbelief is really a form of disobedience.

But strong meat belongeth to them that are of
full age, even those who by reason of use
have their senses exercised to discern both
good and evil. (Hebrews 5:14)

I would venture to guess that we would immediately assume that the difference between a mature and an immature believer is his ability to understand doctrinal truths, but this passage tells us that the qualifying difference is the ability to discern good and evil – a principle very likely we all assume is something that is birthed inside us as soon as we are born again. Yes, we do have the ability to distinguish right from wrong, but we have to mature into understanding the difference between the things that are good (advantageous) and the things that are evil (detrimental) for our spiritual lives.

December 17

Know No Man After the Flesh

Wherefore henceforth know we no man after the flesh...if any man be in Christ, he is a new creature: old things are passed away; behold, all things are become new. (II Corinthians 5:16-17)

It's interesting that we almost always apply the "new creature in Christ" principle to ourselves, helping us to develop a new self-image after our conversion; however, if we read the passage in its full context, we'll recognize that Paul's original intent was that we apply that principle to others. There is nothing wrong with using this verse as part of our own personal renewal, but we must always keep in mind that the real intent is to develop a mentality of seeing others as they are in Christ rather than as the flawed humans we have found them to be.

It's amazing that three and a half millennia later, we still refer to Rahab as a harlot rather than referring to her as the great-great-great-grandmother of Jesus. And even more amazing is that Thomas is still identified as a doubter even though the doubting period of his life was only seven days in length.

One of my college friends was the big drug dealer on campus before he was born again. He was immediately transformed and became an energetic evangelist among the same students that he once supplied with all sorts of illegal substances. Yet, in spite of his very evident regeneration and his passion for the Lord, his pastor still introduced him as the "drug dealer." I'm sure that the pastor's intent was to draw attention to the change that had occurred, but my friend was devastated each time he was introduced that way – he wanted to be known as who he was in Christ!

December 18

Go Figure

But go ye and learn what that meaneth, I will have mercy, and not sacrifice: for I am not come to call the righteous, but sinners to repentance. (Matthew 9:13)

The context of this passage is immediately after the call of Matthew – who was a tax collector, a despised profession that was generally filled by thieves and extortionists. Upon Matthew's selection as a disciple, Jesus joined his new follower and his comrades for a meal. When the religious leaders saw the teacher sitting with these suspect characters, they questioned His motives and integrity. It was at this point that He told them to go figure out the very motives and integrity of God Himself. (Hosea 6:6)

Jesus was trying to show them that His motivation and action were exactly the same as God the Father. (John 5:19) His point was that when they were looking at Him, they were actually seeing the Father Himself. (John 14:7-9) He was actually explaining to them that He was Emmanuel – God Himself with them in the flesh! (Matthew 1:23)

However, He wanted them to go figure it out for themselves because they were blinded by the veil of tradition and bigotry (II Corinthians 3:14) and they would not even be able to see the kingdom as long as that veil remained (John 3:3).

That is why we have Christmas, the celebration of Emmanuel – not so we can stuff ourselves with all sorts of delicious dishes (something that we should do as part of the celebration) or exchange gifts (something else we should do in honor of the great gift God had given), but to take time to reflect on what it means that God is actually with us!

December 19
Immanuel
And he said, My presence shall go with thee,
and I will give thee rest. And he said unto
him, If thy presence go not with me, carry us
not up hence. (Exodus 33:14-15)

I find this passage very intriguing in that Moses essentially disregards what God has just said to him and also seems to ignore the pattern that has already been demonstrated for twenty chapters in the book of Exodus. In the first verse of today's reading, God specifically spoke to Moses saying that His presence was going to be with him as he traveled further. Additionally, God had already proved Himself by accompanying the people visibly with a pillar of fire each night and a pillar of cloud each day since they set foot out of Egypt.

We have to wonder why Moses would feel it necessary to insist again that God would be with him. It seems that Moses had lost faith because the people rebelled and made a golden calf to worship. He apparently felt that God would back out on His end of the bargain since the people had failed in theirs. The thing that Moses discovered was the grace of God demonstrating His unconditional acceptance.

For wherein shall it be known here that I and
thy people have found grace in thy sight? is it
not in that thou goest with us?...And the Lord
said unto Moses, I will do this thing also that
thou hast spoken: for thou hast found grace
in my sight, and I know thee by name.
(Exodus 33:16-17)

This is Immanuel – God with us, full of grace and truth. (John 1:14)

December 20
Mental Filters

Finally, brethren, whatsoever things are true, whatsoever things are honest, whatsoever things are just, whatsoever things are pure, whatsoever things are lovely, whatsoever things are of good report; if there be any virtue, and if there be any praise, think on these things. (Philippians 4:8)

Hopefully, all of us have filters on our computers to keep out the junk that would otherwise be pumped into our homes and minds. Such filtering devices allow us to set varying levels of protection, and I always set mine at the very highest degree possible. These tools are wonderful modern innovations, but the principle has been around for centuries. In fact, Paul described a seven-level filtering system of the things that we should allow into our minds.

First, he says that we should filter out anything that is not true. I think that most Christians are at least aware of this filter in that we are always trying to identify the lies of the devil so that we can reject them. Unfortunately, since we are not aware of the complete system that God has made available for us, we often falter at this initial step. For example, the doctor runs some test and says that you have cancer. If you react with, "Well, that's a lie of the devil! I'm not receiving that!" you've actually made a fool of yourself in that it was pointless to go to the doctor in the first place if you are going to call him a liar. Additionally, you are looking at hard evidence and denying that it exists. The biblical pattern is to acknowledge the truth of the cancer, but filter it out on the fourth and fifth tiers by the virtue that cancer is not lovely nor is it of a good report.

December 21

Crèche

I guess that I'm just a bit of a "county bumpkin" because I had never heard of the "crèche" until I was actually a senior citizen. Of course, I could tell from the context in which people were using the word that it was a fancy name for the nativity scene in which there are little figurines arranged depicting Mary, Joseph, the baby Jesus, shepherds, wise men, camels, sheep, angels, and maybe even a cow. But I decided that I should look up the word before I ever used it myself – I didn't want to embarrass myself, just in case.

Well, when I went to the dictionary, I discovered that a crèche is, indeed, a nativity scene, but that is not the first definition. The first meaning of the word is a day care center where adults take care of children in place of their own parents. When I read that, I was impressed that this is a very appropriate idea. After all, Jesus was not the actual child of Mary and Joseph; He was the Son of God.

I also found a second definition that comes from the discipline of zoology. In this case, the word refers to animals that take care of young that are not their own. Please don't take this in the wrong way; I'm not degrading the Holy Family to the animal level, but I immediately thought of the mythological stories of how wolves raised Romulus and Remus (the founders of the city of Rome) and the fictional Tarzan being raised by apes. What I envisioned was the irony of an intelligent human being under the care of a wild animal. I think that the parallel should be immediately apparent that the very Creator of the universe was under the care of His own creation.

Lastly, I discovered the definition of a point worth taking. Well, enough said!

December 22

Closed Doors

In two different parables, Jesus spoke of closed doors. One was in the story of the ten virgins. Five of them discovered that they were out of oil and had to go buy more; unfortunately, the festivities began before their return and they found themselves locked out of the banquet hall. (Matthew 25:10) The other locked door was in the parable about a man who received an unexpected visitor and had to go to his neighbor's house at midnight asking for bread to offer to his guest. The answer that came from inside the house was, *Trouble me not: the door is now shut, and my children are with me in bed; I cannot rise and give thee.* (Luke 11:7) Of course we all know how the two tales end – in one, the man was finally granted entry; in the other, girls were left standing out in the cold. But that's not a subject that we can pursue today.

In today's meditation, I'd like to consider another closed door – the one at the inn in Bethlehem on the first Christmas night. When Mary and Joseph arrived at the establishment, they were greeted with a "No Vacancy" sign and were told that the only room available for them was the cow stall. But that was only the beginning of the closed doors that Jesus was to encounter in His earthly sojourn. John 1:11 summarizes the continual rejection He experienced in less than a dozen words, *He came unto his own, and his own received him not* – He encountered one slammed door after another. But the most disturbing closed door is the one portrayed in His letter to the Church at Laodicea, *Behold, I stand at the door, and knock.* (Revelation 3:20) Somehow, He has been locked out of His own church. Let's make sure that the door is unlocked and flung wide open for His entry!

December 23
A Penny Saved

Seventy-three-year-old Otha Anders of Louisiana has always taken a moment to bend over and pick up any lost pennies he happens upon. He considers found pennies to be a reminder from God to always be thankful. Forty-five years and fifteen five-gallon plastic water jugs later, Anders finally cashed in his half-million-plus pennies – over five thousand dollars' worth, including those he otherwise saved – to pay for some dental expenses.

This little story can speak to us on so many different levels. First, it shows us the importance of recognizing the value in small things. Who would ever have imagined that pennies would become significant enough to cover a senior citizen's dental bill? Next, it speaks to us about the necessity to recognize value where others do not. To all those half a million individuals who dropped their coins, a penny was not worth taking the time to pick it up, but Otha saw value in those stray coins – and we see that his evaluation eventually paid off. Another message that this story sends to us is that everything has a purpose and we need to be careful not to overlook it. Certainly, pennies have a purpose or the government would stop minting them. I understand that it actually costs more to make a penny than it is worth and that the government has considered stopping their production; however, they decided to continue making them because they see that there is a need for them.

Jesus came to seek and to save that which was lost – men who seem so worthless that we throw them away and don't even think of it as a loss. To Jesus, every soul has value and significance, and He is building His kingdom with these "lost pennies."

December 24

God's Favorite Bible Verse

The Lord said unto my Lord, Sit thou at my right hand, until I make thine enemies thy footstool. (Psalm 110:1)

The New Testament quotes from the Old quite often – over twenty-three hundred times. But there is one particular verse that "takes the cake" – if you will permit that expression – compared to all others.

The second most frequently-quoted verse is Leviticus 19:18, *Love your neighbor as yourself,* and is repeated seven times in the New Testament, but Psalm 110:1 is quoted or alluded to twenty-three times in eleven of the twenty-seven books of the New Testament and by seven of the nine New Testament authors.

The message that Jesus has been invited by the Father to sit in dominion is one of the major themes of the books of Ephesians and Colossians where He is portrayed as seated at the right hand of God far above all the demonic forces. But the wonderful thing about this message is that He has invited us to be seated with Him there and share in that triumphant victory.

The fact that this one verse finds its way into so much of the New Testament is a clear testimony to the fact that God intends for us to see that we are presently living in divine victory – we do not have to wait for a future kingdom to manifest itself. Yes, there is a millennial kingdom coming and then the reconstruction of the entire heavens and earth under God's manifest rulership, but Satan has already been subdued and Jesus has already received all power and authority in heaven and on earth. Right now, we are living in the completed work of the cross and resurrection.

Take hold of it!

Christmas

There It Is!

I remember seeing an old grainy, black-and-white picture of myself that was shot with my dad's little Brownie camera. It was a scene from Christmas morning when I was about two or three years old. There I was in my pajamas with my arm stretched out and my finger pointing toward the Christmas tree. My mother explained that the picture was taken when I had just crawled out of bed and had come into the living room to discover under the tree the rocking horse that I so desperately wanted. She went on to describe how it had thrilled her so much to see the excitement on my face and hear the joy in my voice as I exclaimed, "There it is!"

Our Heavenly Father is just like that with His children. He is always thrilled when we finally wake up and realize what He has done for us and what wonderful gifts He has given to us. One of the most powerful prayers in the Bible is recorded in the first chapter of Ephesians where the Apostle Paul prays that we would have a spirit of wisdom and revelation and that the eyes of our understanding would be enlightened so that we could get a grasp of all the riches of the glory of His inheritance that He has prepared for us and how exceedingly great is His power that is working in us. This prayer is the answer to the oft-quoted passage in the second chapter of I Corinthians about eyes having not seen and ears having not heard what God has prepared for His saints. When the prayer in Ephesians is answered, our eyes will be opened so that we can see all the rocking horses and other treasures under the Christmas tree. And, when we do, we'll shout, "There it is!" All the blessings have been there all along; we've just been asleep!

December 26
God is on the Move
Be silent before the Lord, all humanity, for he is springing into action from his holy dwelling. (Zechariah 2:13, NLT)
Quiet, everyone! Shh! Silence before God. Something's afoot in his holy house. He's on the move! (Zechariah 2:13, MSG)

What an inspiring thought – God is springing into action; something's afoot because God is on the move! That must have been the way that the shepherds felt when the angels appeared to them and told them that a baby had been born in Bethlehem and how the wise men reacted when they saw the star that miraculously guided them to the Holy Family. Yes, God had sprung into action and He was on the move!

However, the message of Christmas is that He is continually on the move and is perpetually springing into action. That's why He chose to send His Son into the world as a baby – so that we would see Him as having the potential to deliver rather than as a final remedy. Had Jesus appeared in some supernatural way – say as a triumphant warrior splitting the heavens asunder as He will in His Second Coming – everyone would realize that this was the once-for-all deliverance. On the other hand, since He came as an infant, we had to wait for Him to mature into adulthood to begin His ministry. Then we had to wait for Him to travel from one place to the other in order to heal the sick in the various locations. On top of all that, He gathered around Himself a group of men who were to carry on His work after His departure, and told them that He would send His Spirit to work through them. Each day, every day – even today – God is springing into action.

December 27
Spiritual Hypochondriacs

A hypochondriac is a person who thinks that he is sick even though there is actually nothing wrong with him. We see many people like that in the physical world, but the spiritual world is basically populated with spiritual hypochondriacs. By that, I mean that most Christians think that they are sick, weak, and powerless when they are actually more than conquerors in Christ.

I remember hearing a preacher who was trying to encourage the congregation to be in all the services that the church held during the week. He said that it was important for them to come to the midweek service in order to get an extra boost to get through the rest of the week so that they could make it all the way to Sunday. When I heard him say that, everything inside of me rebelled. I wanted to stand up right in the middle of his service and protest that he was training the people in his church to be spiritual weaklings who were dependent upon him rather than the Greater One who was alive inside every one of them!

The sad truth is that this is not an isolated situation with this one pastor. The majority of Sunday sermons focus on survival techniques rather than the supremacy of Christ and His authority inside us. When we continually think of holding on, holding out, and pulling through, we make ourselves feeble, anemic, ineffective, and pathetic.

Hypochondriacs love to take pills for their supposed maladies. I suggest that the only pill we Christians need is a good dose of the "Gospill"! It will help us realize that we are more than conquerors, overcomers, continually victorious, prosperous, healed, healthy, strong, energetic, vibrant, and anointed.

December 28

The Right Equipment

A woman was touring an art gallery where a photographer was displaying his most recent pieces. When she had the opportunity to actually meet the artist, she commented on the quality of his work and added, "You must have some very professional cameras and lenses." It turned out that the lady and the gentleman became friends, and she eventually invited him to her home for dinner. After the meal, he complimented her on the delicious food and added, "You must have some very expensive pots and pans."

Obviously, we all know that it takes the right tools to get the right results. I often say, "There is no limit to what a man can do if he has the right tools." However, even with rudimentary tools, the person with the right skills can still do an excellent job. I remember traveling in Nepal when the country was still very primitive. At that time, it was unsafe to eat in the little teahouses and rest stops outside the major cities. Therefore, we hired a cook to travel with us. In fact, the cook that we were able to find was a professional chef who at one time had worked in the kitchen at the king's palace. Along the way, his portable kitchen equipment was lost or stolen, and all he had to work with was my little camping stove. Amazingly, he was able to prepare splendid meals for our whole team with just that single-burner butane hotplate. He never complained, he just kept on task and produced quality meals. It's a bad workman who blames his tools.

As Christians, we have exactly the right tool – the Word of God (II Timothy 3:16-17); we just need to learn how to use it properly (II Timothy 2:15).

December 29
The God of Hope and Peace
Now the God of hope fill you with all joy and peace in believing, that ye may abound in hope, through the power of the Holy Ghost.
(Romans 15:13)

We often like to think of God in all His triumphant manifestations as a great warrior, defeating His enemies with the breath of his nostrils (Psalm 18:8), but, today, let's remember some of the other characteristics attributed to our God. At least three times, He is described as the God of hope (Psalm 71:5, Romans 15:33, I Timothy 1:1) and, at least four times, He is called the God of peace (Romans 16:20, Philippians 4:9, I Thessalonians 5:23, Hebrews 13:20) – terms that paint a much different picture from the one we see when He rises up in fury to defend His people and slay His enemies. These terms convey a message – at least to me – of sailing peacefully along no matter what the circumstances may be. I envision the voyage across the sea when Jesus fell asleep in the boat. It is likely that the seas were calm when they set sail, but the situation turned violent. When the disciples woke Jesus, His reaction was to question why they were disturbed. He felt that they should have maintained their tranquility all during the journey because they had the God of peace with them, and they should have anticipated a successful outcome because the very God of hope was riding in their boat.

As we prepare ourselves for a new year, we have no idea what may await us – what joys, what sorrows, what challenges, what victories, what successes, what disappointments – but the one thing we can be assured of is that the God of hope and peace will be with us through it all.

December 30

Deliverance – Past, Present, Future

*Who delivered us from so great a death, and
doth deliver: in whom we trust that he will
yet deliver us.* (II Corinthians 1:10)

At this time of year, we always find ourselves living in three different dimensions. We look back at the past year as we collect all our receipts and financial documents in preparation for filing our taxes. We live in the present as we are still in the holiday mode connecting with friends and family that we don't get to see during most of the rest of the year. We anticipate the future as we are thinking ahead for the coming year – maybe reorganizing our finances based on our end-of-the-year pay raises, or planning our summer vacation knowing that we have to put in for our desired weeks off as soon as we report back to work after the New Year holiday.

As we live in those three worlds simultaneously, we have the powerful promise that God is continually right there in each of those dimensions perpetually delivering us. In fact, Jesus described His entire ministry as one of deliverance, *The Spirit of the Lord is upon me, because he hath anointed me to preach the gospel to the poor; he hath sent me to heal the brokenhearted, to preach deliverance to the captives, and recovering of sight to the blind, to set at liberty them that are bruised.* (Luke 4:18) As we have seen Him protect, deliver, care for and supply for us in the past and as we realize that He is our total support in the present, we can face the future in full assurance that His grace will be sufficient no matter what tomorrow may hold. No matter what may come, He will deliver us from, through, and in it. (Psalm 34:19)

December 31

Grace Be with You

The grace of the Lord Jesus Christ, and the love of God, and the communion of the Holy Ghost, be with you all. Amen. (II Corinthians 13:14)

At least fifteen times, the New Testament writers offer the benediction that the grace of God would be with us. (Romans 16:20, 16:24; I Corinthians 16:23; II Corinthians 13:14; Galatians 6:18; Philippians 4:23; Colossians 4:18; I Thessalonians 5:28; II Thessalonians 3:18; II Timothy 4:22; Titus 3:15; Philemon 1:25; Hebrews 13:25; II John 1:3; Revelation 22:21) At first, we could assume that this was just a simple expression of blessing and not an actual theological statement; however, if we hold to the persuasion that every word of the Bible is inspired of God, we have to look a little deeper than to just assume that this phrase is only a nicety.

If we do hold that there is an actual message in these words, we are faced with a bit of a dilemma since we know that the grace of God is "standard equipment" with our salvation; it is not an optional add-on. However, the phrase doesn't imply that we don't have the grace of God; it specifically states that we would always have it <u>with</u> us. I keep a pouch of restaurant coupons in the glove compartment of my car; however, occasionally, my wife and I will decide to eat out when we are driving her car. In those cases, I have to pay full price for our meals because I do not have the coupons <u>with</u> me even though I <u>do</u> own them.

The apostles are praying that we will always have access to the grace of God – that unbelief, fear, or simple negligence will not rob us of its wonderful benefits. May God's grace be with you this new year.

Teach All Nations Mission

Teach All Nations Mission (TAN) is a global evangelical educational ministry birthed from the teaching ministries of Delron and Peggy Shirley. The name for Teach All Nations Mission was chosen to carefully indicate the exact heart of the Shirleys' mission. TAN's commitment is to establish a solid biblical foundation in national pastors and leaders so they can help enrich their own people. This vision is being accomplished by holding national leadership conferences and publishing and distributing Christian teaching materials in English and their local languages.

Someone accurately observed concerning the revival that is occurring in many parts of our world today that it is a mile wide but only an inch deep – the result of energetic evangelism by both missionaries and local Christians. Sadly, there is a marked shortage of teachers who are taking the next step in fulfilling our Lord's directive to teach them how to observe all that He has commanded. Therefore, Teach All Nations Mission has literally taken the words of Christ from Matthew 28:19, "Teach all nations," as its motto and mission statement.

TAN's commitment is to deepen that revival by training the pastors and leaders who then go back and strengthen their congregations. TAN pays for the travel and lodging of handpicked leaders because Delron and Peggy want to invest into their lives but know that these third-world saints could never afford to come at their own expense. TAN always provides the meals for all the guests during these conferences. The ministry also furnishes solid Christian literature in their local language or in English for those who understand the language.

Delron and Peggy realize that the challenge is much bigger than what they can accomplish in person; therefore, they have determined to expand the scope of their vision. One area of expansion includes a scholarship fund that will allow selected individuals to obtain a formal education in solid Christian colleges and Bible schools or through correspondence courses. The ministry has also assisted in building a Christian school in Zimbabwe and a Bible college in Nepal. Additionally, Teach All Nations assists the pastors and leaders they work with in times of need such as the tsunami in Sri Lanka, the earthquake in Nepal, and hurricanes in Belize and in the Turks and Caicos Islands. More recently, the ministry supported suffering Christians in twelve different nations who lost their source of income during the shutdowns during the COVID-19 pandemic.

Your gifts to and prayers for Teach All Nations will help the Shirleys continue their outreach to Christian leadership around the world.

Teach All Nations Mission
3210 Cathedral Spires
Colorado Springs, CO 80904
719-685-9999
www.teachallnationsmission.com
teachallnations@msn.com

Books by Delron & Peggy Shirley

Women for the Harvest
You'll be Darned to Heck
if You Don't Believe in Gosh
You Can Be Healed
Your Home Can Survive in the 21st Century
Your Part in the Grand Scheme of Things

Available at:
teachallnationsmission.com

www.ingramcontent.com/pod-product-compliance
Lightning Source LLC
LaVergne TN
LVHW051037080426
835508LV00019B/1565